THE SINO-SOVIET CONFRONTATION SINCE MAO ZEDONG

Dispute, Detente, or Conflict?

by

Alfred D. Low

SOCIAL SCIENCE MONOGRAPHS, BOULDER
DISTRIBUTED BY COLUMBIA UNIVERSITY PRESS
NEW YORK

1987

SOCIAL SCIENCE MONOGRAPHS

Copyright © 1987 by Alfred D. Low
Library of Congress Catalog Card Number 87-60628
ISBN 0-88033-958-6

Printed in the United States of America

Previous books published by the author:

Lenin on the Question of Nationality, 1958

The Soviet Hungarian Republic and the Paris Peace Conference, 1963

The Anschluss Movement, 1918-1919, and the Paris Peace Conference, 1974

Die Anschlussbewegung in Österreich und Deutschland, 1918-1919, und die Pariser Friedenskonferenz, 1975

The Sino-Soviet Dispute. An Analysis of the Polemics, 1976

Jews in the Eyes of the Germans. From the Enlightenment to Imperial Germany, 1979

The Anschluss Movement, 1918-1938: Background and Aftermath. An Annotated Bibliography in German and Austrian Nationalism, 1984

The Anschluss Movement, 1931-1938, and the Great Powers, 1985

TABLE OF CONTENTS

ABBREVIATIONS

Beijing Review	B.R.
(formerly Peking Review)	P.R.
Central Committee	C.C.
Current Abstracts of the Soviet Press	C.A.P.S.
Current Digest of the Soviet Press	C.D.S.P.
Communist Party of China	C.P.C.
Chinese People's Republic	C.P.R.
Communist Party of the Soviet Union	C.P.S.U.

ACKNOWLEDGEMENTS

I am most appreciative of having been allowed the use of the files of *The Current Digest of the Soviet Press* (Translation copyright by The C.D. of the S.P., published weekly at Columbus, Ohio. Used by permission), and also grateful to *Beijing Review*, to the publisher of my previous study, *The Sino-Soviet Dispute. An Analysis of the Polemics*, Fairleigh Dickinson University Press, 1976, for permitting references to it, to B. N. Garrett and B. S. Glaser, *War and Peace. Views from Moscow and Beijing*, Institute of International Studies, Berkeley, 1984, for some quotes from and references to their interviews in China and Russia in 1981 and 1983 with some foreign policy experts, and to Mrs. Jeanne Hsu for permission to use the map from her late husband's, Kai-Yu Hsu's book on *Chou En-Lai*, Doubleday and Co., N.Y., 1968. As previously, I am indebted to my wife Dr. Rose S. Low for numerous kinds of help rendered and to Professor Stephen Fischer-Galati of the University of Colorado, editor of the series "East European Monographs."

I am grateful for the assistance given to me by the library staffs of several Universities, especially the University of Wisconsin and Milwaukee, that of Marquette University and its interlibrary service, and the staff of the East Asian Library of the University of Washington, Seattle, where during the past summers I had the privilege of working as a Visiting Scholar.

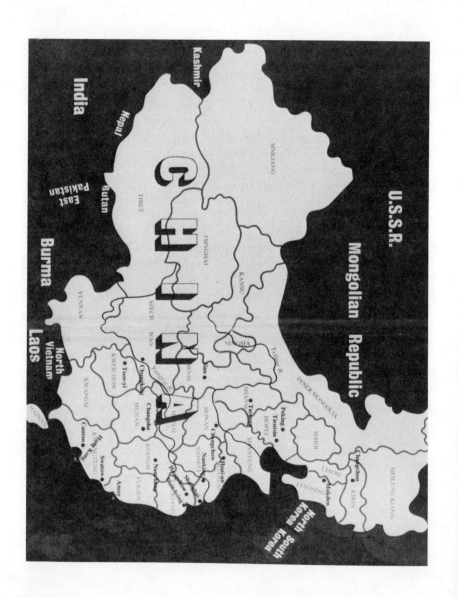

PREFACE

This study is a continuation of my book *The Sino-Soviet Dispute. An Analysis of the Polemics*, (Fairleigh Dickinson University Press, N.Y.) 1976. I have been encouraged to write this sequel, bringing the account and analysis up-to-date, by the favorable response to the foregoing study. Donald S. Zagoria (*Soviet Studies*, July 1980), a pioneer of the study of Sino-Soviet relations, praised the "many virtues" of my book, "keen sensitivity," "avoidance of simplifications," "the balanced judgments and interpretations," and the "accuracy of quotes." He considered my book, "no small achievement," "extremely useful," contrasting it with the works of some social scientists "pretending to outline grand 'theories' and conceptual breakthroughs which turn out to be short on both facts and theory." Though H. C. Hinton's account in the *American Historical Review* (Dec. 1978, p. 1232) was somewhat critical, he too lauded the "remarkable comprehensiveness" of my study, its resting on a "great deal of work in original sources" and my making "a valiant and generally successful effort to understand and convey the topic, which is noted for its obscurity and complexity as well as its importance." *Choice* welcomed it as a "competent work" (November 1976, and also April 1979, in discussing another study on the Sino-Soviet territorial dispute). *Foreign Affairs* (Winter 1978-79) called it "one of the few careful analyses of polemics" between the two Communist giants and endorsed my interpretation of the conflict of both powers being ravaged "by the disease of national chauvinism. "J. E. Thach, Jr. in the *Russian Review* (vol. 37, Nr. 4, Oct. 1978, pp. 475f.) considered it especially valuable for its "analytical perspectives" of the "apparently ideological-nationalistic split of vast proportions," its instilling "an air of authenticity" into the escalating debate through "considerable public press statements for both sides" and its "excellent" bibliography.

More critical was D. W. Treadgold in J. J. Ellison's (ed.) *The Sino-Soviet Conflict*, 1982, "Alternative Western Views of the Sino-Soviet conflict," (pp. 325f.), though including my

study which he held free of partisanship, among five selected
scholarly works for special analysis. He made the charge that a
term such as nationalism needed to be more fully explained.*
Since, however, I had adequately analyzed the nationality
situation in the USSR as well as in the CPR and in their border
regions, it should have been clear that the nationalism
involved on both sides was imperialistic and, in the view of
both Moscow and Beijing, also affected their national security.
Both states, being multinational in character, strove far
beyond the attainment of a mere nation-state in the nineteenth
century European meaning; they were anxious to retain their
national minorities and to gain additional non-Han and
non-Russian population. The peculiar Great Russian and Han
nationalism was one which merged with expansionist "libera-
ting" Communism; it was marked by a Messianic fervor, a
hybrid of chauvinism and "religious" passion embracing the
universe. This analysis, to a large extent, still holds true for
both Communist states, though especially Chinese pragmatism
and the growing time-gap between the Russian October
Revolution and the present have blunted the ideological ardor.

   The importance of the foregoing topic for the study of
international affairs has in the meantime not diminished,
though the two parties involved have for various reasons
decided to tone down their polemics. The divisive issues are
still in existence, not to mention mutual suspicion and massing
of troops on both sides of their long frontier. The Chinese
claims on Soviet territory, never clearly formulated, have not
been relinquished, though they may not be vigorously pressed
at the present time. But the aggression by Vietnam, a Soviet
ally, in Kampuchea (Cambodia) and the Soviet invasion and
occupation of Afghanistan as well as the USSR's over-all policy
in Asia, its maritime encirclement of China and its policy
toward Japan are of major Chinese concern. The ideological
dispute, extending to domestic and foreign affairs, has been
somewhat muted, but has not vanished beyond the horizon.
The CPR and the Soviet Union have exchanged their relative
position in international Communism, the first veering from

* See my review of Ellison's book in *Canadian Review of
Studies in Nationalism*, IX, 1, 1984, pp. 174-76; Treadgold
made the same charge against Zbigniew Brzezinski.

an ultraleftist position to a rightist and revisionist one, the latter moving into the opposite direction, while castigating the "alliance" between the CPR and US imperialism as well as with West European and Japanese capitalism. Yet despite this striking change of position, the hostility between Beijing and Moscow, at times softpedaled for tactical reasons, remains as deep as ever. The deliberate attempt of both sides to avoid extensive discussions of partly esoteric ideological differences and to shelve ideological issues between them-growing out of the conviction that they are insoluble—has by itself not resulted in abating the conflict between them. The ideological switch by the two Communist rivals, has little affected the depth of the controversy; they are still poles apart. If the dispute has been somewhat muted, this, most likely, must be ascribed to tactical considerations rather than to the diminution of ideological and other differences.

I may be permitted to repeat here part of the next two paragraphs from my earlier book: "There is an abundance of articles and journals, of pamphlets and, during the last decade, also of books both in Russian and Chinese pertaining to this topic. This writer has been able to make use of Chinese sources only in English translation. Russian sources, often directly consulted, have been made accessible also through the invaluable aid of the *Current Digest of the Soviet Press.*

In treating the subject matter I have deliberately chosen a combination of the chronological and topical approach. Since the dispute by its very nature took the form of a dialogue, I have also attempted to preserve this framework in order to give the debate between the two world capitals of Communism the character of authenticity and immediate reality. This effect, I believe, is enhanced by numerous quotations to convey to the reader the arguments and the frequently heated atmosphere of a direct confrontation" (p. 10).

While the Chinese and Soviet press and periodicals, a major source for this study, are revealing to various degrees, not all of them are of equal value. The highly important pronouncements of Soviet Party leaders such as Leonid Brezhnev, Yuri Andropov, Konstantin Chernenko, and Mikhail Gorbachev aside, the Soviet newspaper *Pravda* and the government paper *Isvestia* and major journals such as *Kommunist Krasnaya Zvezda* (Red Star), *Literaturnaya*

Gazeta (Literary Gazette), *Novoye Vremya* (New Times), *Mezhdunarodnaya Zhizn* (International Affairs), which government officials and Soviet experts on the CPR use extensively to express official and semi-official views, as well as radio broadcasts constitute significant sources.

On the China side, *Beijing Review*, which is published only in foreign languages, was used again as a major source for Chinese policies, news, and government statements. It also reprints significant articles which previously appeared in the *Journal of International Studies*, the organ of the Ministry of Foreign Affairs, and the *Journal of Contemporary International Relations*, published by the Institute of Contemporary International Relations; its pieces are often written under pseudonyms. Articles on sensitive foreign policy issues are carefully analyzed by the editors to make certain that they represent authoritative views and conform to the government's and the Party's opinions. Governmental views are presented in *Renmin Ribao* (People's Daily) and in the Party's theoretical magazine *Hongqi* (Red Flag), both frequently quoted or reprinted by *Beijing Review*. This is also true of declarations or statements by *Xinhua* (New China News Agency), which are also authoritative.

Among various commentaries, private interviews with government officials and scholars in both Moscow and Beijing, such as used by Banning N. Garrett and Bonnie S. Glaser, *War and Peace, Views from Moscow and Beijing*, Institute of International Studies (Berkeley 1974) constitute a unique supplementary source which this writer has found most useful. These interviews were arranged by the two foregoing authors both in 1981 and 1983, at six Chinese Institutes in Beijing and Shanghai and six Institutes in the Soviet Union. According to the interviewers, some of these scholars clung closely to the Party line, while others occasionally digressed somewhat from government and Party positions. Many Soviet experts on China and Chinese experts on the USSR entertain close relations with government and Party officials of their respective countries. In both states, perhaps contrary to expectations, the views expressed about the other are not necessarily uniform; at times they represent a considerable range of views and opinions. While some of these statements are authoritative, other opinions expressed and views entertained are controversial and are contradicted by their own colleagues.

There can be little doubt that the views and assessments both of the Soviet and Chinese officials and experts about each other have shaped to a significant degree their countries' policies and views on the international balance of power and their assessment of the West European powers, of Japan, and of the Third World. It is evident that Soviet and Chinese perceptions of each other and other outside forces, not to mention of their own situation, are major factors influencing their opinion on international affairs and policies. Perceptions are of course highly subjective and may contain erroneous beliefs. Fear and suspicion, and wishful thinking, may distort the clarity of vision and adversely influence or determine policies. The perception of the third triangular power, the USA, both by the CPR and the Soviet Union is no less important than the perception each has of the other. It was and is Moscow's fear of "collusion" between Beijing and Washington of having to face a possible two-front war which looms behind the alleged "China threat." Similarly, it was Beijing's later view under Mao that the U.S., despite having half a million troops in South Vietnam, was a declining power that, strangely enough, helped to create the vision of a potential alliance with it against the Soviet "threat from the North."

The Soviet push into Afghanistan in December 1979, the Soviet support of Vietnam in Kampuchea, and the USSR's preoccupation with and interference in Poland, contributed substantially to the continuing Sino-American rapprochement. This in turn increased Soviet fears of encirclement. Actually, America's search for alliances was largely the response to the Soviet Union's aggressiveness along her borders and far beyond them.

This book, like its predecessor, is intended primarily for students as well as the general reader. While the literature in the field of Sino-Soviet relations has grown rapidly especially during the last decade, there are still relatively few studies of an introductory, general, and comprehensive character. Most scholarly articles in the USSR and the CPR as well as in Anglo-Saxon countries are written primarily for fellow-scholars rather than for the general public and deal frequently with highly specialized aspects of the Sino-Soviet confrontation.

Though the present work focuses largely on the last decade since Mao's demise, I have considered it necessary to give a bird's eye view on Sino-Soviet relations since the end of World War II to provide the proper background for this study. My previous book fulfilled this need also for the post-World War I period. It is still imperative, as it was before, to attempt to trace the record of the Sino-Soviet relationship and to reach even the most tentative judgment about its nature.

While generally the name "Peking" has been used for the earlier period of this study, the name "Beijing" has replaced it especially for the last decade or so.

November 1986

Alfred D. Low
(Professor Emeritus,
Marquette University)
Bellevue, Washington

I

THE DEVELOPMENT
OF THE SINO-SOVIET DISPUTE

A. An Overview of the Dispute. 1945-1976

The USSR and the Last Phase of the Chinese Civil War

While Nazi Germany in 1945 was in its death throes and the outcome of China's war against Japanese imperialism was no longer in doubt, the Seventh National Party Congress of the C.P.C. was held in Yenan from April 24 to June 11, 1945. On the eve of its meeting an Enlarged Plenary Session of the Sixth Central Committee produced an important document, "Resolutions and Questions in Party History." These resolutions, passed only four days before the opening of the Seventh Congress, were a triumph for Mao, sanctioning all of his policies and warning of past "right" and "left" deviations in the C.P.C. The resolutions proclaimed that the practice of the Chinese Revolution during the last twenty-four years had proved that the line represented by Mao was "entirely correct."(1)

It was on August 8, 1945, that the entry of the U.S.S.R. into the Far Eastern War occurred. In a quick nine-day war Russia occupied all of Manchuria, with the exception of the province of Jehol in the southwest. The Allied High Command, instructed on highest authority to have Chiang Kaishek decide upon the disposition of all Allied forces in China, responded to his demand for lifting his troops into the regions occupied by Japanese troops. These troops, which still controlled all the cities in Northern and Eastern China and many along the Yangtze, and their puppet Chinese units, were ordered to surrender only to the Kuomintang forces, not to the Communists. This American policy appeared to the Communists as an outright intervention in behalf of the corrupt Kuomintang, which was thus able to extend its operations to the north and was anxious to halt the land reform and other reforms that the Communists had introduced. In the immediate postwar period many Chinese, especially the educated class, already alienated from the Kuomintang but not yet ready to endorse Communism, preferred a coalition government to a reoccupation of the North by Chiang's forces; such an occupation might only unleash full civil war.

The U.S.S.R. could have turned over Manchuria, the most industrialized province in China, intact to the Communists. Had Russia adopted this policy, the Communists, who already controlled the rural areas in the north and east of China, would have been able to lay their hands on a considerable industrial potential and could soon have defeated the Kuomintang.

Yet the Soviet Union kept the Chinese Communists at arm's length. The U.S.S.R. was not to recognize Communist China until 1949. In 1945 she negotiated only with Chiang and his government. Contrary to the belief in a worldwide Communist conspiracy, which then and for years to come dominated Western public opinion and political thinking, the Soviet Union and the Chinese Communists were by no means working hand in glove. The U.S.S.R. gave full support neither to Chiang nor to the Communists, but pursued a contradictory policy which left most bystanders puzzled.

It has been suggested that Russian lack of knowledge of China and of the Far East, Stalin's prejudices, and his fears of Communist China's likely independent stance and of her future competition with the USSR were responsible for this policy. To this must be added the lack of any long-range Soviet policy planning and resort to improvisation, as well as the consistent underestimation of Mao and the C.P.C. The Chinese Revolution had gone on for more than a generation and the likelihood that the Communists were on the eve of winning the civil war appeared only slight to Stalin.

The Russians began gradually to evacuate Manchuria, turning the cities over to the Kuomintang troops who were flown in to take control. But the Manchurian countryside was occupied by Chinese Communist troops from North China. Even if the Soviets had been genuinely interested in preventing the latter occupation, they would have been unable to do so. By returning the cities to the Nationalists and leaving the countryside to the Communists, they followed what was probably the line of least resistance, considering their relations with the West and with Chiang, a course likely to produce the least friction with their allies. At the same time, however, the Soviet troops, by stripping Manchuria of industrial equipment and carrying it off, gratified their own national desires, though definitely weakening the C.P.C. in its continuing struggle for power. Though the Chinese Communists did not criticize Russian policy in Manchuria, it must have bitterly disappointed them. The agreement reached later between Stalin and Mao to return Manchurian industrial equipment to China was both a vindication of the justice of China's claims and an embarrassment to the Soviet Union, since she had to admit having taken this equipment illegally. By having deprived the Communists of these materials at a crucial stage in their combat with Chiang, the Soviet Union served ill the interests of an allegedly close comrade-in-arms.

In 1947 Chiang failed to conquer Shantung, to establish the connection with the north, and to expand control of the Kuomintang in Manchuria. Still, in July 1948 at a communist conference in South Hopei, Liu Shao-ch'i, who had returned from Russia, expounded Stalin's recommendation that the Chinese Communists refrain from mounting a major offensive to bring the civil war to a rapid conclusion and rather continue guerrilla war. Other Chinese leaders, including Chou En-lai, held however, that the war should be pressed till final victory was won. Actually, within a few weeks the Nationalists lost all of Manchuria and North China. After the fall of Mukden, Chiang left Beijing. On February 3, 1949, the Communists entered Beijing; no Soviet weapons were seen when the Communist troops paraded through the city.

The Treaty of Alliance, 1950, and Economic and Cultural Exchange

In earlier days Mao frequently attempted to justify his "leaning-to-one-side," leaning-to-Russia policy. He claimed that Communist China had "no other choice," since the U.S.S.R. was "our best teacher from whom we must learn."(2) Communist ideology aside, the C.P.C. repeatedly underlined the systematic and rapid industrialization of the U.S.S.R. and especially of Siberia, which because of its proximity made a special impact upon the C.P.R., as a case in point. Also, American hostility to Communism and Communist China in particular had become quite obvious during the last phase of the civil war.

The Moscow-Beijing alliance, forged in February 1950, seemed in the best interests of both the Soviet Union and Communist China. It furnished the Soviet Union a junior partner against the United States. The U.S. had led the resistance against further expansion of the U.S.S.R. in Europe and had established N.A.T.0. as first line of defense and a means of containing Soviet Russia. The United States was also the dominant nation in the Pacific and, as occupying power in the Japanese islands, a virtual neighbor of the Soviet Union in regard both to the Far Eastern Province and Sakhalin. Thus the alliance with China would strengthen the U.S.S.R. against the American threat of encirclement in Europe and in Asia. The alliance promised to end the Soviet Union's isolation in the world and especially to protect the vulnerable long Siberian coast line.

As far as the CPR was concerned, she probably needed the alliance even more than the U.S.S.R. In 1949-50, Communist China, though she had won the civil war, appeared dangerously isolated and in urgent need of a powerful military ally. Her political and military gains at home might again be challenged by the United States. China needed help in the creation of a modern military establishment. The alliance with the Soviet Union might enable Communist China to learn more quickly about Western science and technological "know-how." By sending technicians and experts, the Soviet Union might help China to bridge the gulf between its underdeveloped condition and the rapid and advanced industrialization that was its goal. A strengthened China would be able to regain influence in the lost border regions and to restore the traditional power that its predecessor, the "Middle Kingdom," had exerted in these strategic areas.

The Sino-Soviet Treaty of February 1950, called a Treaty of Friendship, Alliance and Mutual Assistance, pledged the two partners to far-reaching cooperation for at least three decades along ideological, political, economic, cultural, and, last but not least, military lines. The very preamble of the treaty asserted the determination of the two signatories to oppose jointly the rebirth of Japanese imperialism as well as aggressive moves of other states in collaboration with Japan. This, unmistakably, was aimed against the United States. Though Communist China was not a member of the United Nations, the preamble of the treaty promised that the two powers would always act in conformity with the aims and principles of the world organization. The following articles were of primary significance. Article 1 pledged the two signatories to come to each other's military assistance in the event that peace should be violated by Japan or any state collaborating with her directly or indirectly. Both sides promised in Article 3 not to take part in any coalition or action against the other signatory. Article 4 required the two Communist powers to coordinate their foreign policies and the Soviets to support the entry of Communist China into the United Nations. Article 5 finally pledged both powers to develop and strengthen their economic and cultural ties. Yet economic assistance must be "in conformity with the principles of equality, mutual benefit and of mutual respect for the national sovereignty, territorial integrity and non-interference in internal affairs" of the other party. In theory at least, the treaty was based upon the assumption of full equality between the two communist powers. Though defensive in form, many believed they discerned in the treaty a grand plan to expel the United States from the mainland of Asia and even from the western Pacific.

In a covenant signed simultaneously with the Sino-Soviet Treaty, the U.S.S.R. renounced its old sphere of influence in Manchuria. Though the Chinese Eastern Railway and the South Manchurian Railway, Port Arthur, and Dairen were not turned over to China forthwith, the USSR pledged to do so within the next years. This pledge, however, was somewhat qualified: The Soviet Union, jointly with China, could use Port Arthur for conducting joint military operations in the event of aggression by Japan or any power that might collaborate with Japan. Still, there could be little doubt that the USSR had been compelled to promise to return shortly to China most of the gains she had wrested from Chiang in 1945. The Soviet Union's far-reaching privileges in the Far East, which she had acquired after the turn of the century, had soon lost to Japan, but recovered in 1945, now had to be returned to the Chinese comrades. No comparable concessions — excepting perhaps the return of some Finnish bases acquired during and after World War II — were made by Soviet Russia to any of her European neighbors and comradely Parties.

Of special significance for China was the Soviet pledge to turn over to China the Manchurian "war booty" that the U.S.S.R. had seized from the Japanese in 1945. This was to be done without compensation, just as the Manchurian railways were to be returned without any indemnification — clear admission that Soviet seizure of these properties from the Kuomintang govern- ment had no legal or moral basis. There were also to be established joint Sino-Soviet stock companies to operate in Manchuria and Sinkiang, and a rather niggardly loan of 300 million dollars was to be granted to Beijing.

In an exchange of separate notes, Communist China acknowledged "the independent status of the Mongolian People's Republic." Here was one area that the U.S.S.R. had effectively detached from China in the nineteen twenties. The Mongolian People's Republic had gained independence in 1945, an arrangement quite favorable to the Soviet Union. Communist China failed, however, to regain it in 1950. The Soviets no doubt could hide behind the assertion that the final separation of Outer Mongolia in 1945 had not led to its incorporation into the U.S.S.R. but to its independent status, and that it was beyond the power and outside the jurisdiction of the Soviet Union to reverse a process that affected only Outer Mongolia and China, and not herself. Actually, in the mid-fifties, Krushchev, when confronted by Mao regarding Outer Mongolia, advised the Chinese leader to deal with Ulan Bator directly. The Sino-Soviet Treaty of February 1950, concluded after a stay of unusual length by Mao and the Chinese Delegation in Moscow, and only a few months after the proclamation of the C.P.R., left no doubt about the actual inequality between the two Communist partners.

On October 11, 1954, another Sino-Soviet treaty was signed which elaborated and partly implemented the earlier pact of February 1950. The treaty contained, however, some concessions to Beijing. While under the earlier agreement China, through joint stock companies, close technical and thus economic supervision and military control in some strategic areas was in a state almost approaching tutelage vis-à-vis the U.S.S.R., the new treaty pledged Soviet evacuation of Port Arthur by the spring of 1955 and the dissolution of the joint stock companies. The "unequal treaty" of 1950 was substantially modified. In Chinese eyes, however, it was merely a beginning.

The period after the conclusion of the Sino-Soviet treaty of February 1950 had been marked by an enormous increase in cultural, economic, technical, military, and political exchanges between Moscow and Beijing. They were based upon China's eagerness to learn as much as possible from the Soviet partner, to strengthen her economic and military stance in the world at large, not excluding that vis-à-vis the Soviet Union itself, and to bridge as rapidly as possible the gulf between itself and the technologically advanced countries of the world. They were also rooted in the Soviet Union's willingness to help less-fortunate China in the expectation that its own eminent stature as the Mecca of world Communism and as the economically and culturally leading country in the Communist bloc would be enhanced by the spectacle of seemingly selfless comradely help.

To further Sino-Soviet relations, Beijing sponsored the Sino-Soviet Friendship Association. Founded on October 5, 1949, only five days after the proclamation of the C.P.R. itself, it was headed by Liu Shao-Ch'i. The Association claimed a membership of 40 million, distributed articles praising the U.S.S.R., and published a surprisingly large number of special magazines and books year after year. It sponsored and organized numerous speeches and rallies in behalf of Sino-Soviet collaboration and distributed Soviet films and plays. It helped arrange tours through China for Soviet trade, technical, political, and sport organizations, and artistic and theater groups. It was responsible for programs in the Russian language over Beijing radio and encouraged the adoption of Soviet educational methods and curricula in the country's schools. With its counterparts in the U.S.S.R., it provided for a continuous exchange of cultural delegations, scientists, lecturers, writers, and actors between the two countries.

The War in Korea

Following the proclamation of the C.P.R. in Beijing in
October 1949 and the flight of Chiang to Taiwan and the
establishment there of his government, the United States
under President Truman refused to give support to Chiang
and, in the words of the President on January 5, 1950, to
become involved "in the civil conflict in China." Both the
President and Secretary of State Dean Acheson considered
Taiwan an integral part of China. Though the United States
did not move toward recognition of Mao and his government,
neither did they at first contemplate furnishing aid or advice to
Kuomintang military forces on Taiwan.

In a speech on January 12, 1950, Secretary Dean Acheson
drew a line of America's primary defense in the Far East,
clearly differentiating between regions of primary and
secondary interest to the United States. He significantly did
not include Korea within the American "military perimeter."
(3) At the very time Acheson gave his address, Mao was in
Moscow for a visit that lasted two full months. In another
speech, on March 15, 1950, again about Asia and the Pacific,
Dean Acheson suggested no changes in regard to America's
defense perimeter in Asia. For the moment, tension in Korea
neither abated nor increased and both North and South Korea
continued to display aggressive hostility. In mid-June, John
Foster Dulles, on a personal mission to Asia in behalf of
Secretary Acheson, visited the 38th parallel, also without an
inkling of the coming attack.

The attack came on June 25th. President Truman
responded immediately by declaring that the United States
would defend South Korea. Because of the United Nations'
refusal to seat Communist China, the Soviet Union, boycotting
the Security Council, was absent when the attack on South
Korea started. Thereupon the Security Council denounced
North Korea as aggressor. The War in Korea was in full swing.

America's responses were based on the assumption that
behind North Korea stood Communist China, not the
U.S.S.R. In a note to Moscow President Truman pleaded with
the Soviets to persuade the North Korean leader Kim Il Sung
to withdraw his invading troops from the South. After the start
of the Korean War the American President promptly gave

Chiang full support—which he had so far refused to do. He ordered the Seventh Fleet to sail into the Taiwan straits to protect Taiwan from a mainland attack. At the same time military aid was dispatched to the Philippines. The President even sent a military mission to Indochina to lend assistance to the French, who were already in dire straits. All American moves seemed to be designed to block China on all sides. But was there sufficient reason to assume that China had plotted and abetted the Korean attack and was at the point of plunging into further adventures?

It can hardly be assumed that North Korea undertook the attack without advance notice to the Soviet Union, without having consulted her and having received the promise of help if it should be needed. Kim Il Sung, who had spent many years in Russia, was a confidant of the Soviets and had been placed by them in power in Pyongyang. Though Soviet troops had been withdrawn from North Korea in January 1949—earlier than American troops from South Korea—numerous Russian advisors were left behind to continue training the North Korean troops. In 1950 North Korea was still, for all practical purposes, a satellite of Moscow. By the time of the outbreak of the Korean War, the regime of Communist China was less than a year old; it had not even yet established diplomatic relations with North Korea. Such ties, however, were knit in August 1950, two months after the outbreak of the Korean War.

It appears most likely that the North Korean attack was agreed upon in Moscow by the North Koreans and Russians, probably after Mao's visit to the Soviet capital. The Communist victory in China was probably interpreted in North Korea as a defeat of the United States, Chiang's friend and ally, and may have given encouragement to her own aggressive designs. It is quite likely that the North Korean attack caused as much surprise in Beijing as it did in Washington, D. C.

At the time of the outbreak of the war, Stalin held strong positions in North Korea, Mongolia, and Manchuria. He had his own man, Kao Kang, in control in strategic and resource-rich Manchuria. Beijing accused him later of having aspired to establish a separate "kingdom" of his own in Manchuria and to detach the province from China, and denounced him as a traitor. (Not long after Stalin's death, Kao Kang was to commit suicide.) In 1949, before the C.P.R. was proclaimed, Kao had indeed attempted to set up the Northeast China Region. He then had rushed to Moscow and signed a treaty for Manchuria as if the latter were an independent country. The Northeast China Region for a time survived the proclamation of the C.P.R. in October 1949.

Seen against the background of Soviet interests in the Chinese border regions, stretching from Sinkiang to Manchuria and beyond it to Korea, the outbreak of the Korean War had special meaning and significance. A control of Korea through Stalin, according to Harrison Salisbury, would "place Mao in a nutcracker."(4) Obviously, Stalin proved to have been mistaken. He did not anticipate the American and the United Nations' intervention. When in the course of the war all of North Korea seemed to be lost and Americans were approaching the Yalu river, the Soviet Union, which had furnished arms and equipment for the North Koreans, continued to hold back Russian troops and specialists, except for a few. Surprisingly enough, it was China that intervened, thus transforming the Korean conflict into a Sino-American war. And at the end of the fighting, it was China that appeared as the most loyal and trustworthy ally of North Korea, as her savior.

After Stalin

The death of Stalin on March 5, 1953, was to have a decisive impact upon the further development of Sino-Soviet relations. Mao himself did not attend Stalin's funeral. Perhaps he recalled grievances nurtured earlier with regard to Stalin's imperious attitude toward China and Chinese Communism, or he might have wished to demonstrate his new status vis-à-vis the new ruling group in the Kremlin—mere epigones as compared to himself, a charismatic and undisputed leader in his own Party and country, now a senior Communist in the world Communist movement. He sent Chou En-lai to the funeral, while he himself remained in Beijing. On the other hand, the new Soviet leaders, in order to boost their relative position in the struggle for power, attempted to create the impression of being on best terms with Mao. Beria and

Malenkov, riding high in the first days after Stalin's death, displayed a photograph depicting the signing of the Sino-Soviet alliance on February 1950 that placed Malenkov next to Mao himself. The alleged closeness of the Chinese Communist leadership to the new rulers in the Kremlin was to give an air of legitimacy to themİ As late as February 1955, Molotov referred to the socialist camp as being "led by the Soviet Union and China,"(5) a statement that gave China an unprecedented and, as a matter of fact, never repeated recognition.

The years between 1953 and 1955 witnessed the emergence first of a "collective leadership" in the Soviet Union and the gradual rise of Khrushchev to the headship of both Party and state. During this period, when a struggle for power gripped the Soviet leadership, a decisive change in the Sino-Soviet relationship was not in the offing. Also, after the end of the "hot" war in the Far East, the U.S.S.R., deeply involved in the cold war with the West, faced then problems of greater importance in Europe than in Asia. In 1954 she energetically pushed her plans for the introduction of an international socialist division of labor in the Council for Mutual Economic Assistance (CMEA) and was deeply concerned about the German problem and the West's attempts to integrate Bonn militarily into N.A.T.O. and, economically and ideologically, into the West European system.

After the end of the Korean War, the consolidation in the C.P.R. and the diplomatic successes at Geneva in 1954 and at the Bandung Conference in 1955 that were to come her way, Communist China's self-confidence grew by leaps and bounds. Despite her inability to crush the boastful and hostile Taiwan regime, the C.P.R. displayed a new pride and self-assurance. The adoption of a new constitution in September 1954 by the First National People's Congress was as much an expression of her revolutionary ardor as of her nationalist exuberance. Her nationalist intransigence now showed itself in increasing toughness during the negotiations with the U.S.S.R., in her insistence for the modification of numerous clauses, if not entire treaties, that had been concluded with the Soviets only a few years before. Communist China clearly flexed her muscles. Mao had become increasingly critical of the value of the "mixed companies" that the U.S.S.R. had established in China, just as she had in her East European satellites. The

C.P.R., jealous of her "sovereign" economic rights and resentful of the "privileged" position of any foreign power in China—even though it was that of a friendly, "comradely" state like the U.S.S.R., the fatherland of socialism itself— pressured the Soviet Union into relinquishing some of the concessions granted to her earlier.

Chinese self-confidence found full expression in a joint Sino-Soviet communique, signed in Beijing in October 1954. It ominously stressed that after the termination of the war in both Korea and Indochina the "defense potential" of the C.P.R. had been strengthened, and announced the withdrawal of Soviet military forces from the area of the Port Arthur naval base. The C.P.R., which in 1949-50 had been anxious to conclude the military treaty of alliance with the U.S.S.R. against Japan and any power allied with Japan, had met the enemy on the Korean battlefield and thereafter felt confident enough to ask for the liquidation of the Soviet military establishment on Chinese soil. Thus Communist China was on the march to assert her economic and military independence; in her infancy, when she had been weak and the United States hostile, she had been compelled to mortgage it to the Soviet Union.

Khrushchev's activist policy toward the Third World, which commenced immediately after the Bandung Conference, testifies to Soviet concern over Beijing's making headway among the underdeveloped countries. This new worldwide activity of the U.S.S.R. under Khrushchev was for Beijing an unwelcome contrast to the more limited and cautious Soviet foreign policy under Stalin; Beijing could hardly appreciate what threatened to develop into a brisk competition. Still, after its long perilous voyage, the ship of Sino-Soviet friendship seemed finally to encounter good weather conditions.

Even the Bandung Conference in 1955 did not appear to disturb the basic relationship of the U.S.S.R. and the C.P.R. as comrades and allies, though China's sudden rise to diplomatic eminence and her apparent claim to leadership in Asia and Africa must have produced angry shock waves in the U.S.S.R. After Chou's role at the Geneva Conference, his star performance at the Bandung Conference no doubt aroused envy and concern in Moscow, even if, as some assume, between 1950 and 1955 Moscow and Beijing did arrange between themselves some sort of division into different spheres of influence and activities.(6)

In any case, between 1949, when the C.P.R. was proclaimed, and 1955, when the Bandung Conference was held, Communist China appeared to have completed a full circle. Starting out with a revolutionary foreign policy sharpened by the early confrontation with the United States in Korea, she ended by eagerly embracing the principles of peaceful coexistence and actually reconciling herself to the domination of imperialism in many parts of the world. At Bandung Chou hobnobbed with the representatives of bourgeois Asian and African states, already hopeful of becoming in due time, their champion and leader. Chou attempted to persuade the neutralist countries that the C.P.R. was a firm believer in "peaceful coexistence," trying to make them forget that she had ever talked, or acted, to the contrary. To the surprise of many participants at the Conference and other observers, Chou outshone even Nehru. The U.S.S.R., though also an Asiatic power, was not represented at this Afro-Asian conference, probably to her lasting disadvantage.

Were the preoccupations of the U.S.S.R. with Europe responsible for the neglect of her interest in Asia? After West Germany joined the N.A.T.O. pact, the U.S.S.R. was busily engaged in taking appropriate countermeasures. In May 1955 there was created the Warsaw Pact, providing for mutual defense and military aid among the Eastern bloc countries. The same eight countries that formed the economic group called the CMEA (Council for Mutual Economic Assistance) now pledged mutual military defense to the Soviet Union and to each other. China, however, was neither a member of CMEA nor of the Warsaw Pact. Distant from Europe, the C.P.R. was also in other respects in a category sui generis, in a situation that was not comparable to that of any of the European satellites of the U.S.S.R.

The Twentieth Congress of the CPSU, February 1956, and the Eighth Party Congress of the CPC, September 1956

The year 1956 represented a turning point in the domestic history of both the U.S.S.R. and the C.P.R. It was the year of the Twentieth Congress of the C.P.S.U. at which Khrushchev

denounced Stalin, and the year of the Eighth Congress of the
C.P.C. which, half a year later, reaffirmed the basic policies of
Moscow and diminished Mao's exalted stature. Though it
represented a stage of apparent agreement between Moscow
and Beijing, in the light of subsequent developments it proved
to be one of the last fleeting moments of harmony and
concordance.

The Twentieth Congress of the C.P.S.U., which opened in
February 1956, launched a two-pronged program, the policies
of so-called de-Stalinization and peaceful coexistence, both of
which had large domestic and foreign implications. De-
Stalinization produced the effect of a bombshell in the
U.S.S.R., shocked the Communist world to its foundation,
and was also to affect adversely Sino-Soviet relations. The
other theme of peaceful coexistence,(7) taking account of the
worldwide longing for peace, had obvious propagandistic
significance, but also reflected the Soviet desire to avoid an
unnecessary war; it was to have a decisive impact upon
Soviet-Western as well as Soviet-Chinese relations.

The downgrading of Stalin had already begun soon after
his death, but it was an embarrassed, stealthy, and ambiguous
undertaking, rather than an open criticism of Stalin and frank
admission of the errors and crimes the Soviet government had
committed under his leadership. Therefore Khrushchev's
blunt and uninhibited accusations against Stalin at the
Twentieth Congress, even though coming three years after his
death, represented a bold, unprecedented move and ushered
in a revolution in the political and intellectual climate of the
U.S.S.R. Beijing, however, was to become increasingly
suspicious of de-Stalinization.

The theme of peaceful coexistence, though proclaimed at
the Twentieth Party Congress, had at various earlier moments
been given greater emphasis, most recently by Malenkov at the
Nineteenth Party Congress in October 1952, at which Stalin
was still present. In the years immediately thereafter, Beijing
too seemed to have endorsed the principles of peaceful
coexistence, which were also incorporated in an agreement
between China and India signed on April 29, 1954. In April
1955, at the Bandung Conference of Afro-Asian states, Chou
repudiated the concept of war with the United States and
declared his readiness to enter into negotiations with the

American government for purposes of lessening tension in the Far East. Beijing did not spurn the concept of peaceful coexistence.

But Khrushchev's views, as expressed at the Twentieth Party Congress, were sharply criticized by Beijing, especially his concept that transition from capitalism to socialism could be effected "through the parliamentary road." Khrushchev, according to Beijing, had also questioned the continued validity of Lenin's teachings on imperialism and on war and peace. Distorting Lenin's correct principle of peaceful coexistence between countries with different social systems, Khrushchev, Beijing asserted, had in practice excluded from the foreign policy of the socialist countries their mutual assistance and cooperation as well as their assistance to revolutionary struggles of the oppressed peoples and nations. He had sacrificed these struggles at the altar of "peaceful coexistence."(8)

Khrushchev's speech, as well as the resolutions of the Twentieth Congress of the C.P.S.U., revealed, according to Beijing, a paternalistic attitude toward Communist China. No threat to the Soviet Union's undisputed preeminence among the Communist-led nations was yet in sight. The concepts of peaceful transition to socialism — all soon to be questioned by Beijing — were here elaborated. At the Twentieth Congress of the C.P.S.U., the C.P.R. evidently stood out clearly among all People's Republics. She was given credit for her pioneering experience, her role in international affairs, and her likely importance for the further expansion of Communism among the peoples of the East. Yet the generous assistance given by the U.S.S.R. to the C.P.R. and to fraternal Communist Parties and underdeveloped nations in general was not forgotten.

When the Twentieth Congress of the C.P.S.U. opened its doors, Chou, the Chinese delegate to the congress, read a message from Mao that praised the C.P.S.U., "created by Lenin and reared by Stalin and his close comrades-in-arms."(9) Ten days later, Khrushchev, then leader of the C.P.S.U., denounced his predecessor and master, the man who had "reared" the Party. Moscow's apparent lack of previous consultation with Mao must have been most embarrassing to the Chinese delegation. Or was Mao's praise a last-minute

attempt to halt the impending criticism by Khrushchev? The
Chinese opposition to the Soviet denigration of Stalin, in
combination with the still strong Stalinist influences in the
U.S.S.R. and the unexpected repercussions of de-Stalinization
in the revolt in Hungary and Poland in 1956, compelled
Khrushchev to retreat significantly the following year.

But a few weeks after Khrushchev's denunciation of Stalin,
Pravda, on March 28, 1956, had openly attacked the "cult of
the individual." It criticized it as an "inordinate glorification
of individuals ..., making them almost miracle-workers and
worshipping them. Such incorrect conceptions of man, and
specifically of J. V. Stalin, which are alien to the spirit of
Marxism-Leninism, developed and were cultivated among us
for many years."(10)

The Chinese view of Stalin and of Khrushchev's criticism of
him at the Twentieth Party Congress was expressed in an
article of *People's Daily*, "On the Historical Experience of the
Dictatorship of the Proletariat," on April 5, 1956. Its author
called Stalin "an outstanding Marxist-Leninist fighter,"
though he had "erroneously exaggerated his own role and
counterposed his individual authority to the collective
leadership," as a result of which "certain of his actions were
opposed to certain fundamental Marxist-Leninist concepts."
(11) Though *People's Daily* underlined that the masses were
the "makers of history," it claimed at the same time that,
according to Marxism-Leninism, leaders played a "big role in
history." It was "utterly wrong" to "deny the role of the
individual, the role of forerunners and leaders. . ." In spite of
its deceptive appearance of objectivity, the article was an
obvious attempt to cling desperately to the elusive phenomenon of Stalin's pervasive greatness, conceding merely a few
weaknesses.(12)

As Beijing revealed later, in 1963, the attack against Stalin
appeared to it as criticism of a foe rather than that of a
comrade-in-arms and friend, as complete negativism and as an
attack against the dictatorship of the proletariat and the
Communist movement itself. Beijing apparently feared that
Moscow's attempt at self-purification would irretrievably sully
revolutionary socialism.

Only a few months after the Twentieth Congress of the
C.P.S.U., on September 8, 1956, the Eighth Party Congress of

the C.P.C. convened.(13) The de-emphasis of Mao and the
implied criticism of "personality cult," the insistence on Party
democracy and, in foreign affairs, the stress on peaceful
coexistence—all this was of course quite in line with the
policies proclaimed by the Twentieth Party Congress of the
C.P.S.U. earlier that year. The Eighth Party Congress of the
C.P.C. seemed to be a worthy sequel to the Congress of the
C.P.S.U., reaffirming some of its basic policies and toeing its
line. Mao personally may not have liked this course, but the
C.P.C. clearly ranged itself at the side of the C.P.S.U. Both
parties and countries seemed to march shoulder to shoulder
and to follow a more "liberal" Communist line. Moscow then
approved of Beijing's course and continued to do so even later,
though its own policy was to become less "liberal." The
C.P.C.'s Eighth Party Congress has always pleased the
C.P.S.U., since it acknowledged the theme of "peaceful
coexistence" with the West, recognized Moscow's leadership
within the Communist bloc, and assigned a more modest role
to Mao than the Seventh Congress had done.

*China's Intervention in the Polish and Hungarian Crises and
the U.S.S.R., October-November 1956*

After Stalin's death both the U.S.S.R. and its satellite
Empire went through a period of prolonged crisis. Khrushchev's denunciation of Stalin at the Twentieth Congress of the
C.P.S.U. had unleashed a veritable storm, and giant waves
swept throughout the Communist world. In October 1956 both
Hungary and Poland were gripped by revolution, Moscow was
faced with one of the most crucial decisions in its history—
military intervention or defection of Hungary—and China, in
a stunning turn of events, was called upon to play the role of
moderator.

On October 31, 1956, *Pravda* published a "Declaration by
the Government of the U.S.S.R. on the Principles of
Development and Further strengthening of Friendship and
Cooperation between the Soviet Union and Other Socialist
States," bearing the date of October 30.(14) The declaration,
referring to the Polish and Hungarian events of late October
1956, freely admitted that in the process of the rise of the
system of people's democracies after the Second World War

many different unresolved problems and downright mistakes, "including mistakes in the mutual relations among the socialist countries," had occurred—"violations and errors which demeaned the principle of equality in relation among socialist states." In reference to Hungary in particular, the Soviet Government voiced its "deep regret" for the bloodshed that had taken place. This declaration by the Soviet Government was hailed in the people's democracies and in the C.P.R. On November 2, 1956, *People's Daily*, the organ of the Central Committee of the C.P.C., in the article "Long Live the Great Unity of the Socialist Countries," called the Soviet declaration a highly significant document.(15) Simultaneously with this authoritative article was published the official Beijing Statement on the Declaration of the Soviet Government on Relations Among Socialist States, November 1, 1956. The Statement drew the conclusion that leading members of the Beijing government and the people of the entire country must at all times be vigilant to prevent the error of big-nation chauvinism in relations with socialist countries and others, and carry out appropriate education. Thus Beijing seemingly refrained from adding its own criticism to Soviet self-criticism. But under the guise of approving the most recent Soviet statement, the C.P.C. actually castigated Soviet policy. Referring to the Soviet-Yugoslav dispute of 1948-49, it expressed the view that the errors that led to the crisis in Poland and Hungary were of long standing and that the post-Stalin regime had not improved on Soviet conduct with socialist states; it was actually guilty of an unforgivable crime—of "bourgeois chauvinism," of "big-nation chauvinism."

Beijing had not challenged the U.S.S.R. at the moment of acute crisis in Eastern Europe; on the contrary, it had appeared fearful of its possible consequences for the entire socialist bloc, including Communist China. But it came out strongly for the just demands of the peoples of Hungary and Poland and for their "democratic independence" and equality. Beijing held that these demands could be satisfied within the socialist bloc without destroying its unity.

The Chinese leaders appear to have given encouragement to the movement of the East European peoples for greater autonomy from Moscow. Mao is alleged to have urged the Poles not only to develop greater "autonomy," but also to model their social system after the Yugoslav pattern. During the October crisis, after Khrushchev's sudden appearance in the Polish capital, Warsaw quickly appealed to Beijing, and with apparent success. Beijing let Moscow know of its opposition to Soviet armed intervention in Poland. Communist China's position toward the Hungarian and Polish revolutions was, however, an ambiguous one. On the one hand, Beijing was favorably inclined toward polycentrist tendencies in Communism which, if successful, were likely to strengthen her own position vis-à-vis the U.S.S.R. On the other hand, as a major state with vast human, natural, and geographic resources, the C.P.R. was in a different position from that of the smaller East European satellites of the U.S.S.R. and might have anticipated the time when she herself would be the center of a satellite empire, similar to the one the U.S.S.R. had created in Europe after World War II. She also might have feared the impact of a successful Hungarian and Polish challenge to the Soviet Union and of the possible defection of either from the Socialist camp.

Communist China, taking advantage of the crisis in Europe, threw, to the amazement of the entire world, her weight into the European scales. She thus accomplished an unprecedented feat, one of the great diplomatic revolutions in modern times. China's voice suddenly was attentively listened to in Europe. Beijing then appeared to some as the very champion of national equality in the Socialist camp. Her role, however, due to the generally obsequious tone and behavior toward the U.S.S.R. and continuing recognition of her overall leadership, was apparently not resented by the latter.

Moscow was probably not entirely happy about China's continued forays into Europe, but might have considered her diplomatic and comradely ventures in East European affairs helpful to a degree. Poland, at least, seemed to be appreciative of China's role as a reliable "good and tried friend," though Hungary's hopes for Chinese assistance were rather disappointed.(16)

"Long Live Leninism"

An article published by *Red Flag* on April 16, 1960, and possibly authored by Mao himself, was the first in a series entitled "Long Live Leninism."(17) The publication was to play a major role in the unfolding of the Sino-Soviet dispute. In publishing this series, Beijing still deliberately refrained from openly criticizing the C.P.S.U. It was rather against the imperialists and the Yugoslav revisionists that it seemed to direct its strongest arrows. But actually it was Moscow which, in its view, created "serious confusion" in the ranks of the international Communist movement and was the real target.

The major thrust of the article was a criticism of modern revisionism, as exemplified by the doctrines of Tito. The C.P.C., it was asserted, was the true heir of Lenin's legacy, while the C.P.S.U. was held as having betrayed it, jettisoned it as mere cumbrous ballast. The world was once again assured that socialist countries "never permit themselves to send, never should and never will send their troops across their borders, unless of course they were subjected to aggression from a foreign enemy."

The U.S.S.R. was given full recognition for being the first socialist state, now "headed by comrade Khrushchev," in which a great period of extensive building of communism had definitely begun. Among China's accomplishments, despite their already apparent failures, were mentioned the Great Leap Forward and the People's Communes, since they had inspired the initiative and revolutionary spirit of the Chinese masses.

A prompt answer to the first articles in the series "Long Live Leninism" was Kuusinen's speech on the anniversary of Lenin's birth, delivered at a formal meeting in Moscow.(18) Just as Beijing's criticism was still restrained and of an indirect nature, Moscow's reply followed the same pattern; both parties carefully avoided criticizing the other openly. But Kuusinen's emphasis on peaceful coexistence, his praise for Khrushchev as its champion, his virtual omission of war in his prognosis of outstanding trends for the rest of the century and his support of aid to underdeveloped, including non-socialist countries, ran counter to some of the main theses of the recent Chinese publications.

The conflict between Moscow and Beijing took on new aspects during the summer and autumn of 1960; it grew in intensity along both political and economic lines. Once again Moscow apparently underestimated Chinese pride, determina-

tion, resourcefulness, and her resistance to economic mishaps
— the "Great Leap" and the unexpected natural calamities,
especially bad weather. These reverses, in combination with
Soviet pressure, resulted in stiffening Communist China's
resistance and deepening her resolve to persevere in her
theoretical position and political isolation.

During the autumn of 1962 Soviet and Chinese foreign
policy thrusts deepened the differences between Beijing and
Moscow and set the stage for the explosive war of words
between the two Communist rivals that was to erupt in 1963.
Divisive issues that dominated the stage and were to extend
into 1963 and even beyond it were the Soviet-Yugoslav
rapprochement, the Cuban missile crisis and, simultaneously
with the latter, the Sino-Indian border conflict.

The Cuban crisis and the outbreak of the Sino-Indian war
virtually coincided. The first crisis pitted the U.S.S.R. against
the United States of America, the second juxtaposed
Communist China against the next most populous country in
the world, India, leader of the uncommitted Third World.
Chinese criticism of Soviet policy in the Cuban confrontation
and Soviet criticism of Indo-Chinese hostilities were bound to
deepen the chasm between the two "fraternal" parties and
leave permanent wounds.

Peaceful Coexistence - with the West and with each other

After attempting to show that the settlement in the
Caribbean had allegedly been reached on the basis of mutual
concessions and exemplified peaceful coexistence in action,
Pravda continued trying to prove that such coexistence did not
prevent the progress of the national-liberation movement and
of the class struggle in capitalist countries. The paper seemed
especially sensitive in regard to the accusation that Soviet
Communism was prepared to sacrifice revolution for the sake
of "bourgeois" comfort and experience. There followed a
sharp attack on those who gave no thought to the consequences
of modern war, who underestimated or simply dismissed the
deadliness of nuclear weapons. Vast destruction of productive
forces in a nuclear war would make it extraordinarily difficult
to build a new society on the ruins left by a nuclear war. Yet
the socialist revolution has no need to have the way paved for it

by atomic and hydrogen war, for the final goal of the working class is not to die 'gallantly' but to build a happy life for all mankind.(19)

To eliminate any doubt, *Pravda* then recalled that while the Statement of 1960 had considered "revisionism"—then crystallized in the Yugoslav deviation—the "principal danger" to Communism, it had already warned that "dogmatism and sectarianism" could at some stage also become the greatest peril. In Moscow's eyes, Communist China was the leftist bugaboo, representing the heresy of "sectarianism and dogmatism, just as in Beijing's view Moscow, in addition to Belgrade, had become the very incarnation of "revisionism." Moscow, of course, as always, claimed to follow the correct Marxist-Leninist course, avoiding the pitfalls of both right and left deviation, of revisionism and dogmatism. *Pravda* claimed that it was "more complicated" to expose left opportunism, since it hid behind "ultrarevolutionary phraseology" that played on the feeling of the masses. The paper stressed the need for waging an uncompromising struggle against any distortions of Marxism-Leninism. Thus, Moscow cleared the deck for the ideological battle with Beijing.

Even before the Sino-Soviet dispute erupted into the open, the sessions of the World Peace council in Stockholm and in 1963 in Moscow already reflected serious disagreements on national liberation and disarmament. During the year 1963, the Sino-Soviet rift soon enveloped other international organizations and Communist Parties everywhere. Sharply different points of view by the partisans of the Moscow and Beijing positions were voiced at the meeting of the Presidium of the World Peace Council in Malmö in March 1963 and at another one at Warsaw, which was held between November 28 and December 3, 1963.

The Chinese paper, rather than hiding its "factionalist" support for adherents of Beijing's point of view in other Parties, proudly acknowledged it, and even offered theoretical justification for it. The Sino-Soviet struggle, by affecting the organization of the Communist party, the very instrument of the class struggle and of the fight for socialism, had reached the point of no return. In the political life-and-death struggle with Moscow, Beijing contemptuously discarded established Communist rules relating to the type of infighting and political maneuvering, rules which were permissible and those which were prohibited. In the struggle for political survival and against political heresy, everything was allowed.

Escalation of the Polemics, June-July, 1963

In the Spring of 1963, Beijing battered Moscow with the dispatch of three letters of protest against the Soviet agreement to sign a test ban treaty with the West; the last of these letters bore the date of June 6.

The Chinese letter, in the intensity and breadth of the attack, surpassed anything that Beijing had so far unleashed against Moscow.(20)   The former esoteric criticism was replaced by direct brutal attack. While previously "certain comrades"—including, of course, Krushchev—were considered at fault, now "comradeship," without an eye's blinking, was dropped: "certain persons" took the burden of blame and common party ties were suddenly as good as forgotten. The CPSU was accused of paying only lip-service to revolution in capitalist countries and of not moving ahead with the Socialist revolution in the USSR.

The Chinese document warned that a "one-sided" reduction of the general line of the internationaL Communist movement to "peaceful coexistence," "peaceful transition to socialism betrayed the revolutionary principles of the 1957 Declaration and the 1960 Statement. The Soviet leaders were accused of turning the CPSU into a "reformed party," of sliding down the path of "opportunism" and "degenerating into bourgeois nationalists." While they slandered China, claiming that the CPC wanted to extend socialism by wars between states, they were in fact opposed to revolutions by oppressed peoples and nations of the world. They confined the foreign policy line of the socialist countries to peaceful coexistence. No one could ever demand in the name of peaceful coexistence that the oppressed peoples and nations give up their revolutionary struggles.

The Chinese statement then went on to criticize the "preposterous attacks" that, in disregard of facts, were leveled against the C.P.C. The letters from Beijing ended with an appeal to workers and oppressed peoples and nations of the world to unite and to oppose the common enemy—American imperialism. The increasingly virulent rift between the two Communist superpowers was still officially minimized as a temporary misunderstanding between the two fraternal parties which were bound by common ideology and common goals.

On July 14, 1963, *Pravda* finally published Moscow's reply to the letter of the C.C. of the C.P.C. Because of both its content and tone, it cast serious doubt on the possibility of an early resolution of their deep-seated conflict.

The Beijing letter had pinpointed the major differences in theory and practice between the C.P.C. and the C.P.S.U. At the center of the dispute, in Moscow's opinion, were questions involving the vital interests of the people, namely questions of war and peace, the question of the role and development of the world socialist system, problems of the struggle against the ideology and practice of the "cult of the individual," questions of the strategy and tactics of the workers' movement and of the national-liberation struggle.

When the C.P.C. leaders were speaking of "peace and peaceful coexistence," they were, according to the Soviets, merely paying lip-service to concepts that they well understood to be widely popular. The Soviets placed before Communists, "as a first-priority task," the prevention of a world thermonuclear catastrophe. In the Soviet view, under modern conditions "the forces of peace" could, through united efforts, avert a new world war. Though the nature of imperialism had admittedly not changed and the danger of the outbreak of war not been eliminated, a new balance of forces had emerged in the world, among them the "chief bulwark" of peace, the "mighty commonwealth" of socialist states. The Chinese comrades, the Soviet letter continued, did not believe in the possibility of averting a new world war. They actually underestimated the forces of peace and socialism and overestimated the forces of imperialism. Behind the "ringing revolutionary phrases" of the C.P.C. lay essentially lack of faith in the forces of the working class, in its victory in the class struggle. All peace-loving forces, whatever their class background and class interests, were united in the struggle to avert war. They all feared the destructive power of the atomic bomb. To enter upon the path proposed by the Chinese comrades would mean to "alienate" the popular masses from the Communist Parties. The latter had won the sympathies of the peoples through their persistent struggle for peace. And in the mind of the broad masses peace and socialism were "inseparable."

The leaders of the C.P.C. also underestimated the full danger of thermonuclear war. They held the atomic bomb to be a mere "paper tiger," not a terrible weapon. Of course, the Soviets supported the destruction of imperialism and capitalism. Yet, under modern conditions a world war would be a thermonuclear war, since the imperialists would never agree to leave the stage voluntarily. The Soviets, well aware of the destructive power of thermonuclear weapons would never use them first, and would only resort to these "terrible weapons" for defensive purposes. Furthermore, serious differences existed between the C.P.C. and C.P.S.U. on the question of "struggle against the consequences of the Stalin cult."

Another important question keeping Beijing apart from Moscow was, in the latter's view, that of the relation between the struggle of the international working class and the national-liberation movement of the peoples of Asia, Africa, and Latin America. The correct relationship between them was one of the chief conditions of victory over imperialism. According to the theories of the Chinese comrades, "the basic contradiction of our time" was the contradiction not between socialism and imperialism, but between the national-liberation movement and imperialism. According to this "theory," the Soviets maintained, it was not the industrial working class but the national-liberation movement that was the "decisive force" in the struggle against imperialism. The leaders of the C.P.C. apparently hoped to gain popularity with this thesis among the peoples of Asia, Africa, and Latin America. Yet this theory tended to isolate the national-liberation movement from the international proletariat.

In the course of 1963, the Sino-Soviet dispute had run the gamut from indirect and esoteric criticism to all-out and overt struggle along political, organizational, and ideological lines, and even actual confrontation along the border. On both sides, few illusions were left by the end of the year about their mutual relationship, but Moscow, which seemed all set to banish Beijing from the ranks of the true believers, apparently ran into unexpected opposition from some East European Communist Parties, though on other issues the latter firmly sided with Moscow. The unrelenting escalation of the conflict can best be seen in the mounting fury of the exchanges, the ever-widening scope of the accusations, and the type of charges leveled at the opponent. The Soviet accusations focused on chauvinism, imperialism, racism, leadership-cult, and the like, charges virtually indistinguishable from the period of struggle against Nazism during World War II, and against Western imperialism. At times they even exceeded the accusations against the latter. The Chinese accusation in turn centered on Soviet hegemonism and great-power ambitions, collusion with imperialism, abandonment of Marxism-Leninism, alleged restoration of capitalism, and betrayal of the world socialist revolutionary movement and the national-liberation movement. Not only were the forces of Communism weakened and split by the Sino-Soviet rift, but two Communist giants were at swords' point, ready to give battle along all but military lines.

After Khrushchev, 1964-1966

The coup that removed Khrushchev silenced briefly the contending parties in Moscow and Beijing. The personal antagonism between Khrushchev and Mao had been an important element in the dispute between the two sides. But to what extent its disappearance or the departure of one of the two contenders would affect the relationship between the C.P.R. and the U.S.S.R. could not be fully anticipated. Immediately after the coup both sides displayed cautious hope. Since under Khrushchev their relationship had reached bottom, some reasoned that now matters could only improve. But it soon became evident that most of the serious differences that had produced the rift in the first place, and a veritable explosion in 1963, were to continue and that Khrushchev's removal would not result in an abrupt change of course and in the sudden improvement of relations between the contesting parties. Khrushchev's successors, Brezhnev and Kosygin, displayed greater diplomatic circumspection and tactical restraint, but were unwilling to yield on the substance of policy.

Khrushchev had unceremoniously departed from power, and for a short moment Beijing rejoiced. But on the very same

day on which Chou En-lai returned from Moscow in November
1964, there went on sale in the Soviet capital the November
issue of the Russian edition of *Problems of Peace and Socialism*
edited by A. M. Rumyantsev, member of the C.C. of the
C.P.S.U. It contained a large number of articles in which the
C.P.C. was attacked by name. In one of them, Y.P.
Andropov, Secretary of the C.C. of the C.P.S.U., levied
against Beijing the serious charge of promoting splitting
activities in the international Communist movement. The
publication of this issue, several weeks after the fall of
Khrushchev, was an unmistakable sign that the new Moscow
leadership was not prepared to abandon Khrushchev's China
policy, but rather was determined to pursue it. Both sides
remained convinced of the righteousness of their cause and of
the deep-seated hostility of the opponent. Thus Khrushchev's
fall was to give merely a short pause in the relentless war of
words and hostile acts of both sides.

In the early sixties China and Indonesia had suggested
calling a second Afro-Asian conference. The first Afro-Asian
conference had been held at Bandung in April 1955. Though
the Soviet Union had not attended the Bandung Conference,
Khrushchev's successors were anxious that a Soviet delegation
appear at the second Afro-Asian conference. At a preparatory
meeting, held in Djakarta, it had been decided to hold the
conference in March 1965. After the Djakarta meeting the
Chinese delegate, Chen Yi, however, had bluntly asserted that
the Soviet Union, an allegedly non-Asiatic power, had no
business at the forthcoming conference.

The Chinese position was then presented with brutal
frankness by the *People's Daily Observer* on May 31, 1964.(21)
The paper went so far as to dispute as untenable the Soviet
argument that the U.S.S.R., two-thirds of whose territory lay
in Asia, was therefore also an Asiatic country. Each state was a
single entity and could not be characterized as an Asian as well
as a European state "simply because its territory extends over
both continents." The U.S.S.R. was reminded that three-
fourths of the Soviet population lived in Europe and that the
political center of the Soviet Union had always been in Europe.
Also, in 1955 she had abstained from participation in the
Bandung Conference. In the United Nations the Soviet Union
likewise had not been invited to join the Afro-Asian group.

The Asian union republics of the Soviet Union were component parts of the Soviet Union and not states independent of her. Therefore, they could not take part in the impending summit conference of independent Asian-African states. Referring to the principle adopted at Djakarta of reaching unanimity through consultation—meaning giving each consultant the right to a veto—Beijing expressed its opinion that the decision not to invite the U.S.S.R. was irrevocable.

The Soviets, in support of their claim to the right to participate in Afro-Asian conferences, were shying away from obvious geographical, geopolitical, and also legal arguments, and rather stressed pragmatic considerations.(22) They focused upon the tangible services that the U.S.S.R. had rendered in the past and could offer to the national-liberation movement in the future.

Dispute over aid to North Vietnam in its war against the South appears to have developed first during the summer of 1965, though it was not yet publicized at that time. The Chinese also accused the Soviets that their aid was neither in quality nor quantity commensurate with their country's strength. In 1966 and 1967 the Soviet campaign against Chinese obstruction in the matter of overland transit of Soviet military equipment destined for North Vietnam grew in intensity. The Soviet press went so far as to repeat Western allegations of China's having sold steel to the United States to be used in North Vietnam. The United States, Moscow also asserted, would not have dared to bomb North Vietnam if Soviet missiles and anti-aircraft batteries had not been held up in China.

The Chinese were hoping that Soviet aid carried over sea routes to Vietnam might involve the U.S.S.R. in a showdown with the United States of America. Their negative attitude toward all American moves aimed at bringing the conflict in vietnam to a peaceful solution in turn aroused Soviet suspicion. The Soviets accused Beijing of needing "a long conflict in Vietnam" in order to keep up the international tension and to picture China as a "besieged fortress." The C.P.S.U. Central Committee charged that one of the political objectives of the Chinese leaders in the Vietnam war was to provoke a military conflict between the U.S.S.R. and the

United States. They wished the U.S.S.R. to clash with the United States "in order to be able, as they themselves say, 'to sit on the mountain and to watch the battle of the tigers.'"(23)

Communist China's position on the war in Vietnam did hurt her prestige and image in the Communist and non-Communist world. Her verbal bravados were in striking contrast to her cautious passivity, faced with what she did not cease to denounce as a United States imperialist adventure next door. Her "Cultural Revolution" underlined her preoccupation with domestic rather than international affairs. Her growing isolation in the world and in world Communism laid her open to Soviet attacks. The Soviets, themselves a target of continuing Chinese charges of collusion with the United States, angrily countercharged that since the beginning of the "Cultural Revolution" Chinese pledges to Vietnam had gradually eroded. They accused China of being prepared for military action only in the event of a direct American attack upon China. They thus raised the specter of a "tacit agreement" between America and Communist China, of a collusion of their own, as they tried to turn the table on Beijing.

The "Great Proletarian Cultural Revolution" and Maoism

On November 27, 1966, *Pravda* wrote: "What is being done in China under the guise of cultural revolution in fact has nothing to do with it."(24) Several years later the Hungarian Communist Party chief Janos Kadar commented similarly that the "cultural revolution" in China was nothing but the evil spirit of nationalism, anarchy, and devastation that had broken loose in the C.P.R. By giving conspicuous display to Kadar's utterances, *Pravda* and *Izvestiia* obviously endorsed this view.

By May of 1968, when the tumultuous waves of the Great Proletarian Cultural Revolution had already made deep inroads, and when its character, while still baffling people within China and beyond it, had emerged in sharper outlines, *Kommunist*, focusing on "The Nature of the 'Cultural Revolution' in China," described how by 1966 China's grave economic situation and patent failures in the foreign policy field—her loss of international prestige and growing isolation

—had exacerbated discontent in the Party and among the people.(25) Mao had seen in this mood and attitude a direct threat to his autocracy and his political doctrine. To perpetuate his name and become the symbol of the faith of the Chinese people "for tens of thousands of years," he had unleashed the "Cultural Revolution." Its goals were to suppress oppositionist attitudes, to assert Mao's absolute dictatorship, and to excise from the people's consciousness the correct conception of Marxism and Leninism.

Mao and his group, exploiting the nation's illiteracy— more than 300 million remained completely illiterate in China— were, according to *Kommunist*, attempting to rally the people, especially the younger generation, on the basis of reactionary ideas and the concepts of nationalism and alleged racial superiority of the Chinese over other peoples. The cult of Mao, which had been raised to the level of idolatry, was supported by resort to violence and outright reprisals against everyone who was dissatisfied or merely doubtful. "Storm detachments" of young people and the army, "indoctrinated in the spirit of fanaticism," became the chief tools of this violence. Mao had trained an organization of pogromists and its first target became the creative intelligentsia, in particular its Party stratum.

Mao could not strike directly at the leading Party and state cadres. Thus his political campaign had to be camouflaged as having cultural connotations and was passed off as a movement of the popular masses against "bourgeois culture." But thereafter the attack was shifted against the Party and state cadres. Under the guise of wresting power from those who allegedly followed a capitalist path, Mao was able to disclaim responsibility for past setbacks and place it on the shoulders of real or potential rivals. There was no real unity among the supporters of the Mao group. The army and the hung weiping and tsao fan detachments were split and struggled against each other, and the center was no longer capable of controlling events in the localities.

In spite of the sharp Soviet criticism, Beijing pretended to be undisturbed and self-assured and even anticipated a whole series of new Cultural Revolutions in China in the more or less distant future. No member of the C.P.C. nor anyone in China should think that "everything will be all right after one or two great Cultural Revolutions, or even three or four. China must be very much on the alert and never lose her vigilance. Maoism was "a great leap forward" in the revolutionary theory of Marxism-Leninism. According to Beijing's own assessment, the Cultural Revolution, in spite of its name, had large political, social, and foreign policy objectives. Among the latter the most characteristic was unfurling the flag of the C.P.R.'s great-power nationalism and challenging the primacy of Moscow.

When the "Cultural Revolution" began to unfold in 1966, the anti-Soviet course of Beijing intensified. In August 1966, at the eleventh plenary session of the C.C. of the C.P.C., the Maoists scored heavily when their anti-Soviet aims and campaign were recognized as "absolutely correct and necessary." There followed a vigorous, unrelenting campaign against the U.S.S.R. and noisy demonstrations before the walls of the Soviet Embassy in Beijing.

Day after day Chinese propaganda bombarded the C.P.S.U. and the U.S.S.R. with what in the Soviet view were filthy streams of slander. According to Moscow, Beijing seemed even resolved to transplant the "Cultural Revolution" to the U.S.S.R. and to establish Mao's military-bureaucratic dictatorship in the Soviet Union. The volume of Russian-language broadcasts by Radio Beijing, Moscow charged, had increased enormously, and the broadcasts were transmitted over 40 different frequencies. No demonstration, no rally, no matter on what subject, went by without anti-Soviet slogans and appeals. During the "Cultural Revolution" period, Moscow accused Beijing of committing more than 200 provocatory acts against Soviet institutions and representatives. Anti-Soviet propaganda, alternating with military marches and anti-Soviet songs, was ceaselessly broadcast over the radio. The Maoists, the Soviets concluded, were apparently hoping to solve their complicated internal problems by arousing an anti-Soviet hysteria. They raised a false hue and cry about a "Soviet threat" to justify the further militarization of China. They justified the shortages of foodstuffs and other goods by pointing to the alleged danger from Moscow. Even school children were being indoctrinated to the effect that a large part of the territory of the U.S.S.R. in the Far East and Central Asia was once Chinese. *Pravda* reported that Hunshua wire service had circulated a bulletin in the capitals of several African states asserting that the peoples of the Soviet Central Asian republic were seized with a common desire to "enter into a close union with China." According to Moscow, there was thus a Chinese "threat" to the integrity of the U.S.S.R. rather than vice versa.

The "Cultural Revolution" was closely interwoven with personality cult, the idolization of Mao, and the extolling of Mao's thought than any other phase of the recent history of the C.P.C. and the C.P.R. After their own shattering experience with the personality cult of Stalin, the Soviet Union's leadership could look upon the Mao cult only with growing concern.

Moscow, Beijing, and the Middle East

On June 6, 1967, one day after the outbreak of war in the Middle East, *Pravda* published a Soviet government statement accusing Israel of having commenced military operations and committed aggression against the United Arab Republic.(26) In his analysis and comment on the Mid-East War and Arab defeat, which in view of its support of the Arab position deeply embarrassed the U.S.S.R., Jury Zhukov in *Pravda*, while denouncing alleged Israeli aggression, was anxious to implicate the United States in the conflict and to shift the burden of guilt onto her shoulders. He pointed out that imperialism more than once, especially in 1956 and in 1958, had attempted to impede the strengthening of the national independence of the Near Eastern countries. The United States of America was inclined to turn Israel's temporary advantage into a lasting one, as a cover for making a fresh attempt to restore the colonial order in the Arab East. Against this backdrop Zhukov praised the "truly noble role" that the U.S.S.R. and other socialist states were playing in the Near East. He especially recalled the "enormous assistance" the U.S.S.R. had given to the Arabs to strengthen their economy and defense, somehow ignoring the circumstance that apparently all these efforts had borne no fruit. Washington's role had been to stop the national liberation movements. The attempt, however, by Western imperialism to restore colonialism was doomed to failure.

On June 6 Premier Chou sent messages of support to the Presidents of the U.A.R. and of the Syrian Arab Republic and to the President of the Palestine Liberation Organization. Though Beijing did not hold back its vituperative criticism of Moscow, castigating its policy of big words contrasted by small deeds, *Beijing Review* wrote: "The great thought of Mao is the sharpest weapon /!/ with which Beijing's proletarian revolutionaries support the Arab people in their struggle against United States-Israeli banditry."(27) While Moscow offered real weapons, advice, and diplomatic assistance—though refusing military intervention—Beijing offered intermittently the help of 700 million Chinese and the Little Red Book containing Mao's thoughts.

In its later analysis of the Six-Day War, Beijing resorted to obvious half-truths, if not plain lies. It reversed the actual situation by making beleaguered little Israel one of the main culprits, while acquitting the Arabs—in spite of their threatening preparations for imminent war and ignoring their openly proclaimed genocidal intentions. It made it appear that Israel was a mere stooge of the United States and that the latter allegedly pushed Israel into the war. It also distorted Soviet Russia's vast material and advisory support of the Arabs into an abandonment of the Arab cause,(28) merely because the U.S.S.R. retreated from the risk of a war with the U.S. over the Middle East for the sake of Arab "liberation." Once again a major crisis in international affairs, which threatened for a brief moment to bring about a confrontation of the two superpowers, the United States and the U.S.S.R., and to engulf them in war, resulted also in violent and abusive propaganda war between the Soviet Union and Communist China.

Soviet Intervention in Czechoslovakia, 1968, and "Limited Sovereignty."

According to a Tass Statement, published in *Pravda* and *Izvestia* on August 21, party and state leaders of the Czechoslovak Socialist Republic (CSR) had "requested" the Soviet Union and other allied states to give the fraternal Czechoslovak people immediate aid, "including assistance with armed forces."(29) The reason for the appeal, according to

Tass, was the threat posed to the socialist system in Czechoslovakia by counter-revolutionary forces that had entered into collusion with external forces which were hostile to socialism. The exacerbation of the tense Czechoslovakian situation, the statement continued, also affected the vital interests of the Soviet union and the security interests of all states in the socialist commonwealth. The decision of the socialist countries to dispatch troops to Czechoslovakia, it was claimed, was in complete accord with the right of states to individual and collective self-defense.

The first and most authoritative Chinese position on the Soviet invasion of Czechoslovakia was Premier Chou En-lai's speech in the Rumanian Embassy in Beijing on August 23.(30) According to Chou, the Soviet revisionist clique and its followers had brazenly dispatched large numbers of armed forces to launch a savage attack on Czechoslovakia and had perpetrated towering crimes against the Czechoslovak people. The Soviet move was the "inevitable result of great-power chauvinism and national egoism, practiced by the Soviet revisionist leading clique." Discarding all its fig leaves, its so-called Marxism-Leninism and internationalism, the Soviet leadership was trying to create puppets with the help of guns. Chou compared the Soviet invasion with Hitler's past aggression against Czechoslovakia and the United States imperialism's aggression against Vietnam. The Chinese denunciation of the Soviet move against Czechoslovakia could not have taken any sharper form.

A short while after the occupation of Czechoslovakia, Brezhnev and the Soviet leadership produced the so-called Brezhnev doctrine, which aimed at the justification of Soviet intervention anywhere in Eastern Europe, for the alleged purpose of defending socialism against foreign and domestic attempts to overthrow it and to restore capitalism and bourgeois democracy. The Soviets, according to Brezhnev in November 1968, were entitled to adopt "military measures" against a given member of the socialist "community" and carry out armed intervention. Beijing, however, promptly denounced the Brezhnev doctrine as an "outright doctrine of hegemony."(31) The *Beijing Review* castigated the Soviet revisionist press for endorsing the view that the interests of the socialist "community" must be put "in the first place," while the sovereignty of its individual members was "limited." The doctrine of "limited sovereignty, a corollary of the Brezhnev doctrine, also alleged that the "community" had the right to determine the destiny of the individual community members, "the destiny of their sovereignty."

Of all the doctrines propagated by Moscow, none, for obvious reasons, infuriated Beijing more than this one. In denouncing the doctrine of limited sovereignty used by the U.S.S.R. and her satellites against Czechoslovakia—a doctrine that could be used again against any other socialist country, perhaps even Communist China—Beijing of course understood that it was fighting for its own survival.

Soviet Domination of Eastern Europe and New Soviet Expansionism

Beijing accused the "new tsars" of "riding roughshod" not only over Czechoslovakia, but over all of Eastern Europe. For years the Soviet revisionist clique had been pursuing a "social-imperialist policy towards some East European countries, a policy of tight political control, ruthless economic plunder, and arrogant militaristic intervention and aggression. Its fond dream is to build a colonial empire with itself as the overlord and to realize its aggressive designs to redivide the world in collaboration with United States imperialism. The biggest colonial ruler and the biggest exploiter of East European peoples, the Soviet revisionist clique is a gang of new tsars riding on their backs."(32) The U.S.S.R. thus was indistinguishable from any capitalist and imperialist power. After its usurpation of the Party and government leadership in the U.S.S.R., the Soviet leadership had actually betrayed the Soviet people and was restoring capitalism at home. The ruling Soviet clique had also begun to "expand" tsarist foreign policy and even to surpass the Tsars. "Its aggressive ambition is even bigger and more rapacious than that of the tsarist imperialists, and the methods of aggression it resorts to are even more treacherous and vicious."

The East European countries were victims of Soviet imperialism. The Soviet revisionist renegade clique had said the most pleasant things, but done everything evil in order to establish its colonial empire in Eastern Europe. For years it had treated the East European countries as its colonies and dependencies. "Politically, it wantonly tramples under foot their independence and sovereignty and crudely interferes with their internal and external policies; economically, it plunders the wealth created by the working people of these countries, and even sends its troops to engage in military occupation." However, the new tsars in the Kremlin described their out-and-out acts of social imperialism as "proletarian internationalism." They blustered about "mutual assistance and cooperation" with the East European countries for the purpose of building a "socialist commonwealth" in common prosperity. But what they really practiced was "social-imperialism and big-nation chauvinism ... oppression and plunder... Under the signboard of socialism, they are going about their imperialist villainies."

"Coordination" of economic plans of the East Central European satellites meant that the national economic plans drawn up by the CMEA states be based on the principle of "international division of labor,"(33) actually in accordance with the needs of the Soviet social imperialists. Everything was to be geared to the "predatory" demands of the Soviets. Once a supra-state organ for unified planning was accepted, all the countries would be completely deprived of what little independence remained and would be turned into regions or union republics of the U.S.S.R. In accordance with the program of international division of labor, CMEA countries were allowed only to produce industrial, agricultural and mineral products of certain types and specifications. This had deprived these countries of their right to independent development of their economies, had aggravated their lopsided economic growth, and turned them into dependencies of Soviet revisionism.

Beijing's Foreign Policy, Reversal of Isolationism, and the Soviet Assessment

Just as the C.P.C. was fearful of the specter of encirclement by the U.S.S.R., the Soviet Union similarly claimed to fear encirclement by China and the United States in combination with Japan and other European powers. While Beijing castigated Moscow's foreign policies, Moscow had no good word to say about Beijing's foreign policy course; each country charged the opponent with deviation from and betrayal of Marxism-Leninism both in its domestic and foreign policy. A scathing criticism of Beijing's foreign policy appeared in March also in *Kommunist*. According to it, Beijing had long calculated on turning Albania into China's beachhead on the European continent. The Maoists, Moscow charged, sought in the Balkans a clash between the U.S.S.R. and socialist countries on one hand and the forces of imperialism on the other.

The Beijing leadership, according to *Kommunist*, in line with its general policy of aggravating international tensions, had long promoted a deepening of the Vietnam conflict. It hoped that the D.R.V. would wage "protracted war" and draw the U.S.S.R. and other socialist countries deeper into the conflict.(34) On the other hand, practically every stage in the escalation of the aggression in Vietnam had been accompanied by mutual assurances between the United States of America and the C.P.R. that they would not attack each other. Mao had not only rejected unity of action in the struggle against American aggression. He still placed obstacles in the way of shipping armaments and strategic material through Chinese territory from the socialist countries to Vietnam. Mao and his group attempted to prepare the Chinese for the possibility of armed conflict between the U.S.S.R. and the C.P.R. Chinese leaders were taking a direct part in whipping up an anti-Soviet psychosis. On the eve of the 19th anniversary of the C.P.R., Premier Chou remarked at a state reception that "anything can be expected" of the Soviet Union, including an "attack on China."

A comparative analysis of the accusations leveled at Moscow by Beijing and vice-versa is instructive in several respects. Both sides were deeply convinced of the implacable hostility of the other. Each side suspected the moves by the other and its attempt to improve its relations with the imperialist arch-enemy, the United States. Yet, in the emerging war of words, the "socialist" opponent was frequently denounced in more vituperative terms than the imperialist foe. The denunciation of the latter became almost a religious ritual, while the denunciation of the former was both an affair of the heart and a matter of deepest conviction.

Each side feared the attempt of the other at "collusion" with capitalism and imperialism, at military encirclement. Both sides were convinced that they were involved in a struggle that might last for decades and end in war. The Soviet Union had no doubts that the opponent wanted to spread its "cultural revolution" into the U.S.S.R. and the C.P.R. feared that the Soviets wished to transplant "capitalism" to China, which had been "restored" in the U.S.S.R. Both seemed certain that the other side was prepared to assist in the overthrow of its government. Each party of course, charged the other with having strayed from the path of Marxism-Leninism, of staging bloody provocations along the border, of bearing responsibility for the deterioration of their mutual relations, for the weakening of economic and cultural ties linking the two countries, and for carrying on a ruthless diplomatic and political warfare against the other side in the countries of the Third World. The charges of great-power ambitions, chauvinism, social-imperialism, colonialism, and economic exploitation were freely hurled against each other, as were accusations of interventionism and violation of national sovereignty. Comparisons to fascist aggression and Hitler in particular were frequent. It can hardly be assumed that the war of words could be further escalated without becoming physical.

Judging by historical precedent, many a war has broken out with less acrimonious exchange preceding it. In the atomic age, however, the tolerance of even the greatest and most powerful states for absorbing insults and vituperation has apparently increased manifold. With its onset the diplomacy of courteous disagreement has become a thing of the past.

When Communist China terminated the policy of the "Cultural Revolution," she also shed her isolationist skin and once again reached out for the world. During the years 1970 and 1971 the Chinese leadership radically changed its tactics with regard to the United States of America, the United Nations, and the national liberation movement, as well as to interstate relations with the developing countries of Asia, Africa, and Latin America, attempting to increase the "confidence" of the Third World countries in China. It pursued these tactics by resorting once more to the principles and formulas adopted at the Bandung Conference and by establishing all-around contacts with many countries, irrespective of their political, social, or economic orientation.

In the Soviet view, Beijing retained the basic characteristics of its policy, though it partly resurrected earlier tactics and partly adopted some novel ones, thus displaying "flexibility." In Soviet opinion, since the 19th Congress in April 1969 the foreign policy of the C.P.R. had continued to exhibit its strongly nationalist character and great-power ambitions, as both theory — the decisions of the September 1970 Second Plenary Meeting of the Party's C.C. — and practice have demonstrated.

Anxious to reestablish diplomatic and other ties with the outside world, China, according to the Soviets, had to "dampen down" the propaganda of "ultra-leftist" slogans of a "people's war." The Chinese leadership adopted the role of the champion of detente and peaceful coexistence. Actually, Beijing had suffered a number of setbacks in its foreign and domestic policies. Its attempt to introduce the methods of Red Guards' violence and armed pressure into international relations had backfired and had alienated both the liberation movement of the developing countries and the progressive democratic movement in capitalist countries.

Beijing's new tactics, according to the Soviets, were based upon betrayal of the international revolutionary movement. Communist China has become "the Trojan horse of imperialism" in the revolutionary movement. Her diplomatic flirtation with the imperialist countries headed by the United States has resulted in the restoration of her rights in the United Nations, including permanent membership in the Security Council. For this purpose Beijing has thought it necessary to ingratiate itself with the West and to conceal its participation in the activities of pro-Maoist groups in the revolutionary and liberation movements. In radically changing their tactics regarding the United States as well as developing countries, devising new catchwords and resorting to camouflage, they were demonstrating their opportunism and their abandonment of the anti-imperialist struggle.

The very key of Beijing's recent foreign policy was the so-called two-superpowers concept, the two powers being the United States and the U.S.S.R. Against them Communist China was striving to marshal the support of the medium and small countries by manipulating anti-American and anti-Soviet catchwords. Her real goal, however, was to pursue hegemonistic aims and to become "the third superpower" herself. Though playing both melodies, anti-Sovietism and anti-Americanism, the C.P.R. in practice flirted with imperialism, while continuing its anti-Soviet policy. She attempted to strike a bargain with the United States, especially in regard to East and Southeast Asia. Though the United States since 1963 had repeatedly proposed to normalize American-Chinese relations, the Chinese leaders had responded positively to the American initiative only since the end of the 1960s, especially since 1971. Once the military-bureaucratic dictatorship in the wake of the "Cultural Revolution" was established in the C.P.R., Beijing could meet the American "bridge-building" policy half-way.

The New China Policy of the U.S.

Nixon's new China Policy started, according to Henry Kissinger, *White House Years*, (1979), as "a series of improvisations." Despite Nixon's past support by the "China lobby" — which had accused Truman and Secretary of State Dean Acheson, of the alleged "betrayal" of Chiang Kai-shek — President Nixon, Kissinger thought, was "somewhat schizophrenic in the early days" of his administration. He had "no clear-cut plan", though his inaugural address contained a veiled reference to his willingness to talk with the Chinese leaders.(35)

On April 29, 1969, Kissinger, commenting on the Ninth Chinese Party Congress, assured Nixon that Beijing's "denigration of the U.S. was only "pro forma." Following the Ussuri river clashes between the CPR and the Soviet Union, a redirection of American policy vis-à-vis China became imperative. But while the "Chinese option" was "useful to induce Chinese restraint," it could not be pursued, according to Kissinger, "so impetuously as to provoke a Soviet preemptive attack."(36) In June 1964, Nixon modified some American trade controls vis-à-vis China; this was followed by other conciliatory measures on tourism. Within the US administration there were actually two opposing views. While those of the so-called "Slavophile" position argued that any improvement of relations with China would endanger the "top priority" of improving relations with the Soviets, Kissinger himself and the so-called "Slavophile" group in the Administration rather held that U.S. China policy should not be a mere hostage to Washington's policy toward Moscow.

On August 4, 1969, in a meeting of the National Security Council Nixon "startled" it by asserting that of the two Communist powers the Soviet Union was "the more aggressive party" and that it was against U.S. interests to let China be "smashed" in a Sino-Soviet war. In mid-August a Soviet Embassy official in Washington inquired, "out of the blue," about the likely U.S. reaction to a Soviet attack on China's nuclear facilities. After ominous Soviet threats in September, Under Secretary Elliot Richardson let it be known that the US long-run improvement of relations with China was in the American interest. As Kissinger himself writes in his memoirs: "A Soviet attack on China could not be ignored by us. It would upset the global balance of power; it would create around the world an impression of approaching Soviet dominance." At year's end, Kissinger, in a press briefing, stressed that the US had "no permanent enemies" and would judge other countries, including Communist countries, on the basis of their actions, "not their ideology."

After the Cease-Fire in Vietnam. The C.P.R's Propaganda and Balancing

The cease-fire in Vietnam and the apparent end of the war was widely hailed in the Soviet press. The agreement on "Ending the War and Restoring Peace in Vietnam,"(37) signed in Paris on January 27, 1973, was also welcomed by the Chinese press, which especially hailed the prospect of unification of North and South Vietnam. Differently from the U.S.S.R., however, they recalled that the Chinese and Vietnamese peoples were "of the same family."(38) It was evident that Beijing was pleased about the definite removal of the American threat to the south of their border and that it was laying the groundwork for a special relationship with Hanoi, based not only on recent assistance and common outlook, but also on revolutionary militancy, geographic proximity, and racial kinship. The latter claims could not be matched by Moscow.

Racial and ethnic kinship have long been an important weapon in Beijing's arsenal. At a banquet a few months later in honor of Prince Sihanouk, Chou En-lai underscored that the Chinese and the Cambodian peoples belonged to the same ethnic group. Marxism-Leninism, or better, Mao Tse-tung Thought, had come full circle to pay respect to nationalism and racialism!

The struggle to win the favor of the great majority of the peoples and states of the world and enlist their support against the two superpowers remained the main theme of Chinese Communist propaganda. While anxious to remove the threat of an encirclement by Asian peoples gathering under the flag of Asian collective security, the C.P.R. was bent on marching at the head not only of all Asian but also of the African and Latin American peoples against the superpowers. The C.P.R. played up to the Fourth Conference of Heads of State and Government of Nonaligned Countries. In its view, the conference revealed a further "awakening"(39) of the Asian, African, and Latin American peoples, which aimed at independence, liberation, and revolution. In the economic field, according to Beijing, the gap was widening between the rich and developed countries and poor and developing states. Beijing also suggested a revision of the United Nations charter to give stronger expression to the numerous small and medium-sized countries and to the principles of equality of all states, big or small, and to terminate control by the superpowers. Clearly, Beijing saw itself already as leader of the great majority of states, the small and middle-sized, the underdeveloped and poor nations, against the two world powers, one capitalist, the other claiming to be "socialist," but both irretrievably imperialist.

The CPR pointed to Soviet-American differences as the major root of international tension, though on many other occasions it underlined the Sino-Soviet confrontation. The apparent propagandistic need to have, next to Soviet revisionism and social imperialism, a genuine capitalist and imperialist enemy, may account for the careful balancing of Washington and Moscow, the two major foes of Beijing. For Communist Beijing, the hoped-for center of world Communism, a capitalist enemy, next to the Soviet arch-enemy, was plainly an imperative!

In September 1973 Chou Enlai bitterly denounced "the Soviet revisionist clique from Khrushchev to Brezhnev"(40) that made a socialist country degenerate into a social-imperialist country. The ruling group "had restored capitalism, enforced a fascist dictatorship and enslaved the people of all nationalities." Externally, it has invaded and occupied Czechoslovakia, massed its troops along the Chinese border and sent military units into the People's Republic of Mongolia. It had supported the traitorous Lon Nol clique in Cambodia, suppressed the Polish Workers' rebellion, intervened in Egypt, causing the expulsion of the Soviet experts, and dismembered Pakistan. It carried out subversive activities in many Asian and African countries. This series of facts, according to Chou, profoundly exposed the U.S.S.R.'s ugly features as the new Tsar, and also its reactionary nature, namely "socialism in words, imperialism in deeds. The more evil and foul things it does, the sooner the time when Soviet revisionism will be relegated to the historic museum by the people of the Soviet Union and the rest of the world." The speech was one of the sharpest ever directed against the Soviet leadership.

Europe and Asia.

Since Europe, according to an anonymous Soviet writer, has long been regarded as a key area by the two superpowers in their contention for world hegemony, the Soviet revisionists have for many years deployed most of their troops there. Even though since the mid-1960s they have been "stretching their claws into Asia, Africa and wherever they could and carrying out military threats against China"(41) by steadily increasing their forces along the Sino-Soviet border, Soviet troops in Europe, according to the Western press, have since 1968 gone up almost twenty percent and the tactical air force by fifty per cent. Three-fifths of the Soviet ground forces and over three-fourths of their air force were massed now in Eastern Europe and the Soviet Union. It was quite obvious why Beijing was interested in seeing to it that both Soviet preoccupation with Europe and Europe's countermeasures against the rising Soviet threat continued, thus preventing the U.S.S.R. from focusing her expansionist thrusts against China and Asia.

Beijing has continued to denounce Soviet thrusts in the
Mideast and Europe—which are detrimental to the interest of
Western Europe, especially Great Britain and France—and
also her expansionist efforts elsewhere, into the Indian Ocean
through Afghanistan and Pakistan, particularly through the
mountainous regions of Pakistan's Baluchistan province, and
into Southeast Asia. In an article in October of 1973, Novosti
Press Agency voiced the view that the "two Chinas" would
remain a reality for a long time and seemed to favor the
prolongation of this situation. The feverish Soviet propagation
in 1973 of a system of collective security for Asia made Beijing
wonder why the U.S.S.R., "a European country,"(42) showed
such unusual concern for peace and security in Asia.

The Soviet revisionist clique, according to *Beijing Review*,
asserted that collective security in Asia and Europe was
"inconceivable" without recognizing the"immutability of
existing frontiers."(43) It thus opposed all attempts to
redemarcate postwar borders in regard to her East European
neighbors, stubbornly refused all attempts to return to Japan
the four northern islands, and opposed the settlement of the
Sino-Soviet boundary based on unequal treaties, "insisting on
occupying territory seized from China in violation" of even
these treaties. The retention of all her territory was one of the
important objectives in the Soviet move to establish a system of
collective security in Asia. The Chinese contention of being
willing to reach a settlement on the basis of the foregoing
treaties, which they at the same time brand "unequal," has
obviously not enhanced Soviet confidence that cession of some
territories—those seized "in violation" of the foregoing
treaties—would appease China for very long.

*The USSR-China's "Enemy Number One and the Soviet
Rejoinder*

While Beijing's polemics with the Soviets in the course of
1973 became even more bitter, its criticism of the US tended
somewhat to abate. This criticism became increasingly a weak
second to the exacerbation of accusations against the Soviet
Union. Beijing's apparent approval of the strengthening of
Western Europe, which in spite of dissonances in the Western
camp was militarily still tied to the U.S., meant that Beijing no

longer put the US and the USSR on the same plane. The latter, in Beijing's eyes, had become the more dangerous foe. The Soviets have duly taken notice that, in the CPR's view, they have moved up to the number-one enemy of China. It took some developments to arrive at this stage. The C.P.C. had first worked out the "theory of so-called intermediate zones," according to which, between the U.S.S.R. on the one hand, and the United States on the other, there was an intermediate zone that included all other countries. This had put Beijing between the superpowers, assigning to it the natural role of leader of most of the rest of the world. But soon even this theory no longer suited the C.P.R. in its growing dispute with the C.P.S.U. In 1971 and 1972 *Hung Chi*, the organ of the Central Committee of the C.P.C., developed a theory that still assumed two world poles, but placed both superpowers, the U.S.S.R. and the United States, not at opposite poles but rather cozily into one area. At the other end were China and some socialist countries. Two intermediate zones between them included, first, the countries of Asia, Africa, and Latin America, and, secondly, the main capitalist countries of the West and East.(44) In Beijing's view, the two superpowers were now hardly distinguishable from each other — a view that infuriated the Soviet Union.

Defending their own policy of detente, rejecting Beijing's criticism, and levelling an accusation of their own against China's "collusion" with the United States, the Soviets have charged the C.P.C. with having taken the side of reactionary extremists against the U.S.S.R. everywhere. Both sides in the dispute have agreed that it has escalated during the last years and both charged that, while their own ideological and political course had proved steadfast, the other side had made a radical shift to the Right. Each side has accused the other of having set up a fascist, Hitlerite regime.

Both Moscow and Beijing have revealed deep pessimism about the possibility of "converting" in the foreseeable future the opposing side to the true faith, of adopting the correct interpretation of Marxism-Leninism. Yet each Party, claiming to be in possession of the full truth, condemned the alien heresy, though not the mass of the alien heretics. O.B. Borisov and B. T. Koloskov in *Soviet-Chinese Relations, 1945-1970; An Outline* (Moscow, 1972), pointed out that even before 1949 there had always raged a struggle of two lines in the C.P.C., the Marxist-Leninist, internationalist, and the petty-bourgeois, nationalist one, and that this struggle had continued down to the present(45)—which furnishes the Soviets a theoretical base for an optimistic outlook, at least over the long stretch.

B. The Sino-Soviet Confrontation after Mao Zedong

After Mao's Demise

The death of Chairman Mao on September 9, 1976, created a void which "radicals"and "moderates" within the CPC tried promptly to fill, but neither was first successful. On October 7 Hua Guofeng was elected by the Politburo to succeed Mao as chairman of the Party and of its military commission. Simultaneously the four leaders of the "radicals," Mao's widow; Jiang Qing, Yao Wenyuan, Zhang Chunquiao, and Wang Hongwen, referred to in the Chinese press as the "gang of four," were arrested, being accused of having plotted to seize power. In the following months they were charged with having usurped the leadership of the Party and were criticized for adopting "wrong" policies during the Cultural Revolution as well as thereafter, and delaying China's modernization. Later they were accused of ultra-leftism, but it was pointed out that actually they were "rightists." One of the four was denounced as having become in 1954 a follower of Khrushchev's revisionism. Party purges, beginning in 1976 and continued the following year, replaced radical leaders of many provincial organizations of the CPC.(1) They were found guilty of "bourgeois careerist conspiracy and counter-revolutionary double-dealing"; three of them, including Mao's widow, were ultimately given life sentences-after two death sentences had been commuted—and the fourth was sentenced to twenty years. At the same time, in January 1981, Hua's earlier appointment as chairman of the Party was confirmed and Deng Xiaoping regained the posts from which he had been ejected in 1976.

Soviet propaganda had consistently ascribed the CPR's hostile attitude vis-à-vis the USSR to the influence of Mao and the "radicals" within the party and had claimed that the "moderates" did not share their view. The Soviets had placed hopes especially on Zhou Enlai. However, Zhou Enlai died before Mao. A documentary film shown on Soviet television on February 3, 1976, castigated Chairman Mao and his wife Jiang Qing, but did not criticize Zhou. Following Mao's death in September 1976, the Soviet leaders appeared first to set hopes on a rapprochement with China perhaps under new "moderate" Communist leaders; for a time they suspended all anti-Chinese propaganda. However, the Chinese press did not even publish a message of condolence from Moscow on the ground that there existed no formal relations between the two parties. Yet the Chinese learned that several Soviet officials, including Andrei Gromyko, had signed a book of condolence at the Chinese Embassy in Moscow. Also, an article in *Pravda* on October 1, 1976, by A. Aleksandrov,(2) frequently the mouth-piece for the Soviet Politburo, held out an olive branch to Beijing.

The arrest of the radical leaders, "the gang of four," in October 1976 pleased Moscow which considered them less amenable to national and ideological compromise with the USSR. The Soviet journalist and KGB agent Viktor Louis, who was widely believed to reflect official Soviet views, commented in the *London Evening News* on October 12 that the "majority of the leaders, hostile to the Soviet Union, have been removed from power."(3) Soon thereafter, on October 18, 1976, Brezhnev at a banquet in honor of President Tsedenbal of Mongolia, gave an optimistic assessment of the chances for a rapprochement between the two Communist giants and was seconded by Tsedenbal, known for his sharply critical attitude toward the CPR. A few days later, on October 25 Brezhnev in an address to the CPSU's C.C., while conceding that it was "difficult to foresee" China's political line, stressed that "improvement of our relations with China" was "our constant concern."(4) "We are ready," he proclaimed, "to normalize our relations with China on the basis of peaceful coexistence." There were in his view no problems in the relations between the two Communist states which could not be solved in a spirit of good-neighborliness. But he plainly put the responsibility for improving mutual relations on the shoulders of Beijing.

The conciliatory tone of these messages was soon drowned by the renewal of the polemics. The Chinese Foreign Ministry demanded categorically that Moscow admit its errors committed since 1960 and change its political line.(5) The Chinese press itself, however, continued its anti-Soviet diatribes in early 1977, while the Soviet press was reluctant to reply with equal force.(6) Contradictory signals, some pointing to the possibility of reconciliation and others to the resumption of mutual hostility, continued throughout much of the remainder of 1977. Beijing's *People's Daily* subjected the new Soviet constitution which was approved by the Supreme Soviet on October 7 to sharp criticism, "a despicable betrayal of Marxism-Leninism". The biggest gun in the polemics was Hua Guofeng's address to the Eleventh CP Congress in Beijing in mid-August.(7) He denounced the Soviet leading clique, proclaimed it responsible for the "degeneration" in the USSR which had dragged out border negotiations for eight long years. He warned against Western illusions of detente with Soviet revisionists, and considered the outbreak of war in the world "inevitable." Some Chinese actions, however, ran directly counter to the foregoing official criticism. After a vacancy of Chinese representation in Moscow for more than a year, Wang Youping was appointed Chinese Ambassador in June 1977. And on occasion of the 60th anniversary of the Russian October Revolution, the Beijing government dispatched a message to Moscow in favor of normalizing state relations between the two countries.

The "Three Worlds' Theory" and the Soviets

The "three worlds theory", embraced by the CPR already under Mao and clung to by the Chinese Party and state authorities in the post-Mao period ran counter to the Soviet conception, since it placed American imperialism and Soviet expansionism on the same level.(8) Chairman Mao had first put the theory forth in a private conversation with the leader of a Third World country in February 1974. In view of the subsequent internal development of the CPR it is of special interest that Deng Xiaoping publicly formulated the three worlds concept in an address to the Sixth special session of the UN General Assembly and Zhou Enlai referred to it in his report to the Fourth National People's Congress in January 1976. The theory, castigated by the Soviets, was especially embraced by the moderates in the CPR. *People's Daily* alleged on November 1, 1977, that the "gang of four," ultra-leftists, had "frantically opposed" it.(9) After Deng's rehabilitation in 1977, the concept was reaffirmed by Chairman Hua in various reports. The gist of the "three worlds" conception was that the Soviet Union represented the greatest threat both to China and to world peace, legitimized the CPR's close relations with the USA and Western Europe, and also placed China among the Third World nations, underlining its leading role among them.

The three-worlds conception was articulated most clearly in an article in *People's Daily* on November 1, 1977.(10) As it wrote: "Chairman Mao's theory of differentiation of the three worlds is a major contribution to Marxism-Leninism." According to it, it was in the 1960s that the Soviet Union became "an imperialist superpower that threatened the world," just as US imperialism had done, but the latter was in decline. Of the two superpowers, the Soviet Union was the more "ferocious, the more reckless. . .and the more dangerous source of world war." While the Soviets stretched out the hand of rapprochement toward the CPR aiming at "normalization" of mutual relations, Hua Guofeng made an unfriendly response in his report to the CPC Congress on February 26, 1978.(11) About two weeks later the official Chinese reply was as hostile as ever when it denounced the proposed Soviet statement on principles as "hollow" and "worthless." Hua Guofeng's visits in August 1978 to Rumania. Yugoslavia, and Iran, and the signing of the Sino-Japanese treaty of peace and friendship, including a clearly anti-Soviet denunciation of hegemonism, aroused new anger in the USSR. To it must be added an agreement between the US and the CPR to establish diplomatic relations with each other and Deng Xiaoping's visit to the US the following month. Though the Soviets retaliated by claiming that it was China which pursued a "hegemonist" policy, the last months of 1978 noticed a slight improvement of relations beginning with the appointment of Ilya Shcherbakov to the post of Soviet Ambassador to China as successor to Vasily Tolstikov, who had served in this capacity since 1970.

"Liberalization" under Deng and the Declining Role of Ideology

In 1978, the growing "liberalization" of domestic Chinese politics was linked with the name of Deng Xiaoping. Following the reversal of policies, adopted during the Cultural Revolution and promoted by the "gang of four," Hua Guofeng, a close adherent of Mao's policies was replaced as Prime Minister in September 1980 by Zhao Ziyang, a supporter of Deng's policies. In June 1981, Hua Guofeng resigned as Party chairman, being succeeded by Hu Yaobang, also a partisan of Deng. The thought of Mao was officially still given high appreciation, but on the whole his previous extraordinary role was curtailed. Mao's "grave" left error in pursuit of the policies of the Cultural Revolution and his personality cult were now openly criticized. The admission of these errors formed the background for a reversal under Deng of the policy changes during the decade of the Cultural Revolution, all pointing toward liberalization, modernization, and an "open door" policy, permitting foreign companies to operate jointly with Chinese companies, particularly in special economic zones in southeastern China. These reforms resulted in the CPR veering from an ultra-leftist course to a "revisionist" rightist policy. While immediately after Mao's death Chinese dailies denounced both Soviet internal revisionist policies and its "hegemonist" foreign policy, later articles published in 1979 and thereafter made it clear that Soviet foreign policy, not Soviet ideology, was Peking's major concern. This was partly due to the declining importance of Marxist-Leninist theory and ideology in the Sino-Soviet dispute and the CPR's greater pragmatism. The relative decline of ideo- logy as a motivating force determining China's policy can also be seen in the friendlier relations between the CPR and, on the other side, Yugoslavia.

Having embraced "revisionism" itself, it must have appeared ludicrous to the Beijing leadership to denounce the Soviet rival on account of this "heresy." With the decline of Mao's preeminence as the ideological guide of Beijing's policies, including his dominant role as an ememy of Soviet policy and practice, a major reason for reassessing the CPR's policy versus the USSR had vanished. Similarly, while China had first opposed the Soviet belief of peaceful coexistence between eastern Socialism and western capitalism, in the post-Mao era China abandoned the earlier view that war between them was inevitable. It now rather embraced the opposite theory and entertained herself good relations with the West, including the US, and even endorsed for a time the notion of a global anti-Soviet alliance, linking the Western Powers with the CPR.

Actually, at a conference on contemporary Soviet litera- ture held in Harbin on September 12, 1979 (12) — the verbatim account of which, published on December 20, sold out within a few days — a distinction was made between the Soviet aggressive and expansionist foreign policy and its domestic policy, which was conceded to be "basically socialist." Compared to the earlier point of view of Beijing, this seemed to be a major concession; while making clear Beijing's opposition to Moscow, it removed the ideological sting in their relationship.

Similarly, on April 2, 1980, *People's Daily* disavowed a series of nine articles which had attacked the Soviet Union between September 6, 1963, and July 14, 1964.(13) The accusation of revisionism, then hurled against the USSR, was an error, it now admitted. Closely connected with this concession was the circumstance that in the same month the street in Beijing which housed the Soviet Embassy and which early during the Cultural Revolution had been renamed "Struggle against Revisionism Street," received its previous non-political designation. Despite this reorientation, the opposition against the Soviet Union, though on foreign policy grounds rather than on domestic ones, remained as firm as ever, as seen by the sharp criticism of the Soviet foreign policy course both by Hu Yaobang and Deng himself during the same month of April 1980.

Expiration of the Sino-Soviet Treaty

On February 4, 1950, had been signed a thirty-year Sino- Soviet treaty of Friendship, Alliance and Mutual Assistance, which came into force soon thereafter. But on April 13, 1979, Beijing announced that it would not renew the treaty at the time of its expiration a year hence, though it was prepared to negotiate with Moscow on the improvement of mutual relations. The Chinese statement on that occasion stressed that the "difference of principles" between the two states should not hinder the development of normal state relations. The Soviets' rejoinder followed the next day, on April 4.(14) They did not take the announcement lightly, but made it clear that in their view the Chinese leaders' change of thought on the treaty sprang from their own "hegemonistic aspirations." Prior to the expiration of the treaty in April 1980, there was, however, a lively exchange of notes relating to several old and new issues, including principles governing relations between the two countries, Chinese border demands, and recent strong Soviet support for Vietnam. But negotiations were terminated when the Chinese government repeatedly, including in a note to the Soviets of December 31, 1979, condemned the Soviet interventions abroad.(15) On January 19, 1980, on another matter, the Chinese Foreign Ministry warned that the invasion of Afghanistan threatened both world peace and Chinese security in particular and created "new obstacles" to the normalization of mutual relations. These circumstances made it "obviously inappropriate" to carry on Sino-Soviet negotiations. The Soviets made attempts to produce a change of mind by the Peking leadership(16) including, since March 1979, through radio broadcasts in Chinese; they spoke favorably of the Chinese army and were most critical of Deng Xiaoping. (17)

Despite the expiration of the treaty and the apparent eclipse in mutual relations, Brezhnev in his report to the CPSU Congress of February 23, 1981, though critical of the internal development of China over the past twenty years — a "painful lesson" — regretted that Beijing was "aligned with the imperialist powers" and that Soviet-Chinese relations were "frozen." But he assured Beijing that Moscow never wanted any confrontation with China. Various trial balloons, raised to establish in early 1982 new Sino-Soviet contacts were probably linked with the set-back suffered by Sino-American relations over the Taiwan problem.

Border Negotiations in the 1970s; Afghanistan and Mongolia, Bangladesh and Japan

Following the clashes on the Sino-Soviet frontier in the Far East and Central Asia between March and August 1969, the two countries started border negotiations later in the year, but reached no definite solution of the disputed issues. Actually, there occurred numerous border incidents also during the following years. The publication of the political testament of President Ho Chi Minh of North Vietnam, published in September 1969 and featuring his appeal for the restoration of communist unity among the quarreling fraternal parties, brought Alexei Kosygin, who had attended Ho Chi Minh's funeral, on September 11 to Beijing, where he met Chou Enlai. However, Soviet and Chinese versions of the rather casual meeting and of what had been agreed, differed substantially from each other. While the Soviets claimed that it had been agreed to restore diplomatic relations, raising them to the ambassadorial level, and to expand trade, according to the Chinese source both sides consented to withdraw the armed forces from the disputed areas and to preserve the status quo on the border.(18) Border negotiations, though often interrupted, continued until the summer of 1973. One of the reasons for the failure to reach a settlement was the Soviet rejection of the Chinese thesis that the USSR had gained possession of much of Asian territory through "unequal treaties," imposed by Tsarist Russia on weak feudal China. In an interview with Scandinavian journalists, Chou Enlai later pointed to the likely reason for the Soviet claim that there were no "disputed zones" along the Sino-Soviet frontier. In Chou's words, the Soviets were "afraid of a chain reaction on the part of certain other countries," many apparently European.

In June 1973, according to Brezhnev,(19) the Soviet Union offered to China a non-aggression pact, and on October 1, 1974, on the 25th anniversary of the Chinese Revolution, they renewed this proposal. In March 1974 a Soviet helicopter with a three-man crew of frontier guards, was forced to land in China. Beijing claimed that the crew had engaged in espionage, and that numerous intrusions of Chinese air space had preceded it. After a lengthy detention, the members of the crew were finally released. There occurred also serious clashes between Soviet and Chinese troops along the Mongolian border in December 1984.

Moscow and Beijing had resumed border negotiations between February 1975 and February 1977, and continued negotiations over navigation in Far Eastern rivers; at issue at the latter was, in particular, the confluence of the Amur and Ussuri rivers near Khabarovsk. After 1977 there occurred several incidents on both the Central Asian and Far Eastern sectors of the Sino-Soviet border, which resulted in a few deaths on both sides. A new territorial dispute opened up during the summer of 1981 following a border agreement between the Soviet Union and Afghanistan, when the latter recognized the Soviet claim to some territory that had also been claimed by China. That claim was reaffirmed when Li Xiannian in an interview with the Italian Communist newspaper *L'unità*(20) pointed out that both China and the Soviet Union claimed 80,000 to 90,000 square kilometers of territory then occupied by Soviet troops, but apparently excluding the foregoing Soviet-Afghan agreement.

Mongolia too figured in the Sino-Soviet dispute. What concerned the CPR was not only the formal independence of Outer Mongolia after 1945 but her increasing leaning toward and actual dependence on the Soviet Union, especially the stationing of many Soviet troops on the Sino-Mongolian border under a Soviet-Mongolian treaty of friendship, cooperation and mutual aid, dating back to January 15, 1966. At the same time the expulsion of some Chinese influence from Outer Mongolia and discriminatory treatment of others portended the further decline of the CPR's influence in Outer Mongolia. Nevertheless, diplomatic relations improved in 1971 between both countries when ambassadors were exchanged. But the Outer Mongolian government insisted on the presence of Soviet troops; they asserted that they had entered Outer Mongolia at its express request and as protection against Chinese expansionist aspirations.(21)

Fear of expansionism by the Communist rival and of encirclement as well as its own desire to increase its influence and thrust its power beyond its borders, motivated both the Soviet Union and the CPR. The crisis over East Pakistan, which later became Bangladesh, produced the Indo-Pakistan

war of December 1971 in which the Soviet Union took India's
side and China supported Pakistan. China also remembered
the Tibetan rebellion of 1959 which, it charged, India had
encouraged. When India dispatched troops into East Pakistan,
China bitterly denounced this invasion. While the Soviet
Union recognized the new state of Bangladesh in January
1972, China did not extend recognition until August 1975.
Pakistan's defeat and the creation of Bangladesh constituted a
defeat for China, a success for India, and, indirectly, for the
USSR.

The phenomenal rise of Japan's economic power made a
great impression upon the world at large and on Japan's
immediate neighbors, the Soviet Union and the CPR. While
the Soviet Union aimed at preventing an encirclement by
China, Japan, and the US forming an anti-Soviet alliance,
China, no longer fearful of Japanese imperialism, rather
aimed at creating a counter-balance against Soviet imperialism. Japan herself was equally fearful of Soviet expansionism.
It was also involved in a territorial dispute with the Soviets,
dating back to the end of World War II when the USSR
occupied several islands northeast of Japan, namely the
Habomai group, Shikotan, Etorofu, and Kunashiri, which
Japan considered all her own. These "Northern Territories,"
as the Japanese call them, south of the Kurile isles, are not only
strategically vital but also economically important. Soviet
interest in intimidating Japan by its very proximity, through
controlling these bases, is apparent. Neither has Tokyo
forgotten Soviet promises, after World War II, to discuss with
Japan the status of these islands, apparently considering then a
return of these isles to reach some compromise.

Ever since the establishment of diplomatic relations
between China and Japan in September 1972, there loomed
the possibility of more friendly connections between the
erstwhile enemies. The Soviet Union, on the other hand,
warned Tokyo not to enter into closer relations with Beijing by
signing a peace treaty with it. While proposing herself to
Tokyo in January 1975 a treaty of "friendship and goodwill,"
Japan declined the latter suggestion, fearful that such an
agreement before the conclusion of a peace treaty with the
Soviet Union, would close the door to the reopening of the
question of the "Northern Territories." The Soviets were also

concerned about the "anti-hegemony clause" in the proposed Sino-Japanese treaty which it considered, not incorrectly, as a rebuff administered to Moscow, though Beijing officially disavowed such intent.

There were obstacles delaying the Sino-Japanese rapprochement: both Beijing and Taiwan claimed sovereignty over the uninhabited Senkaku islands. By August 1978 China had virtually recognized Japan's control over the islands, which are a part of the Ryukyu islands. Another unresolved issue was a Japanese-South Korean agreement on the development of the continental shelf, which led to protests by China. Nevertheless, a Sino-Japanese treaty was signed by the two foreign ministers in Beijing on August 12, 1978. The Soviets reacted sharply to it, denouncing Beijing's "diktat" to Tokyo; they had long warned of the adverse consequences of such an agreement. The Sino-Japanese treaty of peace and friendship was actually preceded by an eight-year trade agreement between the two countries and was followed by other agreements providing for close economic cooperation.

The "Northern Territories" quarrel aside, Japan was concerned over the naval buildup of the Soviet Pacific Fleet, while the Soviets were anxious because of the increasing rapprochement between Japan on one side and China and the US on the other. Still, in the late seventies and in 1980 the Soviet Union and Japan reached agreement about a number of joint development projects on mineral resources in Siberia and on and around Sakhalin. In the wake, however, of the Soviet invasion of Afghanistan, Tokyo applied sanctions against Moscow. Other sanctions were levelled against the Soviet Union by Japan in retaliation for the martial law in Poland in mid-December 1981, in line with Western policies. The shooting down of a Korean plane off Sakhalin by a Soviet fighter plane on the night of August 31 to September 1, 1983, aroused the world at large and neighboring South Korea and Japan in particular.

The CPR, Vietnam and Kampuchea

Since the later 1970s Indo-China became one of the main areas of confrontation between China and the Soviet Union. In Chinese eyes, Vietnam aimed at the domination of all of

Indochina, controlling already neighboring Kampuchea (Cambodia) and Laos. In view of the close ties between Vietnam and the Soviet Union, the CPR saw in Vietnam's expansion the Soviet hand and was concerned of itself being "encircled." The worsening of Sino-Soviet relations commenced soon after the Communist victories in South Vietnam and Kampuchea. The Soviet Union backed Vietnam, while China supported Kampuchea. The deterioration of Sino-Vietnamese relations increased in 1978 as a result of the flight of 160,000 of the Chinese minority in Vietnam, the end of China's economic support for Vietnam, the latter's admission to the Soviet-controlled *Comecon*, and especially the treaty of friendship and cooperation between Vietnam and the Soviet Union, signed on November 3, 1978. There was also the dispute over the Paracel and Spratly islands situated in the South China Sea.

On December 23, 1978, Vietnamese troops invaded Kampuchea. The latter's capital Phnom Penh fell two weeks later. On January 8, 1979, a People's Revolutionary Council with Heng Samrin as President was set up which was promptly recognized by Vietnam and the Soviet Union and its European client states. The CPR, however, denounced the Vietnamese aggressors and their supporter, Soviet "Social Imperialism," and began to send supplies to the Khmer Rouge. But the Soviets in the UN Security Council accused the Khmer Rouge under Pol-Pot of committing "open suicide," while constructing a "Maoist society."

When on February 17, 1979, the CPR invaded Vietnam, it claimed that its action was a limited counterattack in response to Vietnam's provocations. Suffering heavy casualties, Chinese troops withdrew in March, completing the evacuation by March 16. The Soviet Union accused China of wishing to create a sphere of influence in Southeast Asia,(22) of having brought the Pol-Pot regime to power in Kampuchea and of aiming at transforming this country into a Chinese bridgehead for the encirclement of Vietnam. The article also hinted at the connection between this Chinese aggression and the "normalization" of Sino-American relations.

The CPR sharply opposed the presence of Vietnamese troops in Kampuchea and steadfastly insisted on the withdrawal of Soviet aid from Vietnam as a condition for the improvement of Sino-Soviet relations. The Soviet Union, however, refused to discuss the issue of Kampuchea with the CPR, claiming that this would affect a third country.

Soviet Intervention in Afghanistan

Soviet intervention in Afghanistan at the end of 1979 became a major cause of the growing Sino-Soviet conflict.(23-24) Even prior to this time, the Soviets, apparently laying the propagandistic groundwork for the invasion of Afghanistan, repeatedly accused the CPR of giving aid to Moslem rebels against the revolutionary Afghan government which had come to power in April 1978. In September 1979 President N. M. Taraki was overthrown by a rival communist faction led by H. Amin. When both the internal situation and relation with the neighboring Soviet Union worsened thereafter, Amin was removed from power, executed, and replaced by Babrak Karmal. The Soviet Union claimed that it had been invited to dispatch troops into the country under the treaty of Friendship, in alleged response to threats and provocations from Afghanistan's external foes. By the end of January 1980, it was estimated that the number of Soviet troops in Afghanistan had reached 85,000. On December 29, 1979, the Beijing government, recalling the Soviet intervention in Czechoslovakia more than a decade before, considered the Soviet invasion of Afghanistan the USSR's first intervention in a Third World country. The Chinese Foreign Minister Huang Hua, while on an official visit to Pakistan in January 1980, called upon the West and Japan to render support to Afghanistan's neighbors to resist Soviet aggression and, at the same time, suspended negotiations with Moscow on the normalization of mutual relations. The CPR government was especially aroused over an Afghan-Soviet border agreement which related to the Walkhan Salient, a strategic mountainous strip of Afghan territory which ran toward the Soviet border. The Soviets occupied the area, and, after expelling the few thousand Afghan residents, closed the area's border with Pakistan. Beijing protested the treaty relating to the salient, referring to its own contrary agreement with Afghanistan. Jeane Kirkpatrick, U.S. representative to the U.N. asserted that the Soviet Union had carried out a "de facto annexation" of the Walkhan Salient.

The USSR, to deflect attention from its own aggressive and destabilizing exploits in Afghanistan and to discredit the Afghan freedom fighters operating from Pakistan's soil, has pictured the defensive patriotic Afghan moves as provocatory and counterrevolutionary, serving only US imperialism. In *Pravda* Schurygin, "Staging Area for Imperialist Interference"(25) criticized Pakistan's role in the US Asian policy: "No propaganda tricks by Islamabad and Washington can hide the obvious fact that the Pakistani regime's course of militarization and complicity in imperialism interferes in the affairs of sovereign states." Neighboring Pakistan is increasingly turning Afghanistan "into a hotbed of tension in this part of the globe. This policy poses a serious threat to peace in Asia." Beijing has countered what it considers Moscow's slanderous attacks.(26)

The CPR on East Europe (1969-1984)
and Sino-West European Relations

Opposition to extensive Soviet control over their East European Empire was displayed in the early postwar period even by many Communists of East Central Europe, especially by Tito's Yugoslavia — which had broken ties with Moscow in 1948-49 — and by Ceausescu's Rumania which, defying Moscow's leadership of the Soviet bloc in foreign affairs, had obtained the reputation of being a maverick. Both these Balkan countries and, for different reasons, the CPR often castigated Soviet policy. China, of course, was interested in weakening the Soviets' hold on the allegiance of East European Communist Parties and states, win friends for herself, and divert Soviet interests from Asia to Eastern Europe.

Not only the CPR but also Yugoslavia and Rumania were shocked by the Soviet invasion of Czechoslovakia. China, though previously locked in a bitter ideological dispute with "revisionist" Yugoslavia, improved her relations with the latter after 1968; a similar rapprochement took place between the CPR and Rumania. In June 1971 Ceausescu, accompanied by the Rumanian Prime Minister I. G. Maurer, visited China, meeting Chairman Mao and Zhou Enlai. At that time Li Xiannian praised Yugoslavia's "struggle against interference, subversion, and threats of aggression by the superpowers," and for its policy of independence from these two rivals. The

Soviets did not hesitate to voice their misgivings over Yugoslavia's and Rumania's improving relations with the CPR.(27)

In August 1978, Hua Guofeng visited these two Balkan countries, Rumania at the time of the tenth anniversary of the Soviet invasion of Czechoslovakia. On August 24th, *Pravda* sharply criticized "Beijing's aggressiveness" In December 1979, both, Yugoslavia and Rumania disapproved the Soviet military intervention in Afghanistan. During the following years the CPR cultivated good relations with both Yugoslavia and Rumania, and Party and government leaders further visited each other; a most important journey to these states was undertaken in May 1983 by Hu Yaobang, General Secretary of the CPC. This was quickly followed by a visit of the chief Chinese representative at the Sino-Soviet talks, Qian Qichen, to Hungary, Poland, and East Germany. But in December 1981 China did not condemn Poland's imposing martial law, though the West applied sanctions against the Warsaw regime. Yet the divisive revisionist issue, separating Belgrade from Beijing, had lost its earlier meaning for the CPR. In March 1984, the Chinese Foreign Minister Wu Xuequian referred to the many similarities in China's and Yugoslavia's internal development and in their foreign policy stand. But China lost its consistent supporter in South-Eastern Europe when Albania, long the lone friend of the radical CPR in the Balkan and all of Europe and foe of the Soviet Union, moved early in 1977 farther away from Beijing's pragmatic, seemingly "rightist" and revisionist policies.

During the Cultural Revolution the CPR displayed hostility both toward the Soviet Union as well as toward the West. But the need to find a counterweight to the USSR, considered the "main enemy," and the decline of the ideological hostility to capitalism and Western democracy, nurtured by geopolitical realism, led to a rapprochement both with the US and her West European allies, the politically democratic Second World capitalist states of Western Europe, though sometimes ruled by Social Democratic parties. Geopolitics brought home to Beijing that the USSR, facing both East and West, had to keep its military forces in readiness on two fronts, in Europe and Asia. This created joint interests between China and the West

European states as well as between the CPR and her former foe, Japan.

In 1972 China and the United Kingdom had upgraded their respective diplomatic representation from chargés to ambassadors. On April 3, 1978, the CPR and the EEC signed a five-year nonpreferential agreement, though only a few years earlier the EEC was pictured by China as a mere "American machination." On October 18, 1979, the Chinese Foreign Minster Huang Hua, while visiting France, West Germany, Italy, and the United Kingdom, stressed during a press conference that China "wished Europe to strengthen its cooperation and its defenses": a few days later in West Germany he called for a union of all peace-loving countries against "hegemonist aggression and expansion." As late as May and June 1984, while journeying also to North European countries, he promised China's support to a Western Europe aiming at "becoming strong and powerful."

Brezhnev's Criticism of Chinese Foreign Policy

In his much noted speech in Tashkent in 1982,(28) Brezhnev once again had offered to reopen border talks with the CPR and had strongly appealed for normalization of relations. While he recalled that the Soviet Union had "openly criticized" and con- tinued to criticize "many aspects of the policy (especially the foreign policy) of the Chinese leadership as being at variance with socialist principles and standards," she had allegedly never tried to interfere in the internal life of the PRC nor denied the existence of a socialist system in China. To distinguish Soviet policy from American policy, he also asserted, the Soviets had never supported the so-called "concept of the two Chinas," and tried to assure the CPR that there was no threat to it emanating from Moscow. Nor had the Soviet Union any territorial claims on the CPR (he ignored China's claims on territory held by the USSR). The Soviet Union was ready to continue talks on existing border questions for the purpose of reaching mutually acceptable agreements. The Soviets recalled the time when the two countries were "united by bonds of friendship and comradely cooperation." Moscow was prepared to come to terms,"without any preliminary conditions," to improve Soviet-Chinese relations, though "not to the detriment of third countries"—meaning primarily Communist Afghanistan and Vietnam. But the Chinese Foreign Ministry preferred to see in Brezhnev's remarks only "attacks" which it sharply rejected, and insisted on attaching importance only to "actual deeds of the Soviet Union in Sino-Soviet relations and international affairs.(29)

Soon after Brezhnev's talk, Mikhail Kapitsa—director of the Soviet Foreign Ministry's Far Eastern Department, who was appointed in December 1982 a Deputy Foreign Minister—visited Beijing between May 13-21, 1982. Though the visit was described as a private one, Kapitsa had several meetings with high-placed Chinese officials, some of whom, including Yu Hongliang, director of the Chinese Foreign Ministry's Soviet and East European Department, returned the visit later in the summer. While Kapitsa was in Beijing, an article in *Pravda* on May 20, 1982 by I. Aleksandrov—a pseudonym for semiofficial statements—declared Soviet readiness for engaging in border talks, but rejected Chinese demands for renouncing Soviet support to the Mongolian People's Republic, the countries of Indochina and Afghanistan, the unilateral withdrawal of the armed forces of the Soviet Union from the border with the CPR, and recognition of China's "rights to vast areas of the USSR."(30) The Chinese preliminary conditions amounted to an ultimatum. Hu Yaobang, elected on September 12 to the post of General Secretary of the CPC, came indeed out for some of the foregoing demands, listed in *Pravda*. He may have attempted to make his criticism of Soviet leaders more acceptable to them by accusing in his report to the Twelfth Party Congress on September 1, 1982, both superpowers of "hegemonism." On the other hand, the new Party constitution of September 1, 1982, omitted all references to "the hegemonism of the two superpowers" and to Soviet "modern revisionism." Though *Beijing Review* still insisted that the Soviet Union constituted the "major threat to world peace,"(31) there were ominous indications of some softening of the harsh anti-Soviet rhetorics previously pursued.

During a conversation with the Japanese Prime Minister Zenko Suzuki who was visiting China, the Chinese Prime Minister Zhao Ziyang emphasized on September 27, 1982, China's independence of foreign policy thought and action, stressing that the CPR had no desire to "play the Soviet card against the U.S. or the American card against the USSR."(32-33) Here was a definite change not only of emphasis but also of the contents of policy compared to a few years earlier!

The Sino-Soviet Dispute under Andropov

An outstanding feature of the Sino-Soviet relationship after the death of Brezhnev was the increase of trading, cultural contacts and, despite the Olympic boycotts, even of sporting exchanges. But on the fundamental divisive issues between them — Afghanistan, Vietnam, and the menacing presence of Soviet troops along the Sino-Soviet border — no rapprochement took place; the Soviets insisted on restricting any negotiations to purely bilateral issues, thus excluding geographic areas and Third World nations into which the Soviets were expanding under the guise of other bilateral agreements. Still, everything considered, there was neither a striking improvement nor an outright deterioration of Sino-Soviet relations in this period. After Brezhnev's death on November 10, 1982. there followed the short-term preeminence of his successors, both elderly and sick, first of Yuri Andropov, who died in February 1984, and then of Konstantin Chernenko.

Brezhnev's demise offered an opportunity to both sides to try to break new ground in their relations. Huang Hua, the Chinese Foreign Minister, flew to Moscow for Brezhnev's funeral on November 15 and met both Yuri Andropov and the Soviet Foreign Minister A. Gromyko. After his return to Beijing he expressed optimism about the prospects of improving relations with the USSR. On November 16, V. Afanasyev told Japanese journalists in Tokyo that the Soviet Union would eventually withdraw its troops from Afghanistan. (34) Six days later, Andropov voiced the Soviet desire to better relations with all socialist nations, including "our great neighbor ... the People's Republic of China." In a friendly greeting to Soviet authorities on occasion of the 60th anniversary of the Soviet Union's founding (1922), the CPR voiced its hope for "normalization of mutual relations" and the possibility of the removal of the "obstacles" preventing it. One of these "obstacles" was Soviet support of the Vietnamese invasion of and control of Kampuchea. Beijing, according to Pierre Bauby, political secretary of the French Marxist-

Leninist Communist party, a Maoist outfit, after returning from a visit to Beijing, stated in Rome that Beijing had allegedly forwarded to Moscow proposals for a settlement of the dispute over Kampuchea and the creation of a neutral state.

But China's criticism of Soviet policy continued, though on a lesser scale, to induce perhaps a more favorable Soviet response. Such hopes for improvement of mutual relations, as aroused by an article in the official monthly *Observation Post*, were, however, quickly extinguished by an attack on the Chinese press by the weekly *New Times* of January 14, 1983.(35) There followed other rounds of Sino-Soviet talks, frequently interrupted by the resumption of polemics. Finally, mutual criticisms were voiced by Andropov in August 1983 and President Li Xiannian on the Chinese side. Kapitsa once again visited Beijing in September 1983, where he met Qian Qichen. Perhaps Sino-Soviet relations looked more hopeful than previously: one of four countries which in the U.N. abstained on September 12, 1983, on the draft of a Security Council resolution deploring the destruction of a South Korean plane shot down by a Soviet fighter plane after flying into Soviet airspace, was the CPR! Talks were resumed in Beijing by the representatives of the two Communist rivals on October 6, 1983. The Chinese Foreign Minister at a news briefing on October 5 made clear his opposition to the Soviets deploying SS-20 missiles, removed from the European theatre to the Soviet Far East. Similarly, on November 3, Xinhua was highly critical of the Soviet use of military bases in Vietnam. At the same time *Izvestia* and *Pravda* condemned Chinese support for Japan's claim to the Soviet-occupied islands off northern Japan! The Soviets strongly disapproved of a visit by Zhao Ziyang to Washington D.C. in January 1984, concerned over the possible improvement of Sino-American relations.

On February 9, 1984 Andropov died. The Chinese representative at the funeral was Wan Li, a Deputy Premier and high-ranking Chinese personality, who met on that occasion Konstantin Chernenko, but only briefly. Another round of talks, the fourth, was scheduled in Moscow for March 1984. Prior to it, both Chinese and Soviet statements, however, played down hopes for the lowering of the polemics. Toward the end of March 1984 Tass reported that the talks had occurred in a frank and calm atmosphere, but would not be resumed before October 14.

Reagan's Journey to Beijing and Soviet Response

President Reagan visited China from April 26 to May lst 1984. This was the President's first journey to a Communist country and the first visit by an American President since the establishment of formal relations between them. Among the four protocols signed was one agreement on nuclear coopera-tion, one to resume cultural exchanges, and a tax agreement preventing double taxation of Chinese and US companies operating in the other country. However, the Chinese also criticized the US position on Central America, the Middle East, and Korea and the US policy on disarmament. Reagan's criticism of the Soviets, while on Chinese soil, was censored by the Chinese media on two different occasions. Chinese television broadcasts of Reagan's speech on April 27 deleted his critical comments alluding to the Soviet threat to China, the Soviet and Vietnamese occupation of Afghanistan and Kampuchea respectively, and the Soviets shooting down a South Korean civilian plane. Apparently China was bent on proving to its own people as well as to the Soviets that it pursued an independent foreign policy and that it was not sailing in American waters.

In an extensive commentary of April 29, 1984, *Tass* in turn denounced Reagan's attack against the USSR and criticized China's leaders for permitting themselves being used by the U.S.(36) Five days earlier, Tass had pointed to the virtual identity of American and Chinese views on numerous Asiatic questions. Following a visit of General Zhang Aiping to the US in June 1984, a Sino-American aggreement on selling weapons to Beijing was revealed. On June 6, the Soviet press issued another warning aimed at Beijing and Washington. A planned trip of Soviet Deputy Premier I. Arkhipov to the Chinese capital, already scheduled, was postponed, reflecting Soviet irritation over the steady improvement of Sino-American relations. Following new clashes along the Sino-Vietnamese border and Chinese naval maneuvers aimed against the Vietnam-held Spratly islands, Chernenko openly condemned China's "hostile actions" in Indochina, while Chinese authorities escalated their polemics against Moscow, comparing Soviet endeavors in Afghanistan with "Hitler's atrocities."

While in the summer months of 1984, China continued to spout anti-Soviet slogans, after September 1984 there followed meetings between Gromyko and leading Chinese officials both in New York at the U.N. and in Beijing. The last meeting in that year took place in the Chinese capital between I. Arkhipov, the highest-ranking Soviet leader to visit China for the last fifteen years, and was climaxed by the signing of several agreements on economic, scientific, and technological cooperation, also designed to promote trade between the two countries.

Beijing on Chernenko's "Rigid" Policy

While Sino-Soviet relations under Andropov (November 1982- February 1984) seemed to Beijing on a slightly more hopeful course, under Chernenko relations were marked by "inflexibility in Soviet foreign relations and imperiousness in handling major international affairs." Since Chernenko had taken power, Moscow has "escalated its war efforts in Afghanistan." In Indochina, Chernenko has increased support to the Vietnamese aggressors and strengthened the Soviet base in Cam Ranh Bay to serve the strategic goal of expansion. In April the Soviet Union carried out the first jet-air and naval maneuvers in Haiphong, when the Vietnamese invaders launched a dry-season offensive along the Kampuchean-Thailand border. Though for some time, the Soviet Union has been in a passive position in the Middle East, now the Soviet leaders, according to Beijing, unwilling to be mere onlookers, were trying to increase Soviet influence in the region. The two superpowers have entered a new round of arms race centering on the deployment of medium-range missiles in Europe. Chernenko had "a more rigid attitude than his predecessor." The Soviets wanted to be flexible in the area of economics and trade, refusing, however, to remove key obstacles toward normalization of Sino-Soviet relations. Observers noticed that Moscow had increased its anti-Chinese propaganda. Since March 1984, anti-China reports in Soviet newspapers and released by *Tass* have doubled, as compared with the preceding year. The Soviet attack was not only aimed at

China's independent foreign policy, but also at its domestic policies and principles of socialist construction. Chernenko had even directly attacked China by name on June 11 and 26, when defending Vietnamese aggression.

Persistent Problems in 1985; Afghanistan and Kampuchea. Deng's Assurance of Continuity

The year 1985 heralded no major change in recent Chinese attitudes regarding world affairs and foreign policy toward the US and toward the Soviet Union.

China's stand on Afghanistan "remains unchanged."(37) *Beijing Review* held that the Soviets in Afghanistan were "trudging in mire." In the five years since their invasion of the country, they have only achieved "military frustrations, a heavy economic burden, and isolation in the world." The brave Afghan people "flattened the Soviet blitz." By modest estimates the Soviet army in Afghanistan has suffered 20,000-plus casualties. On January 10, 1985, China denounced military intrusions in the Kampuchean-Thai border area. The condemnation came one day after Beijing rejected Hanoi's call for a lunar new year truce along the Chinese-Vietnam border. Since December 1984 Vietnamese attacks have intensified, causing heavy casualties and material damage. Hanoi's offensive along this border was "doomed to failure." But the day after the funeral of President Konstantin Chernenko, Mikhail Gorbachev, the newly chosen Secretary of the C. C., received Li Peng, Chinese Vice-Premier, who expressed his hopes that Sino-Soviet relations would be improved.(38) Li also conveyed the congratulations of the CPC General Secretary Hu Yaobang to Gorbachev on the assumption of his eminent post.

While on occasion of Chernenko's death diplomatic niceties were exchanged and hopes for improvement of state relations expressed, China through Deng once again voiced warnings, deprecating the past cult of personality in China and its excessive claims both in domestic and foreign policy, exulted a new moderate course, and assured the Chinese people and the world at large of the "continuity" of Beijing's policy. As far as the Soviet Union was concerned, this assurance, however, fell short of Soviet hopes and goals.

While sickness and death have caused uncertainties in the top echelon of Soviet leadership, Deng apparently has preserved his good health, though his advanced age has raised questions about the permanence of his new policies. But Deng has countered such anxieties:(39) "Foreign newspapers stress my role in the Central Advisory Committee. I have a part in it, but most of the work is being done by other comrades." He called the document "Decision on Reform of the Economic Structure" "a good document; but I did not write or review a single word in it. . .Don't try to exaggerate my role. This would only raise doubts in people's minds and lead them to believe that our policy will change, once Deng is gone. The world community is quite concerned about this. Current policy is working. People's living standard is improving and China's international prestige is rising." There were still some tens of millions of peasants in the countryside who do not yet have enough food or clothing, "although things are much better than before." "In recent talks with foreign guests I never fail to assure them that our policy will not change, that they can rely on the continuity of our current policy. Yet they are not thoroughly convinced."

In a report on the US-Soviet summit in Geneva in November 1985, Yi Ming, *Beijing Review*'s News Analyst, concluded that "whether the two superpowers inch closer depends more on deeds than words."(40) Reagan and Gorbachev spawned more hope than most people had ever expected, though the summit did not bring forth a solution to the key problem of the limitation and reduction of arms. In an official statement, a spokesmen of the Foreign Ministry, spelling out the Chinese Government's stand on the summit, welcomed its results,(41) though admitting that serious differences remained on a number of critical issues. Beijing hoped that the two countries would henceforth truly forego the pursuit of military superiority, would not harm the interests of other countries, and would aim at "a genuine international detente." In this context, the Chinese criticism of the Soviet policy and conception of detente, not long ago rather castigated, had virtually abated. In this crucial sector a significant shift of policy by the Chinese Government had taken place.

Some Lessening of Differences

The year 1985 saw some abatement of the Sino-Soviet conflict, though fundamental differences between the two Communist giants remain unchanged. There exists, however, a kind of consensus not needlessly to exacerbate the differences. In January 1985, *Beijing Review* wrote with apparent satisfaction, that the Sino-Soviet border trade has been rejuvenated. The two countries were now conducting a brisk trade along the border, which is one aspect of renewed economic and trade relations between them. It was heaviest along the northern borders of Heilongjiang Province and the Inner Mongolian Autonomous Region, which are adjacent to the Soviet Union. The trade was halted in 1962. But in 1982 the ministries of trade in China and the Soviet Union reached an agreement to restore border trade. The volume of trade in 1984 increased by 70% over the previous year.(42)

The CPR emphasized repeatedly that both its domestic and foreign policy would stay on its new course, whoever would be in control in Beijing. China distanced herself from the U.S., apparently expecting thus to satisfy her own extreme Left and to lessen hostility toward the Soviet Union. The US was actually concerned about the opposite sharply anti-Soviet stance of Deng in 1980. The new stance seemed to accord with the CPR's own national interests, by keeping its growing ties with the United States, while not alarming the USSR. At the same time, the CPR, also after Gorbachev assumed control in Moscow, reiterated its wellknown "conditions" for removing the major "roadblocks" which were hindering the solution of outstanding issues between China and the Soviet Union, the issues of Afghanistan and Kampuchea and the militarization of the Sino-Soviet boundary.

Cultural Exchange and Trade

While in international politics the Soviets maintained an unbending attitude, they demonstrated flexibility toward China in 1985 in matters of cultural exchange, economics, and trade. On April 6, 1986, *Izvestia* reported, the signing of a Sino-Soviet protocol providing for the exchange of two hundred students and apprentices. One day later, Qian

Quichen, CPR deputy Minister of Foreign Affairs, arrived in Moscow for political consultations.(43)

On July 16, 1985, the Chinese Vice Premier Yao Yilin returned from an eight-day visit to the Soviet Union—a return visit for one paid to Beijing the year before. Yao Yilin brought back from Moscow two economic and trade agreements. The two agreements, he asserted, were important to the long-term development of economic and trade relations between the two countries.(44) Yilin cautioned that many things remain to be done to truly normalize relations. There was the presence of one million Soviet troops poised along the border with China and the disputes over Afghanistan and Kampuchea. "None of these problems have been solved despite the six rounds of talks that have been held." Improvement of relations "cannot be determined by the desire of only one side," China's Communist Party General Secretary Hu Yaobang had voiced the same warning earlier in the year.

But despite the foregoing obstacles, economic relations between the Soviet Union and the CPR had improved. During Yao, Yilin's visit both sides agreed that a Sino-Soviet commission on economics, and trade and scientific and technological cooperation would hold its first meeting during the first half of 1986 in Beijing.

Alliance with Vietnam and Other Sino-Soviet Differences under Gorbachev

On the occassion of Vietnam's Le Duan visiting Moscow, Gorbachev referred to the "coordination of our national-economic plans for 1986-90."(45) He regretted, however that "no political understanding of the acute need to move toward normalization" in the most populous part of the world-Asia and the Pacific basin had been reached: "No Sino-Soviet rapproachement had taken place." The US had recently stepped up its preparations in this region. In accordance with the notorious "Pacific doctrine," the US had interfered in the affairs of sovereign people. "The entire edge of this policy is directed against the Soviet Union," Vietnam, and other socialist states in Asia, Afghanistan and Kampuchea. But by its very essence this policy threatened all the peoples of the Asian-Pacific area. Gorbachev did not give an indication of any change of policy in Southeast Asia or of any concessions to either China or the USA.

On June 30, 1985, according to *Pravda* and *Izvestia*, the joint declaration of the Soviet Union and Vietnam had endorsed Soviet aid to Vietnam and support of the Indochinese states "against imperialism and hegemonism." The two sides resolutely condemned the USA's aggressive policy in various parts of the region and Washington's plans to turn the area into another region of political-military confrontation with the socialist countries, and noted the danger posed by the military build-up of the US and its allies in the Far East and by their "efforts to remilitarize Japan and speed up the creation of a Washington-Tokyo-Seoul militaristic alliance."(46) Both the Soviet Union and Vietnam held that the normalization of relations between the USSR, on one hand, and the CPR, on the other, would strengthen peace in Asia and international security. A not so subtle reminder to Beijing that the further strengthening of the socialist camp was contingent on a change of the latter's policy, a greater orientation toward Moscow.

Since Gorbachev has assumed the reins of government, both Moscow and Beijing have exchanged polite words and at times extended an olive branch to the other side. But neither has modified its basic position on the dividing issues, Outer Mongolia, Afghanistan, Kampuchea, the Soviet naval build-up in the Pacific, and the deployment of Soviet troops and weaponry along the Sino-Soviet frontier. Nor has the CPR buried its suspicion that the USSR is continuing the policy of hegemonism. The Soviets apparently doubt that the CPR is going to repudiate its territorial claims on former Chinese and present Soviet territory. Vice Premier Li Peng told a group of visiting American Journalists on April 15, 1986 in Beijing: "We hope that both China and the Soviet Union will become /!/ good neighbors."(47) Moscow and Beijing have travelled a long rocky road: from being allied to engaging in hostile clashes and military confrontation.

II

MAJOR DIVISIVE ISSUES
SINCE THE LAST DAYS OF MAO

Introduction

The Sino-Soviet dispute is, among other things, a struggle for power between Soviet nationalism and Chinese nationalism. It is the more intense since the two countries are geographically neighbors, along the longest boundary in the world. China has often made vague and ill-defined but persistent territorial demands, which are rooted in historical claims, on the other power. The presence of national minorities in their border regions, which are split between the two giant states, has further deepened their mutual antagonism. Ideologically and theoretically dedicated to Marxism-Leninism-Stalinism, and the CPR also to Mao Zedong's thought, they are superficially united by this creed, but, due to their different interpretations of it, actually sharply divided from each other. The Marxist perspective is reminiscent of medieval theological disputes. Each of the two powers looks upon the opposing side as an arch-heretic, though during the last decade, with both states loosening the ideological straightjacket, Marxist-Leninist theory has lost some of its earlier significance.

The power struggle between them extends all over the globe, finding its climax in the attempt of both Beijing and Moscow to gain influence and power, penetrate the other Party, and corral adherents among the Communist Parties of the world, but also to find followers of their policy among Socialists, Social Democrats, "progressive" parties everywhere, last but not least, among the nations of the Third World. Both Parties have come to appreciate the importance of economic progress for domestic and foreign policy considerations, the CPR emphasizing modernization — to which almost every other goal is subordinated — the Soviet Union stressing rapid economic advancement, which has eluded it for many years.

Their political and military power, both sides realize, is to a large extent a function of their economic progress. In view of the absence of democratic and Western parliamentary tradition in both countries, the two sides uphold "strong leadership" by the ruling Communist Party. They are determined to preserve the Party's dictatorship and the one-party state, all ideological and theoretical modifications and pretentious claims to democracy to the contrary. In their competition for power, unceasing propaganda, a tight organization and discipline are crucial to their success; so are gaining political and geopolitical advantages over the adversary in the international arena.

In the period focussed on in this study, roughly the last decade, both the CPR and the Soviet Union have of course not remained stationary in political, social, ideological, and economic respects and in regard to foreign policy and outlook on international affairs. To the contrary, in this time span the CPR has at times veered from one extreme to the other, producing radical turn-abouts in domestic and foreign policy. Even in the period of Deng's leadership, an era of far-reaching change and of probing and testing domestic and foreign policy waters, policies have been modified or undergone substantial alterations, as, for instance, from propagating an outright alliance with the West to so-called "independence" between the superpowers. Changes in the USSR have been less pronounced in this period, but have not been entirely missing. The change in the leadership of the Soviet Union from Brezhnev to Andropov, Chernenko, and Gorbachev may not have produced reversals of policy, but produced changes in style, vigor, and tactics, influenced by the special background, age, and experience of the individual leaders.

A. The Territorial Disputes
Krushchev Remembers

In *Krushchev Remembers. The Last Testament*, (1974), the deposed Soviet leader, devoting many pages to the discussion of China, treats extensively the territorial dispute between the two Communist giants.(1) While some recent analysts have tended to minimize the significance of territorial differences between Beijing and Moscow, emphasizing rather

the broader power struggle as such, in Krushchev's view and
that of the contemporary Soviet leadership, territorial
differences figured large in the growth of the Sino-Soviet
dispute, both under Stalin and during his own stewardship
until his overthrow in 1964. Contemporary critics of the
opinion that the territorial issues were not, and are not, a
major cause of the Sino-Soviet confrontation but rather its
symptom, tend to overlook the importance which both the
leadership of the CPR and the Soviet Union have attached to
these particular issues. Does the contemporary, also geographically distant analyst of the Sino-Soviet confrontation know
more about the causes of the rift and understand them better
than the leading personalities of both countries who were
directly involved in the unfolding of the dispute?

Krushchev clearly revealed the clash of personalities
between the leadership of the two Communist countries which
underlay the Soviet Union-China relationship. Beyond it, in
Krushchev's view, territorial differences between the two
neighbors, ideological differences, plain chauvinism, even
racism, the arrogance which it disclosed, and considerations of
national power figured dominantly. A careful examination of
Krushchev's personal account is therefore essential: it clearly
illuminates the multiplicity of divisive issues between Moscow
and Peking.

Krushchev, generally critical of Stalin, pointed to the
special errors of his China policy, but placed the much greater
responsibility for the developing dispute on China's and
especially Mao's shoulders. In regard to Chinese Sinkiang,
which the Soviets occupied during World War II, Stalin
committed a "serious mistake" when he later suggested to Mao
the organization of an international society for the exploitation
of natural resources, making the CPR think that the Soviet
Union had "certain designs" on the province and that she
intended to "encroach on Chinese territory and independence." Thus Stalin sowed the seeds of hostility and anti-Soviet
and anti-Russian feeling in China.(2) Krushchev shifted the
burden or possible Soviet guilt on Stalin rather than on
himself. Mao in turn came to believe that "Stalin's policy
toward China had much in common with the imperialist
policies of the capitalist countries." Both Stalin and Mao were

"deeply suspicious" of each other's designs and policies—just as their successors have remained distrustful of each other.

When Konrad Adenauer visited Moscow in 1955 to establish West German-Soviet diplomatic relations, Krushchev revealed to him his concern about China. He declared that Red China was the great problem. "Just think, Red China already has a population of 600 million. Its yearly increase is twelve millions. They all live from a handful of rice. 'What,' and he clapped his hands together, 'what will come of all this?'" And Krushchev literally appealed to Chancellor Adenauer: "Help us. Help us to deal with Red China."(3) The long-lasting German danger had suddenly vanished and the threat from a "fraternal" Communist power had appeared on the horizon! Whatever the likelihood of West Germany's possible help to the Soviet Union along her Asiatic frontiers, the anxiety emanating from the urgent plea had the sound of truth.

Krushchev accused Peking's leadership and Mao in particular of "chauvinism and arrogance," all made "manifest" by their territorial claims. As Krushchev put it, "according to our Communist views of the world, all nations are equal."(4) Such Soviet proclamations, of course, ran counter to the reality of Soviet domination of the world communist movement. Despite Krushchev's contrary claims, Moscow was not prepared to offer Mao "an equal /!/ partnership" in the collective leadership of the international communist movement. But Krushchev held that the CPR's ungrateful and impudent behavior toward the leading Communist state undermined the close cooperation and unity of the entire socialist commonwealth.

Despite the concessions made by the USSR especially in Manchuria after Stalin's death, news reached the Kremlin that the Chinese were not satisfied with the Sino-Soviet border, especially around Vladivostok and in Central Asia. (Some of these demands were dropped in later years.) "We were afraid," wrote Krushchev, "that if we started remapping our frontiers according to historical considerations, the situation could get out of hand and lead to conflict."(5) "National borders should pale into insignificance in the light of Marxist-Leninist philosophy which holds that the international revolutionary movement, a force that transcends national boundaries, will triumph everywhere in the end." The Chinese, however, informed Moscow that it should disregard the reports of "bourgeois newspapers" in Hong Kong relating to Peking's boundary claims. (Some of these dailies were actually Communist-oriented.) But despite Soviet entreaties, Peking refused to publish a clarification of its stand on Vladivostok and other border regions, which Moscow asked for at that occasion.

Chinese procedures in raising the border issue were particularly offensive to the Soviet leaders. Everything else aside, it was clear that any far-reaching Kremlin concessions would create numerous other demands by aggrieved neighbors— Communist-ruled incidentally—to revise the frontier with the Soviet Union in their favor. The Chinese, however, may have wished to wean these states away from the West and over to their side by deliberately "dragging out the old question about how the Soviet Union had seized the Baltic States and then annexed certain territories from Rumania and Poland." (They apparently had not mentioned Czechoslovakia or Krushchev might have forgotten it in this context.) To Krushchev, who "did not even bother to reply to such charges," the whole historical border was "nonsense," a "dead issue." Then Peking turned again to "hostile statements about how we'd seized territory from them in the Far East. . .we wanted to put a stop to such talk once and for all."(6)

The Soviets, as Krushchev tells it, could not seriously entertain Chinese claims "to Vladivostok and a substantial area in /Soviet/ and, Central Asia." The Far Eastern Province was not populated by Chinese nor was Central Asia.(7) While the population of the Far East consisted mostly of Russians, in Central Asia it was made up of Kazakhs, Uighurs, and Kirghiz'. An especially troublesome point was the status of the Pamir Mountains, which were not included in any treaty between the Soviet and Chinese governments. However, according to Krushchev, they were inhabited by Tadzhiks and, "therefore quite reasonably," were part of the Tadzhik Republic.

Another divisive territorial issue was in the Far Eastern Province; the riverbeds of the Amur and Ussuri had shifted somewhat. The new islands in these rivers belonged technically to the USSR, since the border, according to the old Nerchinsk

(Nipchu) treaty followed the river bank on the Chinese side. While the Chinese demand for navigation rights along the Amur was reasonable, the Soviets opposed their coming "literally up to the walls of Khabarovsk." According to Krushchev, "we were willing to give a little as well as take a little." This stance, however, ignored the substantial Chinese demand for restitution of territories, considering all that Tsarist Russia had previously wrested from them. Particularly unacceptable was China's insistence that the new treaty was to include a clause specifying that "the new border perpetuated an injustice foisted on China over a hundred years ago." As Krushchev continued: "We would have been tacitly acknowledging that the injustice must be rectified." "To this day the 'inequality' clause has stuck in our throats." And he concluded with the observation that today the Soviet Union was pursuing the same policies which were conducted when I was head of the Government and the Party." Indeed, the Soviet policy towards China, the roots of which were laid in Stalin's era, has worsened several years after his death. Under his successors the relations have deteriorated, despite considerable changes having taken place both in the USSR and in the CPR under Mao and after his demise.

The "Unequal Treaties": Mao and Krushchev

Of the numerous causes and aspects of the Sino-Soviet controversy, the territorial dispute between the two great Communist Powers, as stated, has loomed especially large. During the years 1962-1964 territorial questions played a prominent part in the polemics between Moscow and Beijing. It all began when in March 1963 the government of the CPR stated for the first time publicly that the Russo-Chinese treaties of Aigun (1858), Beijing (1860), and Ili (1881) were "unequal treaties." Thus Beijing compared these treaties with other "unequal" treaties that Western Imperialism had wrested at bayonet's point from China in the course of the nineteenth century. The Beijing government thus suggested that these treaties would have to be abrogated, as had been those concluded by the Western Powers with China. The fraternal C.P. S.U. was subtly reminded to fulfill its long overdue internationalist and socialist obligations in the field of Russo-Chinese relations.

During the years 1962-1964, territorial issues which centered on Sinkiang and Outer Mongolia figured most prominently in the Sino-Soviet dispute. Soviet interest in Sinkiang had been strongly asserted during the governorship of Sheng Shi-ts'ai between 1937 and 1942 and continued until 1949 when the C.P.R. was promulgated. Since 1949 the C.P.C. had reasserted its control in Sinkiang and has attempted to sinify the numerous ethnic groups such as Kazakhs, Uighurs, and others. Communist China had aimed at the fulfillment of this policy by various means: by colonizations with army veterans and civilian Han immigrants from China proper, the resettlement of nomadic tribes, and through the encouragement of Chinese administration and Chinese language and civilization.

Outer Mongolia, a Soviet satellite since the mid-1920s, separated from China formally in 1945 — a separation acknowledged by the C.P.C. in the Sino-Soviet treaty of 1950. Mao Zedong revealed later that in 1954, when Krushchev and Bulganin visited Beijing, he had attempted to reopen the issue, but they had "refused to talk to us."(8) In 1964 Mao told a delegation of the Japanese Socialist Party, which was then visiting Beijing, that there were "too many places occupied by the Soviet Union" and that the Kuriles should be returned to Japan, and Outer Mongolia, "which is considerably greater than the Kuriles," to the C.P.R.

Krushchev disputed Mao's views, appropriately enough, in a talk also with a Japanese parliamentary delegation on September 15, 1964. According to him, the territory of the Soviet Union had "evolved historically" and the U.S.S.R. was a multinational state. The same was true of China. But the independent Mongolian People's Republic had developed as a result of a national-liberation struggle. Krushchev reminded Mao, not especially tactfully, that "another part of the territory inhabited by Mongols is still /!/ part of the Chinese state,"(9) and also pointed out that the majority of the Kazakh people lived in the U.S.S.R., while only some Kazakhs and Kirghizs resided in China. Soviet Russia was in favor of self-determination and wanted disputed issues to be settled on this basis. This was a new ominous threat to China's integrity, though, of course, it was China that had raised the question of territorial revision in the first place. Krushchev furthermore stressed that the Chinese had not lived in Sinkiang "since time immemorial," and that the region was rather made up of Uighurs, Kazakhs, Kirghiz', and other minorities. The Chinese Emperors had waged wars of conquest, just as the Tsars of Russia, and had brought under their control Korea, Mongolia, Tibet, and Sinkiang. All this could not have been too reassuring to the Beijing government. It was obvious that the U.S.S.R., feeling threatened by Chinese claims, resorted to counterthreats of her own and reminded China of her own vulnerability, on both ethnic and historic grounds.

In 1954 a modern history textbook had been published in the Chinese People's Republic with a map of China showing that country before the Opium War. This map showed the following countries as being part of China: Burma, Vietnam, Korea, Thailand, Malaya, Nepal, Bhutan, and Sikkim.(10) In the north, the border ran along the Stanovoi mountain range, cutting the Far Eastern territory off from the U.S.S.R. In the west, a part of Kirghizia, of Tadzhikistan, and of Kazakhistan up to Lake Balkash was also included in China. Sakhalin too was shown as belonging to China. All this apparently had shocked the Soviets back in 1954. It was only a decade later that they let their people share their irritation and anger.

In a recent interview Mao had declared: "The region east of the Baikal became the territory of Russia approximately 100 years ago, and since then Vladivostok, Khabarovsk, Kamchatka, and other points have been the territory of the Soviet Union. We have not yet presented the bill for this roll call." *Pravda* referred specifically to the boundary along the Amur river fixed more than 100 years ago in the treaties of Aigun and Peking. True, the tsarist government had carried out a "predatory policy," but so had the Chinese emperors.(11)

Pravda continued: "Do those who question whether an area of more than one and a half million square kilometers belongs to the Soviet Union think of how these claims will be regarded by the Soviet people who have lived and worked on this land for several generations and consider it their homeland, the land of their ancestors?" The Chinese-Soviet boundary, *Pravda* asserted, had been "historically formed." (This argument, of course, appeared out of place after the foregoing criticism of alleged "historical rights.") The boundary had "been fixed by life itself" — another favorite

Soviet phrase, but actually nothing more than a redundancy. *Pravda*'s justification of the territorial status quo was based on treaty rights: "The boundary treaties of Aigun and Beijing, 1858 and 1860 respectively, are a basis that cannot be disregarded." Actually, the Soviet Union has regarded such rights rather lightly in disputes between other countries, when her own interests were not directly at stake.

Pravda followed up with an account of alleged Soviet generosity toward China after the October Revolution, of the Soviet renunciation of all unequal treaties with China and a reminder that soon after the end of World War II(12) the Soviets had also renounced the use of the naval base at Port Arthur and had turned over to the C.P.R., "free of charge,"all its rights in the joint management of the Chinese-Changchun Railroad. (Of course, if the Soviets were to be credited for these notable postwar deeds, how should one evaluate their wresting these concessions from China in the first place, in the summer of 1945?). Lenin, who was quoted as having condemned the tsarist seizure of Port Arthur and the tsarist penetration of Manchuria, was, significantly, cited again: "Vladivostock is far away, but this city is nevertheless ours." The C.P.C. was lectured about the difference between imperial and Soviet Russia: "The boundaries of Tsarist Russia had been determined by the policy of imperialist usurpers, but the boundaries of the Soviet Union were formed through the voluntary declaration of the will of the peoples on the basis of free self-determination of nations. The peoples who joined the Soviet Union will never allow encroachment on this right to settle their destiny themselves." Thus Russia's boundaries after the October Revolution had received a "democratic" baptism; their Tsarist illegitimacy was thus miraculously wiped away.

The demands of the C.P.R. were of course insulting to the U.S.S.R. since Beijing ignored the power and the prestige of the Soviet Union and dared question the territorial integrity of a fraternal nation, of the leading Socialist state. They were also a demonstration of base "ingratitude" on the part of the C.P.R. and an intolerable challenge to Soviet leadership in the socialist camp. Beijing's demands had been to the Soviets the insolent proclamation of an upstart rival who still lagged behind in regard to economic achievement and military accomplishment. All this aside, the C.P.R. expressed doubts regarding the claim of the U.S.S.R. that it represented a voluntary federation of equal nationalities, a new type of multinational state which, for the first time in history, had solved the age-old and thorny nationality problem. The Chinese territorial claim, painful to Soviet Russia on numerous grounds, embarrassed and hurt especially because in the eyes of the fraternal C.P.C. the U.S.S.R. was a colonialist power that held Asiatic peoples against their will, by force, within her confines; it thus punctured one of the most cherished Soviet myths, the myth of the U.S.S.R.'s granting freedom and equality to all its nationalities. (Actually, Communist China's nationality theory, closely patterned after that of the U.S.S.R., is, like its model, generous only in theory, being oppressive, assimilatory, and imperialist in practice.) To cap matters, the Chinese accusation, by strange coincidence, reiterated the charges made earlier in the West against Soviet nationality policy.

In the foregoing interview, Mao bemoaned the fate of Outer Mongolia which, he charged, the Soviet Union had "placed. . . under its domination." *Pravda,* pointing to the sovereign status of the Mongolian People's Republic for more than four decades, burst with "indignation" about "such obviously wild statements." Mao would like to deprive Outer Mongolia of her independence in order to make it a Chinese province. The paper revealed that the leaders of the C.P.R. had made this very proposition to Krushchev and other eminent Soviet personalities during their visit to Beijing in 1954. Krushchev had retorted that the destiny of the Mongolian people was decided neither in Beijing nor in Moscow, but in Ulan-Bator.

Let us consider whether the Soviet point of view was a consistent one. It was Soviet Russia's position that her own territorial status quo, her boundaries in Europe and Asia and those of her East European friends and allies with "capitalist" neighbors were sacrosanct and their defense imperative; but the support for the territorial status quo elsewhere in the world was an act of injustice and demanded only by the forces of dark reaction. The U.S.S.R. encouraged "just wars" of so-called national liberation which aimed at totally upsetting the territorial status quo, aside from changing the social and political complexion of the new nations. The U.S.S.R., while not inclined to negotiate what was hers, was quite disposed to enter into negotiations regarding territories belonging to her opponents — the latter, of course, being proclaimed reactionaries and imperialists or their tools.

The problem for the Soviets was thus how to reconcile their often contrary positions. As *Pravda* wrote, "One must distinguish the nature of the territorial issues. It is one thing when the matter is a question of the just striving of peoples to eliminate the survivals of the shameful colonial system, to get back old territories populated by the nation concerned and held by the imperialists."(13) The return, for instance, of Goa to India was fully justified, as would be the reunification of Taiwan and Hongkong with China. Yet territorial claims stemming from attempts "to revise historically formed boundaries between states, to force in any form a revision of treaties and agreements concluded after World War II as a result of Hitler's fascism and Japanese militarism, are quite another matter." The people who won victory at the cost of millions upon millions of lives would never agree to it: Soviet great-power nationalism and imperialism — as real as Chinese Communist chauvinism and expansionism — has its peculiar rationalization; it was unable to put forth an inherently consistent and convincing explanation of why the boundaries of other states ought to be changed while its own boundaries were to remain untouched.

In the foregoing interview, Mao also pointed out that the population of the globe was unevenly distributed and hence justice demanded a redistribution of territory. *Pravda* blasted the "evident demagoguery of this thesis." Communists fought precisely to ensure all peoples a better life. In a completely socialist world, state boundaries would lose their significance. But it was harmful to raise the question now when opposing social systems still existed. "History knows many instances in which the most reactionary wars were undertaken for the purpose of enlarging 'Lebensraum'." Mao had predecessors of whom he could hardly be proud. His compliments about "the greatness of Japan" were quite puzzling coming from a Communist. All who cherished the interests of socialism and wished to preserve peace could not but denounce the expansionist views of the C.P.R. leaders. Their designs were "permeated through and through with great-power chauvinism and hegemonism."(14) *Pravda*'s article thus ended by comparing Mao Zedong with Adolf Hitler. The circle was complete.

In a rejoinder, reprinting an article carried originally in the quarterly *Journal of International Studies*, 1981, by the head of the Institute of International Studies, Li Huichun, *Beijing Review* reasserted the well-known Chinese thesis that the present Sino-Soviet boundary was defined in "unequal treaties which had been imposed by tsarist Russia on China.(15) The treaties marked the seizure, to repeat, of more than 1 and 1/2 million square kilometers of Chinese territory. The Soviet government, however, has never admitted this historical fact. The Chinese government, while pointing to the inequality of these treaties, had expressed its willingness to take them as a basis for settling the boundary question. "Though this constituted a major Chinese concession, the Soviet government was not satisfied. It refused to admit the unequal nature of the treaties and, at the same time, opposed taking them as the sole basis for a settlement."

According to Li Huichun, on September 11, 1969, the Chinese and Soviet Premiers, while meeting in Beijing, had reached an understanding which provided a starting point for reopening their boundary dispute. The Soviet side, however, had refused to proceed according to the agreement; instead, it created new big obstacles to the negotiations. The Soviet military threat and hegemonistic policy directed against China constituted the major obstacles to the settlement of the Sino-Soviet boundary question as well as to the normalization of the two countries' state relations.

According to the author, China and the Soviet Union had started boundary negotiations back in 1964, soon after the dispute had burst into the open. Over the past few years, the Soviet side has been very busy churning out books and articles on the Sino-Soviet boundary question, with some articles specially intended for publication abroad, in an effort to convince people that China was to be blamed for obstructing the boundary settlement. The existing Sino-Soviet boundary line, Li reiterated, was determined by a series of treaties signed between tsarist Russia and China, including the Sino-Russian treaty of Aigun (1858), the Sino-Russian treaty of Beijing (1860), the Sino-Russian treaty of St. Petersburg (1881) and a score of protocols on a multitude of boundary surveys. These were historical records of tsarist Russia's aggression against China, treaties which Russia had imposed on China. "But it is on this very point, itself a matter of common knowledge, that the Soviet Government has chosen to provoke a dispute."

Imperial Russia's invasion and seizure of Chinese territory had been denounced by Marx, Engels, and Lenin. The latter had castigated tsarist Russia as a thief for carving up Chinese territory and had criticized this "criminal policy." According to the *Diplomatic Dictionary*, edited under the leadership of Andrei Gromyko (previous chief editor was Vyshinsky), even the Soviet union as late as 1961 alluded to the treaty of Beijing (1860) as an "unequal treaty," imposed by Britain, France, and Russia upon China. The much earlier treaty of Nipchu (1689), considered by the Soviets an equal treaty, has recently been transformed by them into an "unequal" treaty—one concluded at Russia's expense: The Soviet Union had mangled history beyond recognition. Its political and scholarly spokesmen claimed that Russia in 1858 and 1860 "took back only part of the land," that the Qing government had seized from Russia. Russia spoke about "historical rights" which needed to be restored. The Soviet government claimed that China's northern frontier was marked by the Great Wall or, at the farthest, some line north of it. The Soviet government ignored the Chinese concession to consider the Sino-Soviet border as the basis for the settlement of the boundary question and had also refused to admit the unequal character of these treaties.

The Chinese author of the foregoing article also pointed out that Lenin and the Soviet government had favored the abrogation of all treaties signed by tsarist Russia with China. After the victory of the October Revolution the Soviet Government had repeatedly condemned the "crimes" committed by tsarist Russia in "forcibly occupying" Chinese territory and in several declarations, especially one, (Declaration to China, September 27, 1920) promising to restore territory to China "without any compensation and forever all that had been predatorily seized."(16) But in talks between the two sides, held in 1926, no agreement was reached.

After its establishment, the P.R.C. had early presented its claims, not without "meticulous" studies of the Sino-Soviet treaties relating to their present boundary. It declared them unequal treaties, but it also said that the Soviet people bore "no responsibility for them." Also, since "the broad masses of the Soviet working people have been living in these areas for a long time," the Chinese government, out of the desire to maintain friendship between the Chinese and the Soviet peoples, was still prepared to take these treaties as a starting point for settling all boundary questions.

The Soviet government was not satisfied with inheriting the 1.5-odd million square kilometers of Chinese territory tsarist Russia had claimed under the unequal treaties. The fact was, the article's author claimed that "many sections of the boundary line proposed by the present-day Soviet government go far beyond the line" even stipulated in the treaties." Some of the sections represent invasions of China's territory by tsarist Russia and /!/ the Soviet Union in violation of stipulations in the unequal treaties." Since the Soviet Union government cannot find a treaty basis for them, it must therefore dredge up such formulations as "actually defended" and "historically formed." The rhetoric is in conception not only villainous but dangerous and reeks of expansionism and gunpowder.

In the follow-up article by the same author, also taken from the *Journal of International Studies*, "The Crux of the Boundary Question,"(17) Li Huichun, providing additional and new information about Sino-Soviet relations which covers primarily the last decade, dwelled upon the meeting between Premier Zhou Enlai with Chairman A. N. Kosygin at the Beijing airport in 1969. At this meeting, the two leaders had discussed mainly the boundary question, but also had touched on other problems in the relations between their two states. They had agreed that the two countries should not go to war over the boundary questions and that negotiations should be carried on in the absence of any threats; to this end, the two sides should first of all reach an agreement on provisional measures for maintaining the status quo along the border, for averting armed conflict and for the disengagement of troops on both sides in the disputed areas, and then proceed to settle the boundary question through negotiations." The Soviet side, subsequently, however, "flatly denied" that the premiers of the two countries had reached a clear understanding and even went so far as to speak of Chinese "fabrications." But Beijing insisted on the existence of "a verbatim record of the understanding."(18)

The Soviet Government called any reference to the U.S.S.R. as constituting a military threat "a myth." Yet it was known, to the world that "for more than ten years there has been a massive Soviet military build-up in areas bordering China: the deployment of offensive weapons, establishment of the war zone command headquarters, and endless military exercises and other military activities, spearheaded against China. All these constitute an indisputable threat to China.(19)

It was generally known that Soviet armed forces have been stationed in the Mongolian People's Republic since the early years of the 1960s. In 1968 the Soviet Union concluded a virtual military alliance with Mongolia. Soviet military bases in that country placed Soviet military forces only several hundred kilometers from Beijing. In consequence of Vietnam having invaded Kampuchea, controlling Laos and concocting the so-called "Indochina Federation," the Soviets secured military bases, virtually "turning Indochina into an 'anti-Chinese base.'" The invasion finally of Afganistan, which borders West China, and its military occupation constituted a threat not only to world peace but also especially to the security of the C.P.R. "Thus Soviet armed forces threaten China from north, south and west." Yet the Soviet government, in a false countercharge, alleged that China "attempts to influence the Soviet Union through war and blackmail." True, the Soviets had proposed to conclude a treaty of "mutual non-resort to armed forces." But even the existence of the Sino-Soviet Treaty of Friendship and Alliance had failed to prevent the U.S.S.R. from stepping up military threats against China. The article's author concluded that the Soviet government had deliberately tried to confound right and wrong on historical issues and to whitewash the crimes committed by tsarist Russia in its aggression against China. Beijing held it necessary that the boundary in its entire length be accurately determined.

The Beijing government maintained that, considering the interest of the local inhabitants of the disputed areas, both sides should "make necessary adjustments along the border according to the principles of consultation on an equal footing, mutual understanding, and accommodation." But the Soviets countered that no territorial problems divided the two countries, thus ignoring the very essence of China's position. While the Chinese government held that a new and equal Sino-Soviet treaty should be signed "to replace the old and unequal Sino-Russian treaties," it also charged that the Soviets wanted the CPR to sign "a new unequal treaty under which more Chinese territory would be ceded to the Soviet Union."

In conclusion, the Chinese either asserted that it was "the military threats and hegemonistic policy of the Soviet Union against China," which represented the fundamental obstacle to the settlement of the Sino-Soviet boundary question "and the improvement of Sino-Soviet state relations."(20) He did not promise that the settlement of the boundary dispute would usher in an era of great friendship and alliance, but would merely normalize Sino-Soviet relations, not "improve" Party relations!

Western Scholars on the Territorial Aspects of the Sino-Soviet Dispute and Other Causes

Western historians, political scientists, journalists, and military writers have offered divergent views on the significance of the border question as compared to other causative factors of the Sino-Soviet dispute. Few Soviet specialists have denied or minimized the territorial issue, fully realizing its importance for the Soviet Union which faces numerous other potential claims along her extended frontiers. Some China specialists, however, such as J. Gittings, *The World and China*, 1922-72 (1974)(21) and H. C. Hinton, in various writings speak only of China asking for "territorial adjustments," disregarding the C.P.R.'s intensive propaganda to the contrary. This thesis is also at complete variance with Mao's own utterances: "The places occupied by the Soviet Union are already too numerous. . .We have not yet presented them with the bill." Among other causes, Mao's anger had territorial and ideological roots. It was in the false ideology, the "heresy" of the Soviet leadership that was rooted his deep mistrust of the Soviet leaders as well as his nationalist emphasis on the need for complete self-reliance of China.

H. C. Hinton believes that the Chinese were "making a moral and propaganda case rather than seriously and suicidally pressing for the return of large territories incorporated into the Soviet Union."(22) But the evidence adduced appears hardly persuasive. An occasional toning down of Beijing's steady propaganda barrage of demanding "1.5 million square kilometers of Russian territory," ignores the long-range adverse impact of such unrelenting propaganda upon the Soviet neighbor. Can one assume that Mao and his successors were "suicidal" and utterly irrational? Henry Kissinger offered the contrary view on this point.(23) The Chinese insistence that the U.S.S.R. cease to be "hegemonic", return some annexed territory, and abandon her policy of territorial expansion, is a very real and not imaginary cause of the Sino-Soviet split. Hinton, however, is correct in his conclusion that Beijing resisted a comprehensive settlement with the U.S.S.R., if it would involve a "semisatellite status" for itself.(24) Everything considered, only a minority of scholars downplay Chinese territorial claims, holding that Beijing's bark is worse than its bite. It is undoubtedly true that the C.P.R. is hardly in the position of changing forcibly the territorial status quo in the foreseeable future. China, however, may think in long-range terms rather than in terms of years or the next decade.

Henry Kissinger has pointed to several causes of the Sino-Soviet dispute, "national rivalry between two powerful states," ideology, and, last but not least, territorial differences with China. The C.P.R. "demands the return of vast stretches of Siberian territory."(25) Kissinger somewhat qualified the latter assessment, pointing out that in October 1969 China denied that its goal was the return of all territories seized by tsarist Russia in the nineteenth century, but he considered this stance merely a temporary "backing down of Peking in the war of nerves," rather than a significant change of the C.P.R.'s policy.

B. National Disputes under Communism

Personality and National Conflicts: Stalin and Krushchev

In his first journey to China in 1954 already, Krushchev, as he relates, "was put on guard against Mao's chauvinism."(1) Despite Mao's "exceptionally cordial manner, I could sense an undercurrent of nationalism in his praise of the Chinese nation. His words reflected his belief in the superiority of the Chinese race." The Soviet delegation "had to sit through Mao's longwinded lectures on the history of China." Having faced conquerors like Genghis Khan and the rest, "Mao kept stressing the claim that the Chinese people were immune to assimilation by other peoples" (an unmistakable warning addressed to the Russians!). "He loved to tell us how the Chinese are the greatest people in the world, how they have had a superior culture since their prehistoric times and how they have a unique role to play in history." Whereupon Krushchev promptly pointed out to his Soviet comrades that Mao's tendency to equate himself with the Chinese people as a whole and his air of superiority toward other nationalities boded ill for the future." Mao's lengthy lectures on Chinese history, nationalism, superior culture, and Peking's historic mission undoubtedly shocked the Soviet leadership. They in turn, as Krushchev admits, often wounded Chinese self-esteem and national pride. Krushchev also accused Peking of ingratitude for past and continuing Soviet help.

Stalin had strong prejudices against the Chinese people — as well as against numerous other nationalities — and a special dislike for Mao, feelings which were widely shared by the Soviet ruling elite as well as by ordinary Soviet people, and afterwards by Krushchev. Stalin, according to Krushchev's memoirs, was greatly suspicious of Mao and his stance, since he had never been to the Soviet Union until after his victory in China in 1949. Krushchev himself did not trust Mao more: "Mao played politics with Asiatic cunning, following his own rules of cajolerie, treachery, savage vengeance, and deceit."(2) But he realized that communist internationalism and "objective analysis" would not permit "reviling" the Chinese.

During Stalin's lifetime, the "vozhd" (boss) was challenged first by Tito and then by Mao. The personal antagonism between Stalin and Mao persisted under Krushchev. When Krushchev journeyed to Peking in 1954, he made several concessions to the Chinese leader, but resisted his claims to Soviet territory and to Mongolia. For a time, Krushchev in turn relied on Mao's support against domestic rivals. But Krushchev probably conspired against Mao with members of the Chinese opposition, foremost Liu Shaoqui.(3) On the other hand, he accused the C.P.C. of interfering in the internal affairs of the Soviet Union and apparently resented Chinese influence upon some officials in the Soviet military establishment, bureaucracy, and scholarly and research institutes.

Soviet perception that Mao's China aimed at competing with Krushchev's Soviet Union for the leadership of the world Communist movement was well founded. Though the October Revolution had established Russian supremacy among Communists everywhere, China had a much larger Communist party and bigger population than any other country. As one observer aptly remarked: above all the C.P.C. under Mao was "graced with the politically most adept, verbally eloquent, and ideologically elegant leader in the Communist world."(4) Compared with him, the in many respects shrewd but crude personality of Krushchev cut a bad figure. The Chinese leaders, particularly Mao in his "criticism" of the new Soviet leadership, threatened the very self-esteem of the Soviet leaders and their pride in their achievements and accomplishments. They were insensitive by "maximizing all the primitive and elemental feelings of insecurity, inadequacy, inferiority, and paranoia, to which Soviet leaders and Russians have been prone."

Though this psychological analysis is perceptive, the Chinese, on the other hand, imbued with the greatness of their people and its culture, long history, and splendid civilization, must have felt uncomfortable that despite its military feats in the Korean War, China was still militarily inferior to the Soviet Union and also was keenly aware of its economic, social, and technological backwardness vis-à-vis the U.S.S.R. While the growing hostility between Moscow and Beijing had a multitude of causes, the historical-psychological peculiarities of the leadership and the peoples of both countries and their inferiority complexes played a major role in the unfolding of the conflict.

First, Mao, according to Krushchev, masking his true feelings and thoughts about the Soviet Union and its leadership, had gone "out of his way to show his respect, even his humility and deference towards Stalin," notwithstanding that the seeds of antagonism between the two men were already laid. When Stalin suggested to divide spheres of Communist propaganda and agitation in the world at large between the Soviets and the Chinese, Mao first came out against this suggestion, holding that "the leadership role in Africa and Asia/!/ should belong to the Soviet Union." Despite this restraint and unusual modesty, neither trusted the other. According to Krushchev, soon new differences developed between Mao and the post-Stalinist Soviet leadership over several significant issues. Among the most serious differences were questions of atomic war and, especially on the Chinese side, of "national pride and sovereignty."(5) Mao, according to Krushchev, was quite prepared to sacrifice 300 million Chinese lives in an atomic war in order to speed the future proletarian world revolution and insisted that "we /all socialist countries, including of course the Soviet Union/ should not fear war" and atomic bombs—which shocked the Soviets and especially Polish and Czechoslovakian Communist leaders such as Gomulka and Novotny respectively, since their smaller countries had obviously fewer chances for survival. On a different level, Mao also abruptly rejected the Russian building of a radio station in China to keep in touch with the Soviet submarine fleet and also refused the access of Russian submarines to Chinese ports. When he based the relative strength of the U.S. and of the Western Powers on their population size—by implication minimizing also the military potential of the Soviet Union—Krushchev was too appalled and embarrassed by his line of thinking even to argue with him."(6) In the end he could not help warning Mao that the number of divisions would have no effect on the outcome of a battle: a pointed reminder!

In conclusion, a reading of Krushchev's autobiography confirms the belief that Soviet nationalism and considerations of Soviet national and imperial interests and power, played a significant role among several factors generating the Sino-Soviet confrontation. An examination in turn of the C.P.R.'s motivation further strengthens the point of view that imperial and national interests were a decisive factor also on China's side.

Among the major grievances of post-Stalinist Moscow against Beijing was, according to Krushchev, the reckless foreign policy of Beijing, which threatened Moscow with war for extraneous and not vital causes. Mao started war against India in 1959 "out of some sick phantasy"(7) and the apparent Chinese desire to challenge Moscow's leadership in international Communism. The boisterous slogan, "Catch up with England in five years — America in a little bit longer," signified ultimately China's goal of "outdistancing the Party of Lenin" and the U.S.S.R. itself. As Krushchev disclosed, Moscow definitely feared lest the Soviets and East Europeans would, in the end, adopt Chinese slogans and policies, notwithstanding the C.P.S.U.'s criticism.(8) Beijing made a special impression upon Moscow's "Bulgarian friends."

Russian visitors to China apparently fed Chinese feelings of inferiority and caused bitter resentment in the C.P.R. As Krushchev wrote: "I remember when we toured China, we used to laugh at their primitive forms of organization." Chinese policies such as "Hundred Flowers," "The Great Leap," and the "Cultural Revolution," with all its excesses and frequent reversals of policy, its "degradation of human dignity," and Beijing's "personality cult," generated an irrational atmosphere of "witch doctors and mumbo jumbo" in China. Mao acted "like a lunatic on a throne." Of course, Krushchev and his Soviet comrades managed to forget many similar past and present conditions and practices in the U.S.S.R. While Krushchev himself frequently compared Mao with Stalin, not to mention the Tsars, he basically criticized both dictators for having "strengthened their personal dictatorships, . . .those over the proletariat, the Party, and over the leaders' own colleagues;" he revealingly omitted criticizing the dictatorship over the Soviet and Chinese peoples at large.(9)

The Border Regions and its National Minorities

Both Russians and non-Russian nationalities in the U.S.S.R. and its borderlands fear the Chinese for different reasons. But in medieval times Russia was dominated by Mongols, not by Chinese. Today's Soviet minorities, however, fear more the great pressure of the huge Chinese populace and assimilation by Chinese culture than the pressure by the less numerous Slavs with their low birthrate (a lower one than that of the indigenous non-Russian nationalities). Distant neighbors in Asia, even Russians living in the Far East know very little about the Chinese and China. As Krushchev himself admitted: "You might say that China is both close to us and far from us." THe U.S.S.R., of course, has no Chinese minority. Nor has China Russian and Slavic inhabitants. But the latter's claims extend to Soviet Union territory in which ethnic Russians live. The Soviet Union resents that Russian-inhabited cities such as Vladivostok, Khabarovsk, Nikolaevsk, and numerous smaller cities and other locations appear on Chinese maps with distinctive Chinese names—which all underlines China's territorial claims. There are virtually no Chinese in particular in the Soviet Far East, a region which in fact is one of the most Russian in the U.S.S.R.(10) With minor exceptions, the Sino-Soviet dispute does not center on either Russians or Han Chinese minorities, neither of which is engulfed or targeted by the adversary state, but on Asiatic peoples living in the intervening region. While the Soviets often assert that they have great respect for the Chinese people and merely oppose the views and deeds of the present leadership of the C.P.R., the Chinese similarly tend to make a distinction between the Soviet people and the Soviet leaders. But it is unquestionable that the bulk of the Chinese and Soviet populace is overwhelmingly affected by decades of vituperative chauvinistic propaganda from the other side of the border; it has deepened their hysteria, fear, and animosity toward each other, and has alienated the two neighboring peoples.

The Soviet leaders take the Chinese claim to Soviet territory with "deadly seriousness." Though many observers, in view of China's impotence, her inability to seize any Soviet territory, tend to shrug off the imminence of a Chinese threat, the Soviet leaders clearly think of China's future menace. They also feel rather uneasy, since Marx, Engels, Lenin, and even Stalin have denounced Tsarism's perfidy and its ruthless annexations.

The Far East, including the Maritime Province, aside, the Chinese have territorial claims against the former Soviet dependency of Tannu-Tuva, incorporated into the U.S.S.R., the so-called Great Northwest region, which comprises much of the Soviet Republic of Kazakhistan and western Siberia, a strip of territory on the Pamirs which is part of Tadzhikistan, and Outer Mongolia, which gained independence in the early post-World War II era; the latter alone comprises about 600,000 square miles.

Some Western observers hold that the sympathies of Central Asian nationalities and republics lie with China because of their greater racial and cultural affinities with the latter. Others hold that the diverse Central Asian nationalities fear the C.P.R., which is overwhelmingly Han Chinese in nationality, as a greater threat than the Soviet Union, where Great Russians alone are, roughly 50½, probably less of the entire population. Even counting all Slavs in the USSR, they amount only to about 75½ of the population. Thus cultural and national assimilation seems a lesser threat in the more "cosmopolitan" atmosphere of the Soviet Union.

Of the border nationalities the largest Turkic nationality in China are the Uighurs of Sinkiang; only few Uighurs live in the U.S.S.R. On the other hand, the three Soviet Republics of Kazakhistan, Kirgizstan, and Tadzhikistan have substantial numbers of these nationalities, while on the Chinese side of the border these peoples have relatively few other cultural ties with the Chinese, and resent their own suppression by China before and after the Communist seizure of power. Nomadic Kazakhs, Kirghiz', and Uighurs have crossed the border into the U.S.S.R., but it remains doubtful whether they would prefer the Soviet system to true independence, paying obeisance neither to Beijing nor Moscow. Also the intensive Chinese settlement of Inner Mongolia and Sinkiang has not contributed to improving relations between China and the border nationalities and probably resulted in making the Mongolian People's Republic, nominally independent since 1946, lean more strongly toward the U.S.S.R.

The C.P.R. today fears the Soviet Union, its chief rival in international communism, rather than the contiguous non-Chinese peoples of Inner Asia. The latter, invading and conquering China in the past, represented once a threat to it, but hardly do so at the present time. The C.P.R., however, has shown some anxiety lest these national minorities might be attracted by their kinsfolk on the Soviet side of the frontier. Both the Chinese and the Soviets have tried their utmost to use the international ideology of Communism to attract the impoverished multitudes of the repressed minorities of the border regions to their banner and to foster their assimilation, though officially both disavow such a goal for obvious tactical reasons.

The nationalism of the minority nationalities along the border is of late origin, dating back to the early twentieth century. It was especially during the Cultural Revolution that the C.P.R. relinquished its moderate and relatively tolerant nationality policy and steered directly toward suppression and forcible assimilation. Their humanitarian and international claims notwithstanding, the Chinese Communists have never neglected the geopolitical, territorial, and economic benefits accruing to them from the industrial base in Manchuria, the mineral resources in Sinkiang, and the animals and animal products of Inner Mongolia.

Differently from Sinkiang and Inner Mongolia, the non-Chinese minorities in Manchuria were largely absorbed by the Han people in the early twentieth century. After Japan's defeat in World War II and the eclipse of Japanese-dominated Manchukuo, the Soviet government tried to exert its influence in Manchuria, but during the Chinese Civil War after 1945 and during the years 1952-1955, China restored its control over the economically highly developed region. Its sovereignty over Manchuria has not been seriously challenged within the last generation.

In the February 1950 treaty with the Soviet Union, the thirty-year treaty of Friendship, Alliance and Mutual Assistance, the newly-established C.P.R. made numerous concessions to the Soviet Union. The independence of the Mongolian People's Republic, however, which since 1925-1926 had legally a virtually independent status — a status acknowledged by the Kuomintang and reaffirmed by the C.P.R. — has turned out to be permanent as far as International Law is concerned. Under the leadership of the Soviet-educated pro-Russian Premier Y. Tsedenbal, Outer Mongolia has been a client state of the U.S.S.R. But the Sino-Soviet dispute over the Mongolian People's Republic may not have reached its end.

In the 13th century, the Mongolian Empire comprised what was then both China, the Celestial Empire, as well as European Russia. In the twentieth century, squeezed in between Russia and China, Outer Mongolia has become a virtual annex of the Soviet Union, with some Mongolians, however, continuing to live in Inner Mongolia, the Autonomous Republic, the latter being a part of the C.P.R. By the time of the establishment of Chinese Communism on the mainland in late 1949, Outer Mongolia had a primarily pastoral economy. But with Soviet help it has since been transformed into a predominantly agricultural and industrial economy. Despite the recognition of Ulan Bator's independence by Beijing, the C.P.R. has continued to assist in the development of Outer Mongolia.

This assistance took the form of help in constructing a railway between Beijing and Ulan Bator, in the dispatch of thousands of Chinese laborers to work in Outer Mongolia, the growth of trade relations, and in the encouragement of numerous contacts with the Republic by the Inner Mongolian leader Ulanfu. In the late 1950s, with the first signs of the Sino-Soviet dispute surfacing, the Sino-Soviet competition came strongly to the fore also in the Mongolian People's Republic. In 1960, Tsedenbal signed two assistance agreements, one with the C.P.R., the other with the U.S.S.R. That the latter had won out by 1964 was seen by the circumstance that in June of that year, Tsedenbal asked for the recall of the Chinese workers from the Mongolian Republic. (A few years earlier, in 1960, the Outer Mongolian Republic's master, the Soviet Union, had abruptly withdrawn most of its advisers from China.)

The Sino-Soviet competition in the Mongolian People's Republic has manifested itself in many ways, including in different interpretations of Mongolian history, especially of the role of Chengis Khan. In 1954, the Chinese announced plans to construct a tomb for Chengis Khan on the border between Inner Mongolia and the Mongolian People's Republic; it was obviously designed to strengthen cultural and other ties between the Mongols of China and the Mongols of the Mongolian People's Republic in the hope of strengthening not only Mongolian ties, but also Sino-Mongolian links and to weaken Soviet-Mongolian People's Republican ties. While praising Chengis for unifying the Mongols—a unification actually preceding Mongolian conquests in China and European Russia in the 13th century—Beijing also criticized him for his "destructive raids" which disrupted production in parts of China. In accordance with the on the whole positive opinion on Chengis, the C.P.R. organized in 1962 the celebration of the eighth centenary of his birthday. Simultaneously, the Mongolian People's Republic too conducted festivities to honor Chengis and issued a stamp in his honor. The Soviets became quite concerned about the attempts of their client state to arouse nationalist sentiments, which finally led Ulan Bator to purge some Mongol historians.

In 1964 Krushchev, in an indirect reply to an observation by Mao, accused the C.P.R. that it wanted to impose its rule upon the Mongolian People's Republic.(1) The latter's government also charged the Chinese with planning to colonize and overwhelm the Mongols of Inner Mongolia, a view which closely coincided with Soviet opinion on this issue. After breaking with China in 1964, the Mongolian People's Republic became politically and ideologically a virtual adjunct of the U.S.S.R. The Soviets did everything in their power to make up for the loss of Chinese aid to the People's Republic. Beijing accused Moscow that the Mongolian People's Republic was a colony of the U.S.S.R. This was borne out by the fact that in 1972 99% of the Republic's foreign trade was conducted with the East European Communist bloc and about 2/3 of it with the Soviet Union. There were more Soviet troops in the Mongolian People's Republic than there were indigenous units in that state.

As far as Inner Mongolia was concerned, the Chinese were anxious about giving the region some freedom, calling it the Inner Mongolian Autonomous Region. Headed by Ulanfu, a sinicized Mongol who attained highest status not only in Inner Mongolian circles but also on the national level in the C.P.R., the Autonomous Region grew in size by leaps and bounds. One of the largest administrative units in China, its Mongols by the mid-1950s comprised, however, only 15% of the total population. The C.P.R. was leaning over backward not to alienate the Mongol minority through a rigid economic or nationality policy. It made rather certain that they received special treatment. Thus, the economy of that area flourished. During the Cultural Revolution, however, the migration of Chinese colonists increased rapidly in the Mongolian Autonomous region, and the Mongol language and culture suffered correspondingly. Many herdsmen opposed the imposition of communes and the abandonment of the private ownership of animals. By 1960, many Mongol leaders, Ulanfu included, turned to the Mongol language and culture, and fostered a kind of Inner Mongolian nationalism; they had to defend themselves against charges of preaching Mongol nationalism. The Red Guards even accused Ulanfu of being closely associated with Liu Shao-ch'i, prominent Chinese leader and opponent of the Cultural Revolution. After Ulanfu was deprived of his Party and Government posts, national differences in Inner Mongolia were downplayed. After the eclipse of the Cultural Revolution, Mongolian language and heritage were once again appreciated.

Though a part of China, the province of Sinkiang, in many respects closer to the Soviet Union than to the main centers of China's population, was subject to numerous kinds of Soviet influence, Peking had not actually governed the region since the 1911 Revolution. In the midst of World War II and the anti-Japanese War, the provincial authorities of Sinkiang chose the Cyrillic alphabet for the transliteration of some of its languages, a clear sign of Russian and Soviet influence in the area. Transport by air and on the ground linked Soviet Alma Ata through Sinkiang with Peking and other Chinese terminals, and the 1950 Sino-Soviet accords provided for joint stock companies for as long a period as 30 years!

In addition to problems arising out of the proximity of the Soviet Union, China's difficulties in Sinkiang were multiplied by the aspirations of some of the national minorities which challenged Chinese sovereignty in the region. Among them were Kazakhs, Kirghiz' and Mongols. While the latter pursued a pastoral economy, the Uighurs were farmers and oasis-dwellers. In view of the social, economic, and nationally composite character of the area, the Chinese long pursued a cautious policy, believing in the need of giving minorities a favored treatment, in the hope that it would ultimately lead to the sinification of the various ethnic and religious minorities.

The 1953 census had listed 3.6 million Uighurs out of a total population of 4.9 million. The Uighurs were town-dwellers and farmers, while the Kazakhs and Kirghiz' were largely nomads. Chinese immigrant colonists settled primarily in the Kazakh-inhabited district, which has rich natural resources. Former Chinese Communist soldiers established Production Construction corps, working on State Farms and serving as models for the nomadic Kazakhs. Despite some notable successes, the Chinese encountered a revived Kazakh national movement, and in 1957 the Peking government denounced the alleged anti-Communist national movement among the Kazakh leadership, a movement which was nourished by close contacts with the Soviet Kazakhs. To make communication with the Soviet kinsfolk more difficult, Peking decreed the introduction of the Roman alphabet to replace the Cyrillic alphabet for the transliteration of the Kazakh language and to obstruct cultural and other communication with the neighbouring Soviet Kazakhs and the Soviet Union.

In 1958, the establishment of communes to hasten the transformation of the Kazakh economic and social structure, coupled with rapid Chinese colonization, the abandonment of the C.P.R.'s policy of moderation, and increasing fear of sinification, produced a veritable exodus of about 60,000 Kazakhs, fleeing to the Soviet Union; a higher Soviet standard of living and a seemingly more tolerant nationality policy had lured them to cross the border. Beijing accused Moscow of facilitating this flight by instituting propaganda broadcasts and issuing false passports. Though after Stalin's death the Soviets virtually withdrew from the joint-stock companies, they continued close trade relations with the Kazakhs and on ideological grounds sharply criticized the communes on the Chinese side of the border.

Though Chinese nationality policy in Sinkiang toward Kazakhs and Uighurs grew subsequently more tolerant, the Chinese immigration continued and by 1970 the number of Chinese had grown in importance. The C.P.R. authorities pointed out that much territory in Central Asia belonged rightfully to them, since the inhabitants in past centuries had submitted to Chinese suzerainty. The Soviets, however, countered that having offered tribute to Peking did not signify permanent recognition of Chinese sovereignty. After the end of the Cultural Revolution, the position of the Kazakhs and Kirghiz on the Chinese side of the border has shown signs of improvement .

While China's border disputes with the Soviet Union have not ceased and the tense relations with Vietnam have even aggravated since 1978-1979, the C.P.R. has been more successful in settling differences with other neighbors. They agreed on a common border with Nepal in 1963 and in the same year also signed treaties delineating China's borders with Pakistan and Afghanistan. They subsequently reached similar boundary agreements with North Korea, North Vietnam, and Burma. Boundary differences with India, however, led to war in November 1962 in which China worsted India. Their territorial disputes centered on the northwest and northeast section of their common boundary, the Aksai Chin area of Ladakh and the Northeast Frontier Agency. The clashes led to the Chinese establishing control of the Northwest area; but they withdrew from the Northeast region which they already had occupied.

In the interwar period and during World War II, Manchuria has played a major role in Chinese affairs as well as in overall Asian history, and became a major target of Japanese imperialism. But the Soviets, too, had desired to control it. A province of rich natural resources and also important for its industrial development, it had, differently from the foregoing outlying territories of China, largely solved its national minority problems, since sinification of minorities had already made considerable progress. The Soviet Union's attempt, however, to impose domination over Manchuria after World War II failed entirely. A trade agreement, signed in July 1949 by Kao Kang, commander and political commissar of the North-East Military Region, with Moscow represented the high point of Soviet success. It was substantially altered by the Sino-Soviet treaty of February 1950, to which Stalin and Mao attached their signatures in Moscow. Soviet influence relative to the Chinese Changshun Railroad and the ports of Dairen and Port Arthur finally was completely eliminated in 1952, and after the end of the Korean War and the death of Stalin. The boundary, however, between Manchuria and the Soviet Far Eastern province was not clearly drawn.

In the Sino-Soviet relations since 1949 Kao Kang, all-powerful ruler of Manchuria, continued to play the major role even after the C.P.C. scored full victory on the mainland. He was accused of aiming to replace either Chou En-lai or Lin Shaoch'i, aspiring to become heir apparent to Mao, and of wishing to create the "independent kingdom of Kao Kang"; but ultimately he lost out to the Peking authorities and committed suicide in 1954. He seemed to have been a strong partisan of close relations with Moscow—the very reason why the C.P.C. opposed him by all means. The Chinese treatment of India before and after the outbreak of hostilities and the ruthless suppression of the revolt in Tibet, which had enjoyed a great deal of independence between 1911 and 1949, were of course closely followed by Moscow. Having to accept their setback in Manchuria, the Soviets in the 1950s and the 1960s were resolved to press their interests against China in Sinkiang and Outer Mongolia and along the Amur river, based on treaties going back to the 17th and 19th centuries.

The opposing claims of China and Russia in regard to the region alaong the Amur river reached a climax in 1969, and over a relatively unimportant island in the Ussuri River, Chen Pao, which the Russians called Damanski. It appears that the Chinese provoked the first clash and that the Russians retaliaited in a second engagement killing about 800 Chinese, while suffering themselves only 60 casualties. In the same year Soviet troops clashed with Chinese military units also along the border of Sinkiang. It was perhaps no accident that fear of the superior Soviet military power led to Beijing's attempts to improve its relations with Washington in the spring of 1971.

National Policy and Modernization

S. Bialer in "Soviet Perspectives," (H. Ellison, ed., *The Sino-Soviet Conflict,* 1982) holds that Soviet nationality policy is perceived by Central Asiatic peoples bordering the U.S.S.R. as well as by some scholars to be more tolerant and generous than the Chinese nationality policy. But in the same book, D. W. Treadgold in "Alternative Western Views of the Sino-Soviet Conflict" points to the "discrimination or oppression felt by the ethnic minorities in both states."(13) Most scholars hold that both Great Russians and Han Chinese are chauvinistic, imperial-minded, opposed to genuine self-determination and to secession of their border minorities and aiming at their cultural assimilation with the dominant nationality. The ultimate aim of both the U.S.S.R. and the C.P.R. is complete assimilation of the national minorities. Their goal is the emergence of a single culture, language, and nationality, the creation of the one nation-state rather than preserving the contemporary multinational state. For the present, both the U.S.S.R. and the C.P.R. are cautious in revealing their long-range objectives, fearful of the reaction of their national minorities. At present, they are rather sensitive to accusations of suppressing the diverse national cultures and vehemently deny that theirs is an oppressive nationality policy. Both claim that they are true internationalists; but each accuses the opponent of the very misdeed of national subjugation.(14)

Beijing and Moscow have accused each other of having violated the comradely Leninist concept of national equality and of having, under the thin camouflage of internationalism, established the domination of the Great Russians and of the Han nationality in their respective countries. Communists throughout the world have tended to ignore charges of this kind, as long as they originated in "capitalist and imperialist" circles, but they have been unable to continue ignoring these accusations once they emanated from another Communist-ruled nation.

China has never been inhabited only by the Chinese or Han people, as they were called, but by numerous nationalities such as the Chuang, Uighurs, Dungans, Yis, Tibetans, Miao, Manchurians, Bui, Koreans, and many others. Altogether more than one hundred different nationalities and national groups live today in the C.P.R. According to Chinese figures, considered by many scholars untrustworthy, the total of all these peoples was between 42 and 43 million. Mao, in 1957, even put them only at over 30 million. But recently Russian experts have held that there are almost twice as many and that the lands of non-Chinese peoples account for about 60 percent of the present territory of China.

While the Chinese nationality policy was painted in dark colors by the Soviet comrades, it shone brightly when illuminated in Beijing's own light. On March 3, 1972, for instance, *Beijing Review* asserted that people of all nationalities in China were united as never before;(15) large numbers of cadres of minority nationalities were maturing. Their industrial and agricultural production and living standards were rising steadily and their cultural and educational undertakings were advancing rapidly.

Due to the institution of regional autonomy, democratic reform, and socialist transformation, Beijing claimed that the people of all nationalities in China have established and developed a new relationship of equality, close unity, and common progress. Especially since the Great Proletarian

Cultural Revolution, tremendous change has taken place in the country's border regions where the minority peoples live.

According to the C.P.R., striking industrial and agricultural progress has been made in nationality areas such as the Inner Mongolian Autonomous Region, the Tibetan Autonomous Region, the Sinkiang Uighur Autonomous Region, and others. The health and culture of the peoples concerned had also made tremendous strides and large numbers of minority nationality cadres had come to the fore. Continuous feuds among various nationalities before liberation, over land, mountain forests, and water resources in many parts of China, had been replaced by "unity among the people of all nationalities in their common struggle under the guidance of Marxism-Leninism-Mao Tsetung Thought."

In a speech in February 1957, "On the correct handling of contradictions among the people," Mao himself had directed attention to the nationality question in China and to the imperative need for fostering good relations between the Han people and the minority nationalities. "The key to this question" lay "in overcoming Han Chauvinism." But at the same time, local nationalism, "wherever it exists among the minority nationalities, must also be overcome."(16) Both kinds of nationalism were harmful to the unity of nationalities. Still, according to this speech by Mao, it was Han chauvinism that appeared as the somewhat greater danger of the two.

In this analysis Mao followed the pattern of Soviet nationality theory that has always underlined the dangers of both kinds of nationalism, that of the dominant nationality and that of the minority nationalities. In practice, the dominant nationality in the U.S.S.R. and the C.P.R. has seldom been treated as the sinner; but the minority nationalities were regularly accused of indulging in national excesses that were harmful to the Party and the state and to the cause of socialism.

According to Mao in 1957, there had already been a "big improvement" in the relationship among the nationalities in China, though a number of problems remained unsolved. In some areas, both Han and local nationalism, he conceded, still existed "to a serious degree."

Mao was somewhat more willing to admit the continuance of problems in the field of nationality relations and nationality policy than were the Soviets. The latter have, for decades, unrelentingly claimed that the nationality question in their country had been completely solved. However, the Soviet judged Chinese claims of positive achievements in their nationality policy as vastly exaggerated. Actually, Han chauvinism, comparable to Imperial China's maltreatment of and arrogance toward China's national minorities, reigned supreme. The Soviets conspicuously displayed the denunciation of the C.P.R.'s nationality policy by the Party boss of the allied Outer Mongolian People's Republic, Tsedenbal, when on the occasion of the July 1969 Moscow Conference he referred to the "oppression and humiliation meted out to Mongolians, Kazakhs, Tibetans, Uighurs, and other national minorities in China, and the gross violations of these groups' rights and freedoms."(17)

A full-blast attack on Beijing's nationality policy by T. Rakhimov, "The Great Power Policy of Mao. . .and his Group on the Minorities," appeared in *Kommunist* in 1967.(18) After detailing how the Tibetans, the Chuangs, and the Mongols of Inner Mongolia and other ethnic units, though living compactly, had been deliberately divided up into numerous administrative units, the author concluded that the so-called autonomy in China was nothing but splintering of nationalities and the forcible and artificial breaking up of their historically evolved ethnic boundaries." As a result of these administrative measures, the Mongolians were transformed into a minority in their own autonomous region and constituted no more than 8 to 10 percent of its population.

The master recognized, of course, the ways of his disciples. The Soviets themselves have pursued the same policy in their own republics, settled Great Russians and Ukrainians in large numbers in the border republics; they have smothered, if not removed, the natives, redrawn administrative lines to weaken the will and the power of the national minorities, and forcibly speeded up their assimilation.

Rakhimov also charged Beijing with having set forth quite frankly a policy of accelerated assimilation of China's minority peoples. Quoting the magazine *Sinkiang Hung Chi* in 1960, he underlined its views as to the superiority of the Chinese element, asking for "amalgamation" because it was the "inevitable trend" and was "Communist assimilation."

Since the beginning of the Cultural Revolution, Moscow has charged, the lot of minority peoples in the C.P.R. has worsened; the autonomy of peoples, guaranteed by the C.P.C. Constitution, was practically eliminated. During the Cultural Revolution, Moslem mosques and Buddhist temples and monasteries in the national regions were pillaged and religious sentiments of the non-Chinese peoples outraged. National cadres in the outlying regions of China were persecuted and even exterminated. In some areas, outright uprisings and military clashes had taken place, as in Tibet in June and August 1968 and in Sinkiang in January 1969. The policy of assimilation was pressed by various means.

Nationality and Religion

It is not surprising that Chinese accounts of the life of minorities in the C.P.R. differed radically from the foregoing Russian assessment and extolled Beijing's policy, its justice, and its achievements. They especially contrasted the pitiable life for minorities before the "liberation" of 1949 with that after the Communist seizure of power on the mainland.

Lu Yun in the article, "Minority People Living in the Capital,"(19) pointed out that the minority people who had settled in Beijing before liberation were oppressed by the ruling class, kept in a low position, and lived in poverty. Most of them were small peddlers and vendors, rickshaw-pullers, and casual laborers, and were eking out a bare existence in the capital. Since liberation, however, they have enjoyed equality in politics, and their customs and religious beliefs have been respected and safeguarded. Their overall situation, the author claimed, had improved considerably both materially and culturally. For instance, a Beijing Islamic Association has been established in 1979. The association printed the Koran and the *Essential Knowledge of Islam*. No mention is made here that respect for Islam is also a foreign-policy imperative for the C.P.R., in view of the growing influence of Islam and especially of fundamentalist Islam in the Middle East, and its role in the U.N., the close relations of China with Moslem Pakistan, Bangladesh, and the Third World in general, and, last but not least, in view of the numerous Moslem peoples in the U.S.S.R. as well as in China.

Minority ethnic groups in the C.P.R., Lu Yun continued, had generally received "deep friendship and warm concern from the Han people, though some fail /!/ to show enough respect for the customs of some minority nationalities." "Also, some minority people staying in Beijing temporarily may meet with certain inconveniences in daily life or in finding proper food and lodging." While in the past the special needs of minority people went unheeded, today for instance at the Beijing Railway Station one may hear broadcasts in Tibetan, Mongolian, and Uighurian language, in addition to Chinese. And even signs were put up in these languages! Since March 1983, Moslem food was begun to be served in dining cars. When minority people have diseases difficult to deal with in their locality, they often come to Beijing with great hopes of receiving effective treatment. The example cited here of fraternal love in the C.P.R. appears to be shallow and superficial, testifyng rather to deep-seated old biases and to continuing prejudice and a self-congratulatory attitude.

Both in the C.P.R. and the Soviet Union nationality and religion are often closely intertwined, with nationality impressing its character upon religion and the latter creating a strong tie among different nationalitie.. From its start, Marxism was antithetical to nationalism and looked upon religion as an "opium for the people." But both the Soviet Union and the C.P.R., multi-national states, have been compelled to make some theoretical and practical concessions to nationalism, though holding firm to the integrity of their realms and sharply opposing national separatism. As far as religion is concerned, the Soviet Union has made only minor cosmetic concessions, while the C.P.R. has gone somewhat further.

In an article, "Islamic Culture Thriving in Kashi," *Beijing Review* reported for instance that the ancient city of Kashgar in the southern part of Xinjiang (Sinkiang) awakes to the loudspeakers,(20) sending out the predawn message, "Great Lord, now it's time for prayers!" Local Moslems hurriedly get up to start the first of their five daily Mohammedan religious services. The message came from the Id Kah Mosque, the largest of the 15,500-odd religious establishments in Xinjiang. Here the seven million Moslems out of a population of 13 million account for more than half of China's total number of believers of the Koran. There is "friendliness and warmth" with which official China now treats its Moslem minority both in theory and actual practice. It woos it, making certain that the Moslems on the Soviet side of the border fully understand and appreciate the tolerance and friendship of Beijing toward them. What a far cry from Marx's dictum that religion was "opium for the people" and how radically this also differs from the religious policy and practices of the U.S.S.R., though the latter, despite its continued hostility to religion and most religious groups, has been compelled to pursue a more cautious course toward its rapidly growing Moslem minorities! It is forced to take account of the religious fervor to the south of its Asian borders and also of the C.P.R.'s competitive struggle with the Soviets for the sympathies of the strong Moslem population in the border regions.

Moslem leaders, according to *Beijing Review*, can still remember the "traumatic days of the Cultural Revolution when most mosques in Kashgar were demolished and closed down. . .But today religion is thriving as never before in the autonomous region." In Xinjiang alone more than 100,000 copies of the Koran have been sold, and the Islamic Association of the province has published 140,000 copies of a Moslem reader in Uygur and Han language editions to serve Moslems who do not know Arabic. The Beijing government even encouraged pilgrimages to Mecca "as a reminder of the past." In 1985 alone nearly 2,000 Moslems from around China had made their way to Mecca, being provided with cash in foreign currency from the government.

The Chinese Conmunists, in view of their increasingly friendly relations with the West, are anxious to present the C.P.R. in the best possible light.(21) China, as they point out, is a multireligious country: the major religions are Buddhism, Taoism, Islam, and other Christian faiths. Under their constitution, all inhabitants were guaranteed religious freedom. Believers and non-believers alike participated in the administration of state affairs and were politically equal. "Catholicism and Christianity" had about three million followers. Since, however, the Vatican "for decades has followed a policy of hostility towards New China and its Catholic association," the latter had "nothing to do with the Vatican."

*Nationalism in the C.P.R., the Soviet Union, and the East
European Bloc*

The Soviets were disputing the achievements of the C.P.R.
in the field of nationality policy and magnifying their own
accomplishments in that area. The program of the C.P.S.U.
adopted in 1961 and hailed by Krushchev as the "Communist
Manifesto of the present epoch," made the most extensive
claims also in regard to nationality policy.(22) Allegedly, this
policy has led to the full economic and cultural development of
all Soviet nationalities, and has finally brought about the
"solution" of the nationality question, "one of the greatest
achievements of Socialism."

The basic source of weakness of Soviet nationality policy,
and, as a matter of fact, equally so of Chinese nationality
policy, is the absence of genuine national self-determination
and national equality. National inequality and discrimination
affect both the individuals of the various ethnic groups in the
U.S.S.R. and the nationalities of the border regions and of the
interior region in their entirety. What appears to cause great
concern to many a minor nationality in both the U.S.S.R. and
the C.P.R. is that its territory, due to constant influx and
colonization by Russians and Chinese on their respective sides
of the border, may lose its national character and that the
numerically dominant border nationality may cease to be a
majority or plurality. Many a national minority in the Soviet
Union or in China, anxious, like any biological species, to
preserve its character and its cultural and linguistic identity,
fears submergence and opposes assimilation, whether it is
creeping or sweeping, "voluntary" or enforced.

Just as the U.S.S.R. doubted the true Leninist character of
the nationality policy of the C.P.R. and the existence of
genuine national equality in Communist China, so did the
latter deny that the Soviet Union had solved the nationality
question within her boundaries. The C.P.R. has questioned
outright whether the U.S.S.R. was a voluntary federation of
equal nationalities; to the contrary, it has accused her of
imperialism and neocolonialism and the desire to extend the
existing inequality beyond her borders and her East European
satellite Empire.

Beijing has perceived the close connection between the Soviet Union's territorial expansionism and its nationality program. Making reference to the 325th anniversary of Russia's armed annexation of the Ukraine,(23) *Beijing Review* in this context spoke of the actual annexation of the Ukraine by Muscovite Russia in 1654. The leading Moscow clique, the weekly asserted, "took up where the old tsars left off and carried on Great-Russian chauvinism." Its policy of national oppression and the contradictions among various nationalities in the Soviet Union had grown ever sharper. The non-Russian nationalities, whose resistance increased day by day, were realizing more and more clearly that "the new and old tsars are birds of the same feather." In defending the old tsars, the new tsars were defending themselves. The Soviet rulers proclaimed loudly to "support liberation," "reincorporation," and voluntary choice to join "the Soviet family of nations so as to paralyze the non-Russian nationalities' struggle against Great-Russian chauvinism." In 1972, when Brezhnev was speaking about how all the Republics were brought into the Soviet Union, he announced that "the same principle was also applicable to members of the great /Socialist/ community." The ruling Soviet clique's final goal was to incorporate other countries into the union.

The alleged benefits of the Soviet and Han nationality policies for the domestic national minorities are also expected to lure minorities on the other side of the border, where they allegedly are repressed by feudal, semi-capitalist, or "socialist" states: the last-named accusation is hurled by Beijing against Moscow and vice versa. Nationalities along the Sino-Soviet border aside, there are neighbors of the Soviet Union and of the C.P.R. which have become or may become potential targets of Soviet or Chinese ambitions. Afghanistan, for instance, is in Soviet eyes a candidate for membership in the Soviet family of nations.

Nationalism, still a powerful force in the twentieth century, has also retained its strength in the Communist world and affects deeply the relations of Communist-ruled states with each other. In 1985, two Soviet experts on nationalism have given testimony to it, criticizing of course Beijing's nationality policy.

In an article "Great Chinese Chauvinism in Action," the author M. Sladkovsky, corresponding member of the U.S.S.R. Academy of Sciences, raised the question of Beijing's nationality policy in the larger contexts of China's militariza- tion of border regions, the exploitation of national minorities by the Han majority, and made hardly disguised threats against the territorial integrity of the C.P.R.; all this at a moment when China was engaged in hostilities with Vietnam. China, he recalled, was one of the world's largest multination- al states.(24) In addition to the Chinese, more than 50 million people of other nationalities lived there in regions that make up about 60% of the country's territory. Since these were border regions adjacent to the U.S.S.R., this was not so subtle a reminder of China's vulnerability, on strategic, political, and nationality grounds.

Since Mao's death and the subsequent elimination of the so-called "Gang of Four," the Chinese leadership has placed responsibility for violation of Mao's nationality policy on Lin Piao and the "Gang of Four." The facts, however, showed that Peking's nationality policy was a direct continuation of the great Han chauvinistic policy, which in turn aimed at the forcible assimilation of the non-Chinese peoples. The author pointed to the "artificial curbs" on the development of the national cultures and of the development of national languages, both spoken and written. At present, the C.P.R. published literature in languages of five non-Chinese peoples (more than 50 such peoples lived on C.P.R. territory) and this consisted of translation of Mao's works and materials written by Peking propagandists. Attempting to create a dependable base of support in the national border regions, the C.P.R. leaders were pushing the issue of resettlement of Chinese to these areas. Hypocritically, they asserted that the purpose of this colonization campaign was a need to give the non-Chinese peoples "human resources assistance in a planned fashion." Special attention was given to the resettlement of Chinese in such border provinces as Sinkiang, Inner Mongolia, Tibet, and the Kwangsi-Chuung Autonomous Region. Priority was assigned to demobilized soldiers who, according to candid Chinese press accounts, were supposed to "put down roots in the national regions." The current Chinese leaders' policies in the C.P.R.'s national border regions were aimed exclusively at military objectives. In Tibet, for example, the number of soldiers was as high as 300,000, whereas the region's total population was only 1.7 million. More than one million people lived in militarized settlements in Sinkiang.

All national regions were covered with a network of strategic military roads and airfields. In each there were numerous shelters and underground storage facilities and nuclear-missile installations. The Chinese authorities were forcing the indigenous population to take part in the construction of military facilities. All able-bodied men and women were assigned to detachments of the so-called "people's militia." Thus, the national regions were thoroughly militarized. All this coincided with China's policy becoming virtually identical with the policy of imperialism.(25)

In a *Pravda* article, "A Call for East-Bloc Ideological Solidarity," June 21, 1985, O. Vladimirov referred to the April 1985 plenary session of the C.P.S.U. C.C., according to which the Soviet Union was seeking to strengthen mutual ties and develop "cooperation with other socialist /!/ countries, including the C.P.R. "The socialist commonwealth was an enormous achievement of world socialism. But imperialism, trying to export counterrevolution and directly to interfere in other countries' internal affairs, was attempting to weaken the alliance of fraternal countries, to estrange them from the U.S.S.R., tear them away from it, and, ultimately, to try to bring about the erosion of their social system.

While the Eastern bloc faced problems in its economies and its methods of economic management, nevertheless it was a "fact," Vladimirov claimed, that the socialist economic system was superior to the capitalist system, "being the more dynamic of the two."(26)

It would also be wrong to close one's eyes to some shortcomings in the ideological sphere, though the unity and solidarity of the Marxist-Leninist parties had become vividly manifest. "Revisionist and nationalistic views were making themselves felt." They were connected in a large part to the actions of "the imperialist propaganda centers which are raking the Socialist countries' territory with the fire of radio and T.V. broadcasts." The imperialists were using increasingly "sophisticated methods of undermining the unity of fraternal countries."

"Nationalism continues to be the chief hope of the class enemy." The West's propaganda services were trying to capitalize on problems that the socialist countries have inherited from the past to impose "pseudo-patriotic nationalistic sentiments" on them, to cultivate the worship of Western civilization, and to exaggerate "injustices" and "blank spots" in the history of the Soviet Union's relations with a number of fraternal countries.

The experience of socialist countries shows that "deviations from the Marxist-Leninist line are related, in one way or another, to nationalistic tendencies." On the domestic level, this may lead to a narrowing of the influences of Marxist-Leninist ideology, the appearance of modified theories of "national communism," and the exacerbation of the nationalities question. On the level of relations with other socialist countries, nationalistic manifestations are undoubtedly capable of weakening internationalist ties. Nationalism, when it takes the form of covert—let alone overt—Russophobia and anti-Sovietism, undermines the unity and solidarity of the socialist peoples and damages socialism as a whole and each country in particular.

The C.P.S.U. combatted "nationalist tendencies that are at variance with. . .promoting the molding of the ideologically stalwart internationalists, who are devoted to the cause of socialism. It is our common interest for the number of continuers of the tradition of Dimitrov, Thaelmann, Gottwald, and other remarkable Communists to constantly grow in the fraternal parties." None of the Communists listed here is of recent vintage; to the contrary, they are all dead for decades. Are there no recent true internationalists in East European Communism? And, even more important, Chinese Communists, first of all Mao himself, are totally ignored here. All this speaks volumes!

The author, Vladimirov, ended with a declaration that the purity of the political position of every Communist was "especially important now, when various kinds of revisionist, nationalistic, and clerical concepts are coming to the surface of ideological life." Needless to point out that such concepts were considered harmful to the U.S.S.R.: They threatened the integrity of the Soviet Union and of the Soviet Empire and blocked the expansion of Soviet influence and power beyond its borders and spheres of influence.

C. Geopolitics, the Soviet Policy of Detente, and the CPR's Policies: between Alliance and Independence

The C.P.R.'s Military Strategic Problems

Both Beijing and Moscow, other issues aside, have developed a keen eye for geopolitics. That the latter is a major consideration for both sides, deeply involved in a ruthless struggle for power, seems incontestable. The C.P.R.'s geopolitical views were elucidated in an article in the *Journal of International Studies* in 1982.(1) The author conceded that the Soviet push into Afghanistan and, through the Vietnamese surrogate, into Kampuchea, has improved the geopolitical situation of the U.S.S.R. The invasion of Afghanistan had brought the Soviets 500 kilometers nearer to the Strait of Hormuz. In supporting Viet Nam's aggression and occupation of Kampuchea, the Soviets now had Cam Ranh Bay and DaNang as their military bases, thereby enabling their Pacific Fleet to extend its area of activity several thousand miles to the South.

The invasion of Afghanistan was "a very important move by the Soviet Union in its bid to control the Strait of Hormuz in the west and the Strait of Malacca in the east." If the Soviet Union should accomplish its plan, it would then be able to link up the Middle East, the Persian Gulf, the Indian Ocean, and Southeast Asia; and have the oil resources under its control. "It could then cut the routes of oil supply so vital to the Western countries" and to be in "a very advantageous strategic position," producing "dire consequences" in Western Europe, Japan, and the United States.

The Soviet Union pursued "wild ambitions to dominate the world," but it also faced great difficulties. It spent about 8 million United States dollars to support Vietnam "every day." To keep 100,000 troops in Afghanistan was even more costly. These costs constituted serious limitations to the Soviet hegemonists' ambitions.

In conclusion, the journal's editor appealed to countries and peoples fighting against hegemonism to unite and carry out a joint struggle against the Soviet hegemonists. Nothing was said here about whether such a coalition should, or should not, include the U.S. But it was rather apparent that the U.S., if not explicitly included in this scheme of things, would at least be aligned with this coalition against the U.S.S.R. Without the U.S., there would be no genuine balance of power between the U.S.S.R. and the developed capitalist and democratic nations of the world. At many other occasions, though not in recent years, the C.P.R. leaders have come out openly and unqualifiedly for a close global cooperation against the Soviet Union, if not for an outright global anti-Soviet alliance. Though having adopted a stance of neutrality between the two superpowers during the last years, the C.P.R.'s very proximity to he Soviet Union and its threat to China, in contrast to the geographic distance and absence of any threat from the U.S., virtually demand that the U.S. be a counterweight against Soviet pressures on the C.P.R.

The C.P.R.'s Perception of the Changing Global Balance of Power

In a follow-up article in the *Journal of International Studies*, 1983, "Changing Balance of Soviet and United States Power," the Chinese authors Xing Shugang, Liu Yunhua and Liu Yingua asserted that both Soviet and United States military forces had each their strengths and weaknesses, and were roughly equal.(2) In the 1980s, both will try harder to change the balance of power, which will result in their relations continuing to be strained. During the 30-plus years, since the end of World War II, the United States' position of overwhelming superiority had "steadily eroded," while the Soviet Union, "once in an absolutely inferior position," has been "rising steadily," approaching and surpassing the United States in many fields. Soviet economic progress has made considerable progress since the war, but its economic strength is still clearly inferior to that of the United States. In technical and managerial skills the Soviet Union lagged far behind the United States; its industrial labor productivity was only 55% of that of the United States, and its agricultural labor productivity 20% of the United States. In theatre nuclear strength the Soviet Union had gained considerable quantitative and qualitative superiority, an imbalance which the

United States will redress only after the deployment of Pershing II and the cruise missiles. While the United States outstripped the Soviet Union in long-distance air and sea transportability and had a bigger worldwide network of naval and air forces than the Soviet Union, the latter had the advantage that its centers of contention with the United States lay mostly in its vicinity—which made up for the Soviet Union's weaker strategic transportability. As far as the future balance of forces is concerned, it did not appear very likely that the Soviet Union will catch up with and surpass the United States economically and militarily. The declining economic growth rate of the Soviet economy limited Moscow's ability to freely engage in arms expansion.

According to the authors, it appeared almost certain that Soviet-American relations in the 1980s will be more tense than in the 1970s. In the face of mounting difficulties, they will have to make certain compromises in their fierce struggle. But the "detente" of the 1970s will not reappear in the 1980s. The strained relations between the two superpowers "stem directly from the conflict of their hegemonic interest. As long as they do not abandon hegemonism and cease contention for world domination, there will be no genuine detente in their relations, nor will negotiations or summit meetings be of any help. Soviet-United States relations in the 1980s may basically be "characterized by tension; but not head-on collision," by compromise, but no longer by a "detente honeymoon." Secondly, the furious contention between the two superpowers in the 1980s will pose a grave threat to world peace and international security.

While the armed invasion of Afghanistan was "a demonstration of the escalation of Soviet aggressiveness and adventurism," the fact that the United States declared its readiness to consider more areas vital to its interests and to use armed forces to defend the Persian Gulf demonstrated that it has changed its attitude of avoiding military involvement in regional conflicts. Since the Soviet Union's and United States' participation in local wars or behind-the-scenes manipulation of proxy wars had continued unabated over the last decades, the possibility for the direct involvement of the superpowers in military conflicts had increased. Both superpowers will take "advantage of third world turmoil and contradictions to

pursue their own contest," but—and here comes a somewhat
suspect prognosis, revealing a good deal of wishful thinking of
China as an interested party—the position and the influence of
the superpowers in the Third World will "decline further."
The authors point to United States impotence in the face df
the retention of Americans in Iran and to Soviet losses suffered
in Afghanistan and their "hopeless dilemma" in that country;
this, however, contrary to the authors' opinions, has so far not
resulted in a change of Soviet policy.

There is here, as elsewhere, an apparent tendency to boost,
if not China's role, then that of the Third world, of which
China is always declared to be an integral part and a potential,
if not present, leader. The writers claim that the Third World
countries' international status has remarkably improved and
that they were playing an ever greater role in international
affairs. This has allegedly been fully demonstrated in a series
of major international issues such as United Nations debates
and votes on the Afghanistan and Kampuchea questions, on
the conflict between the Arab countries and Israel, on
North-South economic relations, and on the election of the
United Nations Secretary General. To the student of
international relations, this role of the Third World appears
greatly exaggerated. It has resulted largely in a flurry of words
and votes which have not had any tangible impact on any of
the foregoing fundamental disputes or on others such as the
Iran-Iraqi conflict, which is simply omitted.

The major conclusions offered here differed radically from
earlier attitudes. The C.P.R. no longer toyed with the
dangerous and reckless notion of an atomic war between the
superpowers which it used to embrace during Mao's lifetime. It
no longer minimized the terrors of the holocaust which such a
war would produce. Nor did Beijing flirt with the idea of a
Sino-American alliance which it eagerly sponsored in 1979 at
the time Deng visited the U.S. China has settled down to a
policy of an uneasy "neutrality" between the superpowers,
though it still considered the U.S.S.R. "the greater peril" to
itself and to world peace.

The line of the C.P.R.'s neutrality apparently satisfied
China's own extreme left more than a Sino-American alliance,
the Chinese Left being still deeply suspicious of the capitalist
U.S. The new line expressed hostility towards the Soviet

Union, but did not unduly arouse the U.S.—which actually was concerned about the opposite stance of Deng in 1979, when he championed a Sino-American alliance. This "neutral" attitude of the C.P.R. also seemed to be in accord with its own national interests; by keeping some ties with the U.S., it did not unduly alarm the U.S.S.R. At the same time, though reiterating its well-known "conditions" for improving relations with the U.S.S.R., the C.P.R. did not surrender its "principles" and basic foreign policy interests.

According to Chinese commentators, the Reagan administration's foreign policy, guided by a two-poles concept, aimed at achieving military superiority in a struggle with the Soviet Union for global hegemony. It tried hard to check Soviet expansion and to reinforce the role of the U.S. as the world's overlord.(3) Viewed from this angle, they did not deny that President Ronald Reagan has scored some strong points in his first term of office. An important change in the global contention between the two superpowers has taken place in the past four years. Previously, Moscow was on the offensive, while Washington took the defensive. Now they were in a strategic stalemate in which neither side was absolutely on the offensive or defensive.

In Europe, the focus of the superpower rivalry, the United States has gradually overcome its disadvantageous position in the balance of theatre nuclear forces by bringing to deploy more intermediate missiles. The Soviet policy of trying to wean Western Europe from Washington's aid has achieved little; in fact, its weak countermeasures have only aggravated existing disharmonies between it and its allies in East Europe.

In Asia and the Pacific, the political situation was more unfavorable to the Soviet Union, while the United States has considerably strengthened its ties with China. The Soviet Union and Moscow-backed Vietnam were bogged down in Afghanistan and Kampuchea; a rapidly expanding Soviet military build-up in the region has also led to more American and Japanese countermoves. In Central America, the United States invasion of Grenada and the Reagan administration's efforts to isolate Cuba and weaken Nicaragua have caused the Soviets some setbacks. And in southern Africa, the United States' clandestine diplomacy has made some progress, while

Angola and Mozambique have tended to move away from Moscow.

It was only in the Middle East that the United States, allegedly, has suffered "serious setbacks." While United States marines pulled out of Lebanon, President Amin Gemayel subsequently rescinded his country's accord with Israel. Moscow quietly strengthened its position in Syria, expanded its influence among the Gulf nations, and succeeded in exchanging ambassadors with Egypt, after a 13-year break in relations. It was most significant, however, that the United States-Soviet Union global rivalry seems mainly to favor Washington.

Economically, the Reagan administration has succeeded in bringing about an economic recovery in 1983 and 1984. By contrast, the Soviet economy was still in trouble. Taken together with the military situation, the unfavorable United States-Soviet military balance has been reversed as compared with four years ago.

When considering "the new American ascendancy" /!/ over the Soviet Union, one must recognize that the Reagan administration has enjoyed several compelling advantages. First, Moscow has run into great difficulties at home and abroad in the past few years because of its frequent changes in leadership, the unfortunate war in Afghanistan, continuing problems in Poland, and other expansionist activities. Second, conservatives led by Margaret Thatcher, Y. Nakasone, and Helmut Kohl have come to power in key United States allies, Britain, Japan, and the Federal Republic of Germany. And in France, the Socialist government of President François Mitterand has taken an even tougher line towards the U.S.S.R. The establishment of diplomatic ties with China during President Jimmy Carter's term left Reagan in a favorable diplomatic position. There was a resolve now in the United States to negotiate with the Kremlin from a position of strength.

Reagan has taken important steps towards improving Sino-United States relations "by successfully removing obstacles thrown up by pro-Taiwan forces." His 1984 visit to Beijing was also helpful.

The Soviets on the Chinese Foes of Detente

While unprecedented global rivalry between the superpowers dominated international affairs, the Soviet Union has proclaimed its willingness to pursue detente with the U.S. To Beijing detente appeared long ago only as a smokescreen behind which Moscow found it useful to operate. But Moscow has lamented the deterioration of relations with the U.S. and has tried to pin the blame for it not on its own aggressive thrusts in various parts of the world, but on the alleged abandonment of the policy of detente by the U.S. It has considered a "detente" which permitted the Soviet Union aggressive moves preferable to a rigid opposition which blocked any Soviet "progress" around the globe.

The Soviet Union has long posed as champion of detente. *Izvestia*'s political commentator V. Kudryantsev wrote on August 8, 1975: "Everything that happens in Europe is echoed, directly or indirectly, in the rest of the world. This applies to the process of detente. . ."(4) Imperialists, having suffered defeat in Vietnam and Cambodia, "have only shifted the center of their military undertakings from Southeast Asia to... South Korea and Japan." *Izvestia* dismissed the notion that a giant such as the C.P.R. could ever be "isolated" and "encircled." "Only the sick imagination of the Beijing leaders could conceive the idea of naming the Soviet-sponsored collective security plan as aiming at the 'encirclement and isolation' of the C.P.R. One would have to lose all sense of reality to believe that a country with a population of 800 million and an ancient culture could be isolated at all."

At about the same time, in the summer of 1975, *Izvestia* attacked Mao's "new political campaign."(5) This frontal attack on Maoism climaxed in criticism of Beijing's foreign policy course. Virtually the same kind of accusations were hurled by Beijing against Moscow: bourgeoisification of the youth and even of the apparatchiks, pseudo-Marxist ideology, and intensification of dictatorship by a bureaucratic clique. In *Voprosy istorii*, the leading Soviet historical journal, L. S. Peremolov, following the Chinese ideological campaign against Lin Piao and Confucius, criticized not only China's domestic policy and ideological aspirations but also Beijing's activities against Communist Parties, "progressive" regimes in

Asia and other parts of the world,"(6) and of using troops to
seize the Paracel and Spratly islands. Chinese soldiers are
alleged to be in Nepal and Laos, under the guise of road
construction crews. The Chinese leaders were also claiming
"considerable portions" of the territory of Mongolia and the
Soviet Union and, allegedly, also of Korea and Japan, though
the latter charges were not specified in this context.

The C.P.R.'s foreign policy course, castigated while Mao
stood at the helm of the Chinese ship of state, was no less
sharply criticized by the Soviet press after Mao's demise. This
holds true for the C.P.R.'s aspirations to become the leader of
the Third World.

Beijing's Third World Policy and Moscow's Concerns

According to the Soviets, China's repeated assertion that it
is an inseparable part of the Third World, is designed to
"flatter the young developing states and demagogically
portraying itself as a fighter against superpower hegemonism."
Beijing desires "to use the developing states as an instrument in
the realization of great power policy:"(7) actually, it harbors
chauvinist designs. "But these tricks are unavailing." "The
shameful history of Beijing's participation in attempts to
suppress the national-liberation struggle of the people of
Bangladesh, the open act of betrayal with respect to the people
of Chile, as expressed in the support for the bloody fascist
regime in that country, the flagrant interference in the
internal affairs of India and Burma—where to this day
Chinese money and weapons are being used by reactionary
elements and separatists—this is the true face of Beijing!"
"Beijing's line is aimed at fanning military conflict in the Near
East, at disuniting the Arab peoples." This is "another
example of China's leaders' two-faced policy toward the
developing countries. Actually, this propaganda plays into the
hands of bellicose Zionist circles and their imperialist
protectors." What is allegedly involved here, is the forming of
a bloc between Beijing and reactionary militarist-revanchist
forces in Western Europe and Japan. Beijing attempts to pit
the capitalist states against the Soviet Union and other socialist
countries. The Maoists want to create something like a united
front of the enemies of world socialism. China, however,

countered by claiming that its policy was merely to establish a defensive circle around the aggressive Soviet Union.

Moscow followed with concern and dismay the rapprochement between World War II enemies, China and Japan, though its own militant policy in the Far East had been the main catalyst of this development. Beijing's desire to include in the treaty with Tokyo a special point opposing the hegemony of "third powers" in Asia spoke volumes; meant by the "third party" was the U.S.S.R.(8) As *Izvestia* stated, "The Soviet Union is a state, a large part of which lies in Asia. For this reason the state of affairs and of international relations on this continent is by no means a matter of indifference to our country. But there is nothing more alien to Soviet diplomacy of peace than a drive for hegemony anywhere."(8)

Mutual Threats and China's Policy of "Equidistance" and "Independence"

In the late 1970s, Chinese leaders were bent on creating an anti-Soviet bloc, comprising the U.S., Western Europe, and the Third World. But by 1981, the C.P.R. leadership was raising questions about the benefits derived from a closer relationship with the U.S. Aroused by what it judged to be a contradictory policy of Washington toward Taiwan, they have frequently charged the U.S. with pursuing a "hegemonist" policy and have begun to emphasize their own "independent" foreign policy. Far from acting consistently, however, they have simultaneously revived the idea of creating a united front against the Soviet threat. With Beijing threatening to switch Chinese policy toward the U.S.S.R., Chinese political analysts were saying privately that a united front opposing Soviet hegemonism was imperative.(9)

The Chinese hold that the Soviet threat to China was a long-range threat. At the moment the Soviets want to gain only new bases in the Southeast Asian Sea, continue their occupation of Afghanistan, decisively influence Vietnam in her Indochina policy, and encircle the C.P.R. Chinese analysts interviewed in 1983 saw the main thrust of Soviet strategy aimed at Europe and the Persian Gulf rather than toward China herself.(10) While the C.P.R. leadership emphasizes frequently real or alleged Soviet threats against China, at other times they point to Soviet shortcomings which make it unlikely that they will obtain global hegemony. Among these weaknesses are listed primarily their economic difficulties, excessive military expenditures at the expense of improving their living standard, the financial burden of supporting near-by allies in Eastern Europe or distant allies such as Cuba, frequent droughts, and natural misfortunes.

While the Soviet Union, geographically a European and Asiatic state, can, differently from the U.S., switch promptly attention from West to East and vice versa, bringing pressure to bear upon many different neighbors, the U.S.S.R., in Chinese eyes, has also staggering obligations to friends, fellow-communists, and some Third World nations. Their battle lines are overextended and their in some respects "unfavorable" geographic situation compels them to face simultaneously a two-front war.(11)

Many of the Chinese remarks, like those of the Soviet leaders, must be taken with a grain of salt. Some observations are made not only for home consumption but for the nations of the world, and, last but not least, for the Soviet government. They are designed to make the Soviets refrain from escalating threats against the C.P.R. Thus, they frequently warn that China is determined to fight even a nuclear war. They remind the Soviet union that the C.P.R. has a billion-plus population and a land area of over 8 million acres, and try to impress upon her that "China cannot be conquered or digested."(12) While Chinese officials repeatedly demand that the Soviet Union relinquish its hegemonistic policy, they are skeptical that it will accommodate them and radically change its policy; they are doubtful of a genuine improvement in Sino-Soviet relations.

Just before visiting Washington in January 1984, Premier Zhao criticized those who characterized Chinese policy towards the U.S. and the Soviet Union as equidistant between Moscow and Washington. Actually, the C.P.R. neither attached herself to "a certain big power" (the U.S.) nor did it practice "equal distance diplomacy."(13) China was prepared to establish a "steady and lasting relationship with the U.S." and "willing to conduct a dialogue with the Soviet Union." The latter statement actually contradicted the disavowal of equal distance!

Nevertheless, in the eighties China has veered from the policy of building a coalition with the U.S.A., with developed capitalist countries such as Great Britain, France, and Japan, and with Third World nations, against the Soviet Union to a policy which often claims keeping equidistance from the U.S.S.R. and the U.S. These claims are misleading, as both the Soviets and the U.S. well understand. The C.P.R. still considers the Soviet Union its main enemy and threat, but finds it politically opportune to pretend pursuing a neutralist or at least independent course. It thus avoids escalating its differences with the U.S.S.R. and appeases perhaps some of its own domestic opposition, which favors a lessening of tension, if not a rapprochement, with the Soviets. But in matters of substance and major national interest, Beijing differs from Moscow, while it is critical of Washington only on peripheral issues. In private, Chinese analysts argue that the C.P.R. is still vitally interested in a close diplomatic and even military relationship with the U.S. Both the U.S. and the C.P.R. seem to comprehend the necessity for Beijing to cool the inflamed rhetorics between China and the Soviet Union and to criticize some aspects of U.S. policy toward Taiwan, but also toward the entire Third World.

Though the C.P.R. criticized specific American hegemonist policies, especially toward the Third World, it still aims at including the U.S. in a united front against the Soviet Union. It realizes that a front which does not include the U.S.A., is not likely to be sucessful against the U.S.S.R. China's strategy in time of peace is to keep Moscow off-balance. In the event of a war, the C.P.R. similarly will not be prepared to pledge assistance to the U.S.— which the latter has not asked for. China prefers not to reveal its policy in the event of an international crisis. The U.S., in turn, has not made public any promise of assistance to China, should she be attacked by her Communist neighbor. But the Soviet Union cannot take comfort from the circumstance that there is no iron-clad treaty between the U.S.A. and the C.P.R. In the event of a Soviet attack on China, the Soviet Union must by necessity count on the U.S. rushing to the defense of the C.P.R.—which national self-interest may require.

It was, of course, growing Soviet power which brought the U.S. and C.P.R. closer together in 1971-1972. In February

1983, the Chinese Foreign Minister Wu Xue Quian, while in the U.S., pointed out that in 1972 American and Chinese leaders made "an important strategic decision," ending the mutual isolation between the two countries. After a visit of Secretary Shultz to Beijing, a Xinhua commentary noted that the two countries came "close in their analyses of the current international situation."(14) And a Chinese foreign policy spokesman stressed that American and Chinese interests-stretching from Korea to Afghanistan, were "nearly identical."(15)

Beijing's relationship with Washington, conversely linked with that of Moscow, was well illuminated by Premier Zhao Ziyang. Talking to American reporters, he stressed that China's views were similar to or identical with those of the United States on Afghanistan and Kampuchea — where the Soviet Union and its Vietnam mercenary are the opponents. He also pointed to some differences in regard to "rights and interests of Third World countries." He could not help noticing the large military build-up of Soviet forces and stressed the "heavy responsibility" of both China and the U.S. to maintain stability and peace in the area — a basis for a close "understanding, if not military alliance, against a hegemonistic intruder"(16) — the U.S.S.R.

But speaking thereafter in San Francisco, Zhao swung back: "China pursues an independent foreign policy and is ready to establish, develop, and improve relations with all countries, including the Soviet Union, on the basis of the Five Principles of Peaceful Coexistence." But there had not yet been any substantial progress in talks between the two nations, and China's position towards many Soviet policies remains unchanged. "But we have increased trade and economic relations with the Soviet Union," and he added, "we are willing to improve our relations with the Soviet Union, but apparently this does not depend on China alone."(17) Though his remarks on Sino-Soviet relations sounded conciliatory, he did not budge from the usual preconditions posed by Beijing and concluded that improvement of relations was a bilateral affair! But Moscow was not appreciative: with respect to the developing countries, the Maoists, it countered, "were trying to take a hegemonist position" and to discredit the world revolutionary communist movement, attempting "to knock together a pro-Beijing alliance." The goal of Maoist foreign policy was "to turn China into a world center with its own sphere of influence."(18) According to Moscow, Beijing hoped that the provocation of armed conflicts between the U.S.S.R. and the West would bring about war and mutual exhaustion.

Mao and the "Three Worlds"

Since Mao's death, Sino-Soviet relations have been characterized both by great expectation and bitter disappointment. During the last decade there has been a bewildering array of positive and negative developments following and more often accompanying each other.

Behind all these developments still lingers Mao's theory of the alignment of forces in the international arena which, according to *Pravda*, presented a "distorted picture" of the world at large. As the daily had written on March 19, 1975: "All states are divided. . .into three worlds. The United States of America and the U.S.S.R. form the "first world," the developed countries are "the second world," and the developing countries of Asia, Africa, and Latin America constitute "the Third World." Completely denying the existence of the socialist system, the Mao group "provocatively disperses the socialist states among all three worlds," trying to counterpose them to one another. It is apparent that this division of socialist states into political units of different economic development and different national interests goes against the very grain of Marxist and Soviet thought. "This scheme has nothing in common with reality, with Marxism-Leninism, and the first world:" the Maoists were trying to prove that the U.S.S.R. and the United States of America were two "superpowers, allegedly seeking to divide the world between them." According to Moscow, the thesis of "superpowers," originating in the West, was taken up in Beijing primarily with the aim of slandering the Soviet Union. A slanderous label, "social imperialism," was pinned on Soviet foreign policy. The Soviets accused the C.P.R. of wishing to improve relations with the United States, of supporting NATO and striving, as the Western press conceded, to catch the Warsaw Treaty countries in "Sino-American pincers."(19)

The ideological shift from the extreme Left to the "Right" in Communism, from Mao's Cultural Revolution to Deng's pragmatism and drive toward "modernization," has, in Moscow's view, little changed Beijing's foreign policy course, especially not its anti-Soviet orientation. Concerning Deng's speech, while visiting the United States in February 1979, A. Petrov in *Pravda* observed, that it was "permeated with dyed-in-the-wool anti-Sovietism and hostility."(20) Deng disparaged the notion of any U.S. accord with the Soviet Union in the field of disarmament. Revamping the Maoist "theory of the three worlds," he even assigned to the U.S. the role of China's ally.

According to the Soviets, part of the "ten-year nightmare" of the "Great Proletarian Cultural Revolution" was the worsening of the Sino-Soviet relationship. Yet, despite all the changes in the C.P.R., Maoism, as a theory and practice of great-power claims and extolling hegemonism and anti-Sovietism, remains the "foundation" of the C.P.R.'s domestic and foreign policy.

In the Soviet view, Washington has revived the Cold War atmosphere. The latter is partly the result of its policies in the Middle East, in particular toward the Arab states, Iran, and Afghanistan and of the attempt to strengthen its military stance in Europe. Moscow holds that the pro-American Maoist course of Beijing was responsible for the aggravation of the international situation, since it played directly into the hands of Washington.

China's Critique of U.S. Foreign Policy

Even when the C.P.R. strove more determinedly toward the creation of a virtual alliance with the U.S.A. against the U.S.S.R., it never suppressed entirely its criticism of U.S. Policies. There were a number of international problems on which China and the U.S. did not and do not see eye to eye. While the C.P.R. has welcomed the growing American role in Asian affairs—what a reversal from the era of American intervention in Vietnam!—as a necessary counterweight against Soviet pressures, it feared on the other hand being dragged by the U.S. into war with the Soviet Union, notwithstanding its opposition to and sharp criticism of Soviet policies. Beijing has also criticized the U.S. unilateral policy, its failure to consult friends and allies. Obviously, China herself prefers to be consulted rather than face an American *fait accompli*, whatever it may be. Beijing is also critical of U.S. policy toward much of the Third World, a policy which it claims to be insensitive toward the latter and which thus creates opportunities for the expansion of Soviet influence. The same holds true for U.S. procedures in the U.N.

It is noteworthy that these criticisms have a common denominator. By pursuing the foregoing policies, the U.S. weakens rather than strengthens the creation of a united front against the Soviet Union. While Beijing seemed to welcome U.S. rearmament and her tougher policy against the U.S.S.R. under President Reagan, the Chinese leadership and press occasionally expressed the fear that this policy might push China into war with the Soviets. While there is no love lost between the C.P.R. and the U.S.S.R., the former apparently wants to avoid becoming embroiled in hostilities with its powerful neighbor, unless the Soviets would attack it directly. Specifically, Beijing has disapproved the lifting of the grain embargo against the Soviet Union,(21) which Washington saw belatedly as counterproductive. West European allies also were frequently critical of Reagan's policies as being contradictory on this issue, while urging West Europe to curtail the export of high technology to the Soviet Union. The C.P.R. leadership also points to American support of Israel, South Africa, and South Korea. In 1983, Beijing charged that the U.S. thus alienated other Third World countries, which actually deprived her of the support of numerous allies and friends against Soviet expansionism.(22) It is the latter goal, an anti-Soviet bulwark, which, in the Chinese view, must have top priority for the U.S. in her competitive struggle against the U.S.S.R. The same reasoning applies also to the Taiwan issue, which, according to Beijing, is an obstacle to further improvement of relations between Beijing and Washington.

This American position was partly responsible for Beijing's adoption of an "independent" foreign policy. The U.S. alone, it is frequently implied and at times articulated, can not counter the Soviet Union.(23) Occasionally, however, Beijing voiced the fear that a more "flexible" U.S. attitude toward the

U.S.S.R. might lead to an American-Soviet collusion at the expense of the C.P.R.(24) The U.S. is never fully trusted!

Soviet Fear of Post-Nuclear China

There exists some doubt among Soviet military planners that the U.S.S.R. can win a nuclear war or even survive one. (25) On the other hand, others hold that, due to its vast population, the Chinese have very good chances for survival. Therefore, the C.P.R. constitutes a threat to the Soviet Union which, ravaged by a nuclear war unleashed in the West, would be extremely vulnerable vis-à-vis the C.P.R. Considering the Soviet Union's multinational character, national inequalities and dissatisfactions, it might even disintegrate: many of the border nationalities might consider seceding from the U.S.S.R. Thus, Soviet fears of a post-nuclear attack by China, may be real and not be a mere subterfuge. If China herself becomes embroiled in a nuclear war, her losses would be smaller than those of the Soviet Union. The latter, largely devastated and weakened both in regard to manpower, resources, and industrial strength, would face a serious threat from China. As a Soviet military analyst put it, perhaps exaggeratedly, in an interview in 1981," Even if the war is not over China, it would be good for China."(26) As Barrett and Glaser sum it up: "Chinese strategists say privately that China is in a better position to survive a fight and protracted war than is the Soviet Union. They maintain that China's advantages in demography and grain production and its abundant natural resources will enhance its 'revivability.'" (27) The evaluation of China's peacetime strengths by impartial observers is much lower than the assessment of her wartime and postwar power.(28)

The Soviet Union, fearful of encirclement and American-Chinese "collusion" in times of peace and war, aims at reducing the chances of a two-front war, one in Europe against Western Europe and NATO in league with the U.S., and another one in the Far East against China and Japan, also in alliance with America. On the other hand, any Sino-Soviet talks are likely to arouse suspicion in the minds of U.S. policy-makers. The policy of Sino-American rapprochement has been championed by China since the early 1970s. Actually, since 1969 the U.S., in turn, has looked upon the prevention of a Soviet attack on China as a major goal of its foreign policy.

But the U.S., as stated, has also been concerned over the opposite development, a marked improvement of relations between the C.P.R. and the U.S.S.R. There exist, as has been pointed out, geographic areas where U.S. policies and China policies diverge. But the issues in question are peripheral and do not affect vital national interests of the U.S. and China.

Chinese analysts argue that the Soviet concern about an unmanageable post-nuclear threat from China actually deters Moscow from taking forcible actions against the C.P.R.(29) It is therefore not surprising that the U.S.S.R., while repeatedly warning the U.S. against military cooperation with China, has calmed down, especially after Beijing has apparently modified its course, preaching "independence" rather than an outright form of alliance with the U.S.

"Plot" against the U.S.S.R.

Throughout the last decade both the U.S.S.R. and the C.P.R., with the exception of relatively brief periods, have poisoned the air waves with their vituperative campaigns. Chinese propagandists and agitators have ceaselessly talked about "Soviet menace," "Soviet espionage," etc. The Chinese authorities have staged trials of "Soviet agents," thereby implanting in their people both a "spy-mania" and hostility toward all Soviet people working in China. The whole of this campaign was intended to psychologically condition the Chinese people, and above all the young people, to feel hostility and hatred toward all things Soviet.

Though Moscow excoriated Beijing's anti-Soviet propaganda, the Soviets were hardly slow in responding or even starting to blast the Chinese. They were quite adept in turning the tables against the C.P.R., though not likely successful if the situation in Afghanistan was the source of discord. Trying to defend their invasion of Afghanistan, the Soviets have gone to the extremes of accusing the United States and the C.P.R. of waging an "undeclared war" against Afghanistan: together with Washington, Beijing has allegedly been taking part in this war for a long time. "Now international reaction is using Pakistan's territory as a sanctuary and base for bands of

Afghan counterrevolutionaries." The visit by Dezhi, Chief of
Staff of the Chinese Army, to a camp of Afghan counterrevolutionaries in Pakistan, showed that "the strengthening of the
Beijing-Islamabad axis on a militaristic basis threatens
the Asian people's peace and security; and is a direct
source of tension and conflicts in the region."(30)

The Soviet evidence against the C.P.R. and China's alleged
timetable of expansion is rather questionable. The Soviet
picture, on the other hand, of its own invasion of Afghanistan
as mere assistance to a progressive and proletarian brotherly
nation is similarly mere propaganda. At the same time, the
Soviets hold that other neighbors of theirs such as Japan are a
major target of sinister U.S. plans to close the encirclement
around the U.S.S.R. The "'Pacific ring' is intended to join the
NATO and ANZUS blocs and Washington's bilateral alliances
with Tokyo and Seoul into a single chain."

According to the Soviets, Communist China's new
economic policy, opening the door to Western and developed
capitalist countries, in return for anti-Sovietism in foreign
policy, is a dangerous trend for China and the peace of the
world.(31) While Chinese Premier Zhao Ziyang visited all
ASEAN countries — excepting Indonesia, with which China
had no relations — he argued not only for maintaining but also
increasing America's military presence in Asia. At a press
conference in Manila he characterized the Kampuchean
problem as "an important element in the joint struggle of
China, Japan, the United States, Australia, New Zealand, and
the ASEAN countries against global Soviet expansion." That
is, added *Pravda*, perfectly in keeping with Maoist hegemonistic designs. This increased attention to the ASEAN countries
has not just tactical goals but a strategic goal as well: to draw
them into the so-called "Pacific Community" or, as it is
sometimes called, "the Pacific ring." The proposed members
of a regional association of this sort included five developed
capitalist states in the Pacific—the United States, Japan,
Canada, Australia, and New Zealand—the five ASEAN
countries—Indochina, Thailand, the Philippines, Malaysia,
and Singapore—and South Korea.

An attempt was being made to harness the United States
partners together in a simple team by means of various
agreements and to shift part of the police duties in the Asian

and Pacific region onto them. Japan's "self-defense forces" have already assumed a number of day-to-day tasks of the United States Seventh Fleet in the Nort-West Pacific—from Guam to the Philippines. Australia and New Zealand were being more and more actively drawn into the militarization of the Indian Ocean. Australia has been assigned a new major role in the "Pacific Community," that is striving to develop military ties between states of South-East Asia and those of the South-West Pacific, and, in particular, to revive the practice of holding joint military maneuvers with Singapore and Malaysia. In short, the Pacific ring is intended to bring about the encirclement of the Soviet Union.

The Soviets followed closely the development of American-Chinese relations, always a matter of primary interest to them.(32) Many Soviet commentators noted that the particip-ants in the Chinese-American talks sought to play down the existing differences between the two countries—especially on the Taiwan question—in order to focus attention on trade, economics, and scientific and technical ties. But the journey by the head of the Chinese government to the United States had, according to Pravda, still another aspect, a political-strategic one. During the visit, the leaders of the United States administration stated unequivocally that they regarded American-Chinese relations primarily in the context of a "community of strategic goals." United States ruling circles have the major goal of using China's interest in the development of economic, scientific, and technical ties with the United States in order to bind that country to Washington's global anti-Soviet course and to draw it into a "strategic paartnership" that would be in the interests of imperialism.

While verbally condemning "all forms of hegemonism," the Chinese leadership, according to Pravda, at the same time declared its readiness to establish "stable and lasting relaitons with the present United States administration." In receiving Prime Minister Zhao Ziyang, Seacretary of State Schultz said: "We have resumed and continue our strategic dialogue." The Chinese guest, however, backtracked, pointing to similarities as well as differences of the two states on other questions. "In such conditions it is impossible to establish a comprehensive strategic partnership." Quoting from the American journal,

the *Far Eastern Economic Review*, Ovchinnikov held that
Beijing wanted to create the notion that it is "a non-aligned
country and to distance itself from the United States." But the
journal then added that China was loudest in its criticism of
those aspects of American policy that have no direct
significance for Beijing.

But on the issues vital for the U.S.S.R., Afghanistan, and
Indochina, the U.S. and China hold "basically parallel views."
According to Ovchinnikov, the Reagan administration's recent
efforts to "humor" Beijing have been dictated in part by
election-campaign considerations. The author pointed out
that despite pledges to the contrary, the United States persisted
in its imperialistic approach to China's national interests:
Washington politicians tended to "forget" their acknowledg-
ment that there is only one China and that Taiwan is part of it.
Despite Washington's verbal deference to Beijing, its relations
with Taiwan continued unchanged. In an interview, the
Chinese guest to the United States stressed that there had been
no qualitative reduction in deliveries of American weapons to
Taiwan, and their qualitative level had even risen. The United
States administration was not at all interested in the practical
resolution of problems that are important for China.
Washington was seeking to draw Beijing into the orbit of its
influence in order to use American-Chinese relations for selfish
purposes.

The China "Threat" in Past, Present, and Future

The repeated Soviet reference to the "China threat" is not
merely overblown propaganda, but has a substantive core.
Such talk is clearly designed to blunt the C.P.R.'s own
accusation of the existence of a "Soviet threat from the North."
But the widely reported concern of the Soviet population
about the "China threat," which propaganda and official
policy helped to disseminate, is genuine. Even though the
Soviets, realizing the more limited military power of the
C.P.R., may not harbor any fear of the Chinese colossus for
the foreseeable future, they feel that in the long run China
with its industrious and capable populace, far surpassing the
size of the U.S.S.R., constitutes a real threat to the security of
the U.S.S.R.

The traditional Russian concern on her Western European borders is coupled with Soviet concern on its eastern Asiatic borders. The Soviets fear that in the event of a European war, China, by herself no menace, will tie down numerous Soviet divisions along the Sino-Soviet frontier and make any Soviet military response in Europe more difficult. By 1972, the Soviets had already 45 divisions in Asia; a decade later, they had raised their strength to fifty well-equipped divisions. The Soviet Union fears China, if allied with the U.S.A.; it fears the global deployment of American conventional and nuclear forces.

While the Soviets question the chances of improving relations with the C.P.R. in the near future, they realize the propagandistic importance of striking an optimistic pose. Though they denounce the C.P.R.'s policy toward the U.S.S.R., they also claim the existence of "healthy forces" in China.(33) Following the start of "consultations" between China and the U.S.S.R. in 1984, they were cautious not to alienate needlessly the C.P.R. leadership; after Mao's demise, the Soviet leaders and expert analysts, in a pragmatic mood, would modify, if not repudiate, Mao's theories, held to be distinctly anti-Soviet. But despite their overtures, the new Chinese leadership seemed hardly responsive. At the 26th Party Congress on February 23, 1981, Brezhnev gave expression to his disappointment. *Kommunist*, the journal of the C.P.S.U., concluded that the Maoist ideology continued to be "the Party's basic ideological and political platform."

While Deng Xiaoping became the main target of Soviet disillusionment regarding lack of progress in Sino-Soviet relations, others such as the General Secretary of the C.C. of the C.C.P., Hu Yaobang, were considered more friendly to the concept of improving Sino-Soviet relations.(34) Many Soviet experts seem convinced that with China's domestic power struggle coming to an end, Sino-Soviet relations will improve.

After the outbreak of the "Cultural Revolution" in 1966, M. S. Kapitsa, Soviet Deputy Foreign Minister, writing under the pseudonym Ukraintsev, considered Mao the main stumbling block toward the improvement of mutual relations. He pointed out that all pro-Soviet forces in the C.P.R. were wiped out starting in 1966. In 1974, Brezhnev seemed to place some hope upon new forces emerging in China which would also

change Beijing's course toward Moscow. The same view was
expressed by O. B. Rakhmanin (pseudonym for O. B. Borisov)
in two books published in 1981 and 1982, when he prophesied
the replacement of present Chinese leaders and anticipated the
time when China once again will take her place in the great
fraternal socialist community.(35) Such optimism was expressed by many Soviet sinologists who insist that, in the long run,
China will reject Western capitalist influence(36) and will
ultimately return to a Soviet-style centrally planned economy.
They seem confident that Beijing will in the end reject
Western individualism and "bourgeois egoism." In Tashkent,
March 1982, Brezhnev reconfirmed the Soviet conviction that
the Chinese system was still socialism. Yet the Soviet experts
and the Soviet press are often concerned that Western
capitalism will penetrate the C.P.R. and mold Chinese ways.

From the end of the 1970s, Soviet commentators voiced
concern over the rapid military build-up of the C.P.R. In the
early 1980s, however, this fear had largely subsided.(37)
Privately, Soviet experts pointed to China's military inability to
absorb large quantities of foreign technology. Nor did they
seem impressed by the large quantity of foreign weapons which
the C.P.R. had succeeded in importing. They held that the
Chinese leadership emphasized development in agriculture
and industry, science and technology, rather than of military
modernization.(38)

In an article in June 1981, J. H. Aleksandrov—a pseudonym which voices the views of the Central Committee of the
C.P.S.U. —held that the Chinese did not fear nuclear war.
They believed that in the post-nuclear stage China would
emerge as the strongest power on earth.(39) After the U.S. and
the U.S.S.R. had destroyed each other in a nuclear war, China
would emerge as the winner. Many Soviet experts hold the view
that in a global nuclear encounter China, due to the very size
of her population, has greater survivability than either
superpower.

In his memoirs, *Years of Upheaval*, Henry Kissinger
reported a private discussion with Brezhnev in May 1973 when
the latter appealed for U.S. acquiescence to a Soviet attack on
China. He also threatened that any American military
"collusion" with China would result in a U.S.-Soviet war.(40)
Fears of a Sino-American collusion had plagued the Soviet

leadership for a long time. They were greatly concerned when President Carter's National Security advisor Zbigniew Brzezinski, whom they particularly suspected on account of his Polish background and anti-Soviet stance, visited China in May 1978.

Such fears were voiced in the article, "Dangerous Partnership" in *Kommunist* in July 1980, which made no bones about the adverse impact of a Sino-American rapprochement upon world peace. When Secretary of State Alexander Haig journeyed to Beijing in June 1981, an article of Aleksandrov in *Pravda* warned that Reagan had escalated President Carter's decision to sell arms to China, and spoke of an emerging U.S.-China military axis.(41) Other Soviet analysts cautioned that China's long-term global interests and American national interests did not coincide.(42) Similarly, G. Arbatov, Director of the U.S. A. Institute in Moscow and advisor to Brezhnev and later Andropov, warned that the C.P.R.'s nuclear power would soon be able to reach U.S. territory.(43) Others, like Bovin in *Izvestia*, "Partnership with Trust," predicted that in view of fundamental differences between Chinese and American social systems and ideologies the relationship between the two states will "inevitably sour" and China will be "forced to return to the path of detente, dialogue, and agreements" with the U.S.S.R.(44) Wishful thinking has colored some predictions by Soviet leaders and commentators on Sino-American relations.

Alternative Chinese Policies

What, in the Soviet view, were the strategic considerations of both Beijing and Washington in forging their anti-Soviet bonds? According to I. Aleksandrov, the C.P.R. was intent on provoking a military confrontation between the superpowers. (45-46) The C.P.R. was like the monkey sitting on top of the mountains and watching the "battle of the tigers" in the valley. Kapitsa in the foregoing article accused Beijing that it had pursued such policy for the last quarter of the century. After having urged Moscow, especially between 1957 and 1959, to launch a nuclear attack against the U.S.A. over Taiwan, the Chinese more recently had tried to influence the U.S.A. to take through a nuclear strike the military initiative against the Soviet Union.

Other commentators stressed China's modernization goals as its primary motive in bringing about a rapprochement with the West. The West, in return, insisted on a "promissory note of anti-Sovietism." One Soviet analyst argued that China aimed at becoming a powerful state of "independent influence on international relations," taking account of the C.P.R.'s new emphasis on foreign relations. J. Bazhanov, in his book *Motive Forces of U.S. Policy Toward China*, accused the U.S. of wishing "to harness Chinese nationalism."(47-48) Many other commentators pointed to America's self-interest in creating a U.S.-China axis.(49) The Soviet Army newspaper *Krasnaya Zvezda*, after Defense Secretary Weinberger's visit to China in 1983, seemed convinced that American-Chinese military links would become closer.(50) The danger of stronger military ties between them has always preoccupied Soviet leaders.

In January 1980 Brezhnev warned Jacques Chaban-Delmar, presiding officer of the French National Assembly, pounding his desk several times, that the nuclear arming of China would result in a Soviet nuclear attack on the C.P.R. and appeared confident that American leaders would be taken aback by a Soviet *fait accompli*.(51) The Soviet leaders also made abundantly clear that they sharply opposed the delivery of British defense missiles and of other U.S. weapons to China. In 1981, Soviet analysts privately stressed that the "China threat" gripped not only the Soviet leadership but also the Soviet populace.(52) It appears that China's fear of the "polar bear" is matched by the Soviet fear of the "Chinese threat," though the latter applies to a more distant future and arises only in combination with a U.S. alliance with the C.P.R.

By June 1983, fears of China had somewhat receded.(53) Chinese-American relations had apparently not produced the anticipated rapid build-up of Chinese armaments. The most recent interviews also pointed to China's equidistant position between the two superpowers. But the Soviet analysts also emphasized that Beijing's global strategy had not changed.

The basic alternatives of the C.P.R.'s policy toward the Soviet Union are, first, provoking a nuclear war between the two superpowers — which would irreparably weaken the U.S.S.R. — second, an alliance with the U.S.A. — which would deter the Soviet Union from attacking China — or third, the reduction of the Sino-Soviet confrontation to a lower level, a "normalization" of Sino-Soviet relations.

From Brezhnev to Andropov

Despite frequent changes in the Soviet top leadership in the early 1980s, their views on Sino-Soviet relations have remained unchanged, though minor improvements as well as some deteriorations have taken place. At the 24th Party Congress (1971), Brezhnev had observed "signs of a certain normalization in relations" and expressed the Soviet Union's wish not only for normalization but "also for the restoration of friendship."(54) But such hopes vanished into thin air the following years. At the 25th Party Congress of the C.P.S.U. in February 1976, Brezhnev denounced Beijing's "inflammatory policy" and dropped the earlier remarks of "restoration of friendship:" Beijing would have to "return" to a policy truly based on Marxism-Leninism-as interpreted, of course, by Moscow—and abandon its hostile policy against the socialist bloc. The Soviet disappointments with Beijing increased when the post-Mao leadership continued to cling to Mao's anti-Sovietism.

At the 26th Party Congress, Brezhnev accused the C.P.R. leadership of trying to torpedo detente policy in the world and of "aggravating the international situation." Alluding to changes which had occurred in China, he voiced the hope that the new leaders will overcome "the Maoist legacy." In a speech at Tashkent in March 1982, he assured Beijing that the Soviet Union had never denied the existence of a socialist system in China.

A few weeks after Brezhnev's death, his successor Yuri Andropov made his first major statement on China in an interview with *Pravda*.(55) Referring to "the anomalous state of Soviet-Chinese relations over the last two decades, he saw nevertheless some "positive trends" in increased trade and other exchanges. Moscow was ready, he averred, for a political dialogue with China on fundamental questions relating to world development, peace, and international security; but he rejected concessions relating to Afghanistan, Kampuchea, and troop concentrations along the Sino-Soviet border. On the whole, all this did not show a marked change from the policy of Brezhnev. Indeed, in 1983 Soviet commentators concluded that the China policy under Andropov followed Brezhnev's line. M. S. Kapitsa, the leading China specialist of the Foreign Ministry, writing under the pseudonym M. S. Ukraintsev in the Institute of the Far East's *Problems of the Far East*(56) expressed the pessimistic view that China's leaders were not interested in solving the border dispute. China played the role of "imperialism's junior partner." Chinese leaders were only taking some "little steps" to settle differences with the Soviets. But such steps, nevertheless, might improve Sino-Soviet relations.

After the opening of Sino-Soviet consultations in 1982, Soviet commentators cautiously refrained from sharp accusations and polemics so as not to adversely affect the negotiations. But the Soviet press continued to criticize outright anti-Soviet propaganda. When the Chinese premier Zhao Ziyang visited the U.S. in January 1984, the Soviet press once again unleashed sharp criticism of the C.P.R.'s policies. *Krasnaya Zvezda* concluded that China and the U.S. adopted "identical positions" on the question of Afghanistan and Kampuchea.(57)

Moscow as well as Beijing have frequently voiced skepticism in regard to a possible solution of their dispute. According to one Soviet commentator, the outcome of possible talks would be at best, "a mountain giving birth to a mouse."(58) But both sides seemed to agree that negotiations between them will continue. Indeed, since the talks between Moscow and Beijing began in 1982, trade and cultural relations have expanded. But they have not removed the fundamental differences and "roadblocks" to which the C.P.R. never fails to draw attention: Afghanistan, Kampuchea, Outer Mongolia, the maritime encirclement of China, and the massing of Soviet troops along the Sino-Soviet border. To sum it up, Beijing remains convinced that Moscow aims at global hegemony. It holds that Soviet policy towards the C.P.R. was within the framework of this goal. Like the U.S.S.R., the C.P.R. has come to look upon its opponent as a threat, though as a long-term menace, rather than one in the near future.

Persistent Ambiguities

Yet a long-term menace may under circumstances easily turn into an immediate threat. In that event, it may generate excessive caution in the weaker party and limit its policy choices.

Such caution becomes evident in Beijing's article, "U.S.-U.S.S.R. Military Rivalry stirs up in the Pacific" (May 1986). "A match for military supremacy between the Soviet Union and the U.S. in the Asia-Pacific region appears to be escalating."(59) "Now that the European military stalemate is a fact, the Soviet Union and the U.S. are both determined to create a new military hegemony in the Asia-Pacific region." The Soviet Union "aims at breaking up U.S. containment of the area in order to assure its sea traffic through the Pacific Ocean, to the Indian Ocean... The Soviets hope to improve their status in the rivalry by stepping up communications between their eastern and western wings. The U.S. has designated the Far East, Western Europe, and the Middle East as its three major strategic regions. Believing the Pacific to be the best region from which to confront the Soviet Union, the Reagan administration is reconsidering its military designs in the Western Pacific. It is stepping up plans to further its military cooperation with Japan and South Korea in an effort to retain its military advantages in the region and contain the Soviets to their own waters."

Most striking in this assessment is the apparent "impartiality" of the C.P.R., indicating no preference for the U.S.A., despite the repeated proclamation of the "threat from the North" and of the Soviet Union being the "main enemy." Equally puzzling seems China's aloofness from a "military rivalry ... stirring up" the entire Pacific. The C.P.R., it is made quite clear in this context, is neither successfully wooed by the U.S.A. nor does it play an activist role in ranging herself at the side of the U.S., Japan, and South Korea. She plays a sort of "neutral" role—in striking contrast to numerous other utterances and deeds of the last years. Does this outright contradiction constitute a radical shift of the C.P.R.'s foreign policy or is it simply a pose designed to curry favor with the Soviet Union? Is it motivated by fear and caution?

For years, *Beijing Review* continues, the two countries have persisted in setting up new command facilities, have increased their military forces, consolidated overseas military bases, and have furthered cooperation with allies in the Pacific region. The Beijing journal points to the growing strength of the Soviet navy in the Pacific—the total Soviet Pacific fleet had 600 vessels and its tonnage amounted to 1.6 million. The U.S. had now close to 200,000 troops in the Far East or 33.1% of its total overseas forces. At the moment the Soviet Union "has been engaged in active propaganda for peace to soften U.S. military cooperation with Japan, South Korea, Australia, and New Zealand. The U.S. is working hard to build a multinational strategic alliance." Again, the authoritative Beijing journal simply omits to list the C.P.R. as either being interested in or participating in the defensive anti-Soviet alliance, which it energetically pursued until recent times.

D. Maoism, the CPR's Ideological Turnabout and the Soviet Union

The Decline of Ideology. Its Survival

Though both the U.S.S.R. and the C.P.R. have, according to Soviet dissident Andrei Amalrik, *Will the Soviet Union survive until 1884?* (1970), paid "homage to one and the same ideology," the absolute antagonism of their national imperial interests, and the rise of a "revolutionary curve" in China and cautious decline along the same curve in the Soviet Union, made a quick end to "any pretense of unity."(1) Common Communist ideology has indeed not prevented the Sino-Soviet relationship from worsening, while the different ideological and political philosophy of China and the U.S. has not hindered the Sino-American relationship from improving. It may thus appear tempting to discount ideology as a factor determining Sino-Soviet relations and the Sino-American relationship. The C.P.R.'s alienation from the Soviets results largely from their power dispute; the latter has prevailed over "common" ideology. While the U.S. emphasizes its ideological opposition toward the C.P.R., American perception of the Soviet Union as the main danger to Western Europe, Japan, China, and the rest of the world has, in combination with the realistic assessment of the C.P.R.'s conservative and relatively moderate foreign policy, helped to bring about the current Sino-American rapprochement. This parallel outlook of China and the U.S. on fundamental problems of international affairs is, however, not an outgrowth of common ideology. On the other hand, American-Soviet relations are dictated by a combination of national power politics, imperial Soviet ambitions, and ideological opposition, still nurtured by Leninist Messianic fervor on the Soviet side and, on the American side, marked by dedication to preserving the democratic political order and Western liberties and the global balance of power.

In the last decade, the ideological roles of the Soviet Union and of the C.P.R. have been virtually reversed. Since ideology in general has declined significantly in the Sino-Soviet dispute, some students of it have come close to denying the importance of ideology as such, pointing almost exclusively to power rivalry and opposing geopolitical interests. Yet the continued significance of ideology and Marxist theory in the life and thought of both the U.S.S.R. and the C.P.R. is undeniable, notwithstanding their different interpretation and frequent pseudo-Marxism on both sides. Distinguished statesmen, leading politicians, eminent scholars, and observing journalists past and present have acknowledged the importance of ideological motivation in the Sino-Soviet struggle. Henry Kissinger, talking of the "many roots"(2) of the Sino-Soviet conflict, listed among them "ideological disagreement," especially Beijing's claim of being "ideologically more pure than Moscow," a claim hardly changed to this day!

Soviet and Chinese commentators themselves attribute much of the Sino-Soviet dispute to ideology, respectively to erroneous and "heretical" thought of the adversary. But Western writers and commentators have by no means discarded the significance of ideology as a divisive factor. It is, of course, impossible to deny the important role of ideology as long as the educational system in both Communist countries rests on the pillars of Marxism-Leninism.

According to J. Gittings, *The World and China, 1922-72* (1974)—in his analysis of the Sino-Soviet dispute, he seems to lean to the Chinese side—the reading of some of Mao's unofficial writings adds "a measure of depth to the ideological

aspect of the Sino-Soviet dispute which has previously been
lacking."(3) Gittings added: "Whatever some of his /Mao's/
colleagues or many Western analysts—may have believed, for
Mao ideology was never a veneer to cover national interest, but
a bond which united and at the same divided China and the
Soviet Union in the greatest contradiction of all."

Nor has ideology become a minor factor for the U.S.S.R.
In his forward to H. Ellison's (ed.) *The Sino-Soviet Conflict*
(1982), the late Senator Henry Jackson quoted approvingly the
Soviet specialist Philip Mosely's view that the Soviet Union's
long-range ambition was to "reshape the world according to its
own dogma."(4) In this same study, H. W. Treadgold held
that American authors, "even more than others are ready to
discount ideology" and also warned against "explaining it
away," a warning repeated in the same book by Seton-Watson.
(5) Still, the British historian was correct in pointing out that
the Sino-Soviet conflict has "lost its ideological content:" the
C.P.R. under Deng was sponsoring "archrevisionist" policies,
which it had previously denounced.

According to G. W. Gong, "China and the Soviet Union,"
"a significant measure of cultural interpretation /featuring
ideology/"(6) is indispensable to understand China's problems
and politics in their proper context. According to Robinson,
after a decline of ideology in the 1970s, it has, by the early
1980s, reappeared "as an autonomous factor."

The fact remains that both sides still wrap their dispute in
ideological garb. While addressing their own populace and
other Communist-ruled nations and states, they still use
Marxist-Leninist terms. Though ideology may frequently hide
basic differences and antagonisms, it is undeniable that while
one adversary pointed the accusing finger at revisionism of
which the Soviet Union was declared guilty, the other pointed
at C.P.R.'s embracing rigid orthodoxy, disdainfully ignoring
new experiences. True enough, the accusations involving
revisionism have, in view of the major changes in the domestic
policies of both countries, vanished some time ago. But new
ideological changes have surfaced.

Considering the major importance of the Marxist-Leninist
doctrine and the role it still plays in the intellectual,
educational, political, and every-day life of both the C.P.R.
and U.S.S.R., it cannot be doubted that the thinking of the

leadership of both countries was still shaped by seminal Communist doctrine, whatever its interpretation. Despite the divergent interpretations, common Marxist-Leninist writings, like the Holy Scriptures, still create common bonds. Chinese and Russians may both be vulgar-Marxists, but they still worship the same idols. The leaders of both countries, while bending the doctrine to suit their purposes, are themselves, to a large extent, the prisoners of their own Communist teachings.

Stalin, Krushchev, and their successors, as well as Mao and many Chinese leaders, have steadfastly clung to Marxist-Leninist ideology, though Mao has unquestionably "sinicized" it. His successor Deng and many Chinese pragmatists since have reversed many important, even basic, features of it — to an extent that can be described as an actual abandonment. But official Chinese doctrine still claims that it is "purified" Maoism from which only later mistaken notions have been excised. Still, in the broader sense of the word, Marxism-Leninism and, in the C.P.R., Marxism-Leninism-Maoism, continue to be upheld, though with significant qualifications.

As far as the Sino-Soviet relationship during the last decade is concerned, the importance of ideology, as stated, has declined. But previously it was a highly potent factor, shaping decisively the mutual relationship. In the Stalinist era, when Mao was still willing to play a deferential and subordinate role vis-à-vis Stalin and recognized Soviet and in particular Stalin's supremacy in the World Communist movement, he once appealed to Stalin to recommend to him a literate Marxist-Leninist theoretician who could help him to edit his speeches and articles written during the Civil War. Mao was preparing to publish his collected works and wanted someone to check his writings for possible ideological errors. Stalin, according to Krushchev, was "delighted" to help him, seeing therein positive proof that Mao had no ideological, meaning political, pretensions for leadership in the international Communist movement, which, among other qualities, always required theoretical and ideological eminence. Stalin sent P. F. Yudin,(7) former editor of the Cominform journal *For Lasting Peace, for People*'s Democracy, a propagandist and philosopher, who could carry on lofty conversations with Mao, known for being fond of philosophical colloquies.

Ideology and propaganda have been wedded to Soviet as well as Chinese Communism from the moment of their birth as Parties and have continued after the proclamation of both the Soviet Union and the C.P.R. In the article, "Marxism endures as a Beacon," in *Beijing Review,* An Zhigno conceded that Marxism, which came into being a century ago, did have a few conclusions that were no longer valid.(8) But its fundamental principles still upheld today. Since China, according to An Zhigno, has entered its new period of building socialism with Chinese characteristics, many new questions have cropped up for which the classic Marxist literature contains no ready answers. Since 1978, the C.C. of the C.P.C. has put forward a series of policies and principles. They include socialism, the people's democratic dictatorship and the leadership of the C.P.C., Marxism-Leninism *and* Mao Zedong thought, the opening to the outside world, and reform of the economic structure and the development of commodity economy based on public ownership and building material wealth.

Soviet Communist doctrine, differing from the foregoing Chinese version, has stressed the concept of the "state of the entire people, while claiming to nave overcome the people's "dictatorship." It rejects of course "Maoism" in all its forms, has not passed through the isolationist phase to the extent and duration of the C.P.R., and has not engaged in any significant restructuring of its economy.

After the demise of Mao and the apparent de facto de-Maoization which has taken place in the C.P.R., the major reforms in Communist China and some recent more moderate "modernization" in the Soviet Union, theory and ideology have been compelled to make corresponding adjustments. During the last decade, these changes have extended also to Sino-Soviet relations and especially to Chinese Communist thought. Despite the switch from the extreme Left to the Right of Communism and the Soviet Union's assumption of the left position in the international movement, the theoretical distance between the two adversary powers has hardly diminished. But, in view of the switch, the gyrations especially of Beijing's policy, the ideological rift has not lost its depth, though perhaps some of its credibility. It is not surprising that the C.P.R. has long ago dropped its accusation of revisionism against the U.S.S.R. —of which it now could be accused itself.

The charge of "rigid orthodoxy" can hardly be levelled any longer against China, herself deeply involved in the process of "modernization" and experimentation.

On the tenth anniversary of Mao's death, *Beijing Review* found that Mao was still well remembered, "but as a man, not a god to be worshipped." In spite of his mistakes in late life, Mao was considered by many to have been "a great leader of the Chinese people,"(8b) In a compilation of Deng's quotations from his *Selected Works*, extending from 1978 to June 1981, Mao was said to have made mistakes in the evening of his life, particularly during the "cultural revolution." These mistakes brought the nation "many misfortunes." But Deng also said that for the most part Mao accomplished great things and without him the Chinese people would, at the very least, have spent much more time groping in the dark.

While the role of ideology can by no means be dismissed, other factors such as the struggle for power, nationalism, imperialism, and geopolitics have evidently come to play a much larger role in the opposition of the two Communist giants toward each other.

Mao's Foreign Policy Thought and the Soviet Union

In September 1958, Mao, speaking to the Supreme State Conference on foreign policy, noted that of the three "isms of communism, nationalism, and imperialism, communism and nationalism are rather close to each other. And the forces of nationalism occupy quite a large area, the three continents of Asia, Africa, and Latin America."(9) The U.S. and NATO, according to Mao, were allegedly on the offensive against the forces of nationalism and indigenous communism, but not against the socialist camp, though for reasons of propaganda this should not be publicly conceded. On the other hand, China should not be "deluded" by its own propaganda.

"Catching up" with the West was Mao's long-term objective, though he never precisely defined it. It will probably take "50-70 years. . . until we shall succeed in catching up or overtaking the U.S." Though China was "poor" and "'blank'-lacking knowledge, these disadvantages had hidden advantages and should help China, after several decades, to overtake other countries."(10) There were distinct traits of outright chauvinism in Mao's thought. Though he believed that China had made great contributions to humanity, he thought it should have made "still greater" ones. The one made "is far too small. This makes us feel rather ashamed. "(11)

Mao was determined not to be frightened even by nuclear war and mass extermination of the Chinese and other nationalities, not even by the destruction of life on earth itself! In a conversation with Edgar Snow, Mao disclosed that "even if man disappeared from the earth—committed suicide—life would not be extinguished by man's bomb." Pointing to past Chinese history, he recalled that "our population has been destroyed by half a good few times,"(12) but had subsequently recovered.

In 1946, Mao evolved "the theory of the intermediate zone" and, in 1958, revived it. Once again, he underlined the decisive importance of Third World nationalism. While he did not discount the allegedly aggressive character of the wide-ranging American military pacts, he did not think that the aggression was aimed against Communism. U.S. imperialism's main purpose for the moment was to be "the tyrant of the intermediate zone."The latter included at least 90% of the whole world's population.

China's relationship with the U.S.S.R., in theory and practice, was, according to Mao, a complex one, both prior to the seizure of power by Chinese Communism and thereafter. While it deteriorated after 1949, and especially by the late fifties, the seeds of the differences were laid long before this time: the Sino-Soviet relationship worsened in the 1950s, while the four following concepts, pointed to frequently by Mao, played a major role: China should "unite" with the Soviet Union; it should have an "equal relationship" with it; it should "compare" its experiences with the U.S.S.R. Even if the Soviet Union stopped being socialist, China should "learn" from its negative experience. China should unite on equal terms with the Soviet people, but no longer with its leadership.(13)

Mao was impressed, but never overwhelmed, when he had met Stalin for the first time in a face-to-face meeting in Moscow in 1949-1950. As he later wrote: "I argued with Stalin for two months," for the entire length of his stay in the Soviet Union. "The Chinese revolution," Mao continued, "succeeded against the wishes of Stalin." When Chinese Communism, at the Seventh Congress, decided to go all out defeating the Kuomintang, Stalin and Wang Ming warned that the Chinese revolution would "never succeed." Only after the Korean War, Stalin decided that the Chinese revolution was "genuine." But Stalin, who brutally repressed and killed communists at home, was not one to grant Chinese leaders equality. Mao, in turn, was very critical of Stalin's abuses in treating so-called "counter-revolutionaries" and exterminating domestic critics. He also resented it when Chinese artists painted pictures of Stalin and himself, always making him "a little bit shorter" than the Soviet leader. Still, Mao opposed what he considered Krushchev's excessive criticism of the defunct Soviet leader. Everything else aside, Mao, elder Communist statesman, took offense because of Krushchev's denigration of the "cult of personality" in the U.S.S.R; he felt that it indirectly aimed against his own eminent stature in the C.P.R. and in world communism.

In line with the nationalist emphasis on equality between China and the Soviet Union, Mao insisted that China not only learn from the U.S.S.R. but also that the latter learn from China.(14) "We might just as well ask these comrades / the Soviet advisers/ why they did not copy the Chinese?" Besides, Mao repeatedly emphasized that a Communist ought to study not only the Soviet experience in World War II, but also the Chinese experience in the Korean War.

The "Degeneration" of the Ideological Controversy

The Sino-Soviet ideological dispute extended also to domestic policy as well as to that of revolutionary strategy. All these issues and disagreements as to the correct road for "building socialism," found expression in Krushchev's new Party program of the C.P.S.U. in the early 1960s. It enhanced the antagonism between the two rivals. In combination with the Cuban missile crisis and the new Sino-Indian border conflict, it deepened the gulf between the two communist powers.

According to Richard Löwenthal, the Sino-Soviet dispute was "never a primarily ideological conflict," but chiefly a conflict of interests between a superpower and a rising regional power. In view of the reversal of both the ideological and, in important respects, political roles of China and the Soviet Union, the ideology "degenerated" in recent years:(15) from being a major factor in the breakup of the Sino-Soviet alliance, it has turned into "a threadbare cloak for a conflict between the two great powers." Still, Löwenthal does not claim that theory and ideology have completely vanished from the horizon, nor does he hold it unlikely that they may play a somewhat greater role in the future. In view of the past and present "alleged unifying role of ideology," both Communist regimes paying lip-service to Marxism-Leninism and, in China's case, also to some aspects of Maoism—have led them into opposite directions, into an adversary relationship.

In the spring of 1960, Peking accused the Soviet leaders, first in closed conferences, later publicly, of "modern revisionism." What had started out as a conflict of more or less aid and more or less "risk-taking" (relating to the Mideast, to Yugoslavia, the Quemoy crisis, etc.), ended in a clash over orthodoxy and heresy. At issue was also the question of the inevitability of local wars, especially of wars of national liberation. Yet while the Chinese stressed the importance of the "liberation struggle" of the Third World nations, the Russians insisted on the subordination of the interests of the struggle to those of the chief revolutionary force, the U.S.S.R. itself.

In the early post-Maoist period, in 1976 and 1977, the Chinese emphasis was once again on "continuing the revolution under the dictatorship of the proletariat" and the revival in the C.P.R. of Zhou Enlai's formula of the "Great Four Modernizations" (of agriculture, industry, national defense, and science and technology). The inceasing influence and power of Deng resulted in 1979, on the 30th anniversary of the victory of the Chinese Revolution, in the ritualistic reemphasis of the dictatorship of the proletariat, but in practice the main stress was on the primacy of expanding and modernizing production. Admitting that the former exploiting classes had on the whole disappeared, the Chinese leadership concluded that there was no longer a need for class struggles taking the form of "turbulent mass movements." Since this speech by Ye Jiamjing, the Cultural Revolution was acknowledged to be a major error and the "dismantling" of the late

Maoist ideology had begun.(16) The phase of "revolutionary utopianism" had ended and "bureaucratic rationality" had won, as it had previously in the Soviet Union. The "continued Chinese hostility to the Soviet Union" had no longer an ideological justification. It was simply "the response of a weaker but proud and ambitious power to the pressure and threats of a stronger rival."

Soviet ideology of the last decades has remained more or less on the same tracks, but is on the whole weaker than before. In the Chinese case, too, ideology has lost much ground. Not only in public life and inspiration but also in regard to policy motivation, it has grown weaker. While a quarter of a century ago, it was a major factor in producing the Sino-Soviet split, it is today no more than *one* factor in perpetuating the sometimes open, recently often latent, Sino-Soviet hostility. As far as peace and stability of the world order is concerned, China obviously has reversed her role: from a firebrand ready to unleash the firestorm of violent revolution, irrespective of consequences and costs, she has become a responsible conservative force, aware of her limitations and unwilling to sacrifice a substantial part of her huge population on the altar of the liberation" of the Third World and of mankind. Though not having abandoned all its revolutionary rhetoric and especially not its championship of the Third World, it is too undeveloped and weak, as it now realizes, to give substantial economic and technological help, not to mention military assistance, to the Third World. The Soviet Union, on the other hand, is prepared to render significant assistance to some selected Third World nations in exchange for strategic, geopolitical, and ideological gains around the globe. But it is hardly prepared to sacrifice her vital national interests for the sake of non-Soviet Communist interests and of a vague "internationalism," though it continues to unfurl its banner. The U.S.S.R. is probably just as unwilling to risk war over influence in any distant part of the Third World, as it was a generation ago prepared to fight for the "liberation" of Taiwan.

A Soviet Summary; Maoism, Chinese Nationalism, and Militarism

Along with Mao's personality cult and tenacity of nationalist prejudices among the masses, the comparatively unhindered imposition of Maoism on China was, according to Moscow, facilitated "by the historical conditions of China's development, above all the relative weakness of the working class and its inadequate organization, the overwhelming predominance in the population of peasants owning small plots of land, and the low literacy level of the workers and peasants." Nationalism, in one way or another, has influenced the political line followed by all of China's leaders. Unfortunately, in Moscow's view, it has taken the form of shameless anti-Sovietism and great-power aspirations.

It was no accident that the Cultural Revolution was primarily aimed at the destruction of the political structure that had evolved under the influence of the Soviet Union and other socialist states. In the Maoists' opinion, the danger of Soviet influence was considerably more menacing than the influence of capitalist regimes. To Maoists, the "Soviet Union is a more serious threat to China" than the imperialist countries, including the U.S. "According to Mao's recipe, to weaken the U.S.S.R. it was necessary to take all steps up to and including the outright formation of a bloc with imperialist circles."(17) Finally, Maoist propaganda has launched a vigorous campaign for the so-called "restoration of historical justice." "At the same time, the Maoists are keeping quiet about the actual territorial problems they have in relations with the imperialists."

A major article in *Kommunist* makes it clear that, all theory aside, the U.S.S.R. fears that "Maoism forces socialist countries to engage in a confrontation on a second front."(18) In its nationality policy, the Chinese leadership continued to pursue the forcible assimilation of small peoples. The militarization of the C.P.R.'s national regions (particularly of Sinkiang, Inner Mongolia, and Tibet) is continuing. The army had taken control of all aspects of life in the national regions. "Special" detachments for work with the masses have been set up in the People's liberation Army. These units were sent to areas populated by non-Han nationalities to conduct political campaigns." "The growth of popular discontent is a source of weakness, and, in the final analysis, of the inevitable collapse of the military-bureaucratic dictatorship. . ." The army was still the Maoist regime's main bulwark, although there was oppositional sentiment within it as well. After the 10th C.P.C. Congress, a purge took place in the army. This purge, camouflaged by the campaign of criticism of Lin Piao and Confucius, gave rise to covert resistance and discontent among regular army officers, many of whom doubted that Lin Piao was a traitor. In conclusion: "Maoism is an outspoken enemy of socialism, democracy, and peace."

In its foreign policy, Maoism gives now "increasing priority to relations with the capitalist world. The process of expansion of China's contacts with the West has gone beyond an ordinary normalization of relations." The C.P.R. favored American military presence in various parts of the world, including Europe and Asia. The Chinese leaders hoped to make all countries believe that a Third World War was inevitable. Beijing waged a fierce campaign against the Conference on Peace and Security in Europe. "The Chinese leadership masks its open shift to the positions of reactionary imperialism with anti-imperialist demagoguery."

The Maoist "theory" of three groups of states totally rejected the class principle in evaluating the foreign policies of various states. The Maoists declared that the only mainspring of world development was the struggle of the "third" and "second" worlds against "superpower hegemonism." Recognizing that United States imperialism for a time seemed "on the decline," the Maoists insisted that the main threat came from Soviet "social imperialism."

Beijing used economic aid to influence developing states. The Chinese leadership has also resorted to the direct use of armed forces for its expansionist aims. Despite gestures of reconciliation toward India, the Chinese leadership is continuing and intensifying its hostile actions toward New Delhi. The Maoist leadership's regional policy toward the developing countries was at variance with their true interests, "it is directed against the unity of the anti-imperialist forces." In early 1974, Beijing announced: "The socialist camp has already ceased to exist as a result of the emergence of social-imperialism." The latter, it claimed, pursued an annexationist policy toward the Mongolian People's Republic, subjecting it to constant political and economic pressure." "The Maoist attacks on scientific socialist and proletarian internationalism, help to activate anti-communists; all sorts of renegades, Trotskyists, anarchists, extremists, right-wing and "left-wing" opportunists, in their attacks on Marxism-Leninism often side with the Maoists." "Neutralism, or worse still, a conciliatory attitude toward Maoism. . .objectively serve the Chinese leadership's anti-socialist aims."

Beijing varied its tactics toward individual Communist parties. Some Communist Parties in South Asia have become isolated from the international influence of Mao's group. Until recently, these parties followed Beijing's lead. Now, however, following the Vietnam victory, a struggle within these parties was taking place. But the author did not recommend "excommunicating" the Chinese from the world Communist movement.

Maoism and "Deviationism"

Izvestia in an article, "How Maoism nourishes Revisionism," referred to revisionist theoreticians such as the Austrian Ernst Fischer and the Frenchman Roger Garaudy, who use the platform of Maoism to substantiate the possibility of various "models of socialism." In one of his latest public speeches, E. Fischer tried to attribute the sharp deterioration in Soviet-Chinese relations to Moscow's unwillingness to recognize the possibility of different paths in the construction of socialism, while maintaining, as also Garaudy did, that current Chinese practice did not go beyond the framework of a "model for socialism" for backward Asian countries.(19)

According to Moscow, not only rightist but also leftist deviationism was attracted by Maoism. Leftist elements in the West were especially outspoken in making apologies for Maoism. The reason for this is "disillusionment with prevailing ideologies and the inflation of ideological values that is characteristic of some Western intellectuals and of young people; this gives rise to feelings of spiritual emptiness, loss of perspective, and ideological confusion. Under these condi-tions, the demagogic propaganda of the Maoists who offered the outside world cultural revolution packaged for export, was received with great enthusiasm by young leftists."

While beatniks and hippies put on badges bearing Mao's picture and brandished Mao's quotation books "like real Red Guards, without delving very deeply into the meaning of Maoist wisdom, a small segment of young people studying China in Universities developed a wildly enthusiastic attitude toward Maoist practice of recent years." Young people and intellectuals of the West who sympathize with Maoism, naively perceived in Chinese society a kind of "social dynamite of national initiative," saw in it something progressive and revolutionary, and judged Maoism from Chinese propaganda publications.

The foregoing article was of special interest since it linked Maoism at a time when it was sailing in leftist, if not ultraleftist, waters with revisionism! In later years, Maoism swung around to rightist revisionism, leaving thus Soviet Communism to the left.

Maoism, the U.N., and the "Mythical" Soviet Threat

According to *Pravda*, "With Whom are Maoist U.N. Delegates Voting?," it was no secret that the Maoists have not broken off ties with the Republic of South Africa and Southern Rhodesia.(20) To the contrary, Beijing has been flouting numerous United Nations resolutions by stepping up its relations with racist and colonial regimes; this included the support of these regimes' intervention against Angola and pursuing a policy of preserving potential hotbeds of military danger. Beijing's representatives in the U.N. abstain from the vote on crucial Middle East problems, claiming that they could not support the idea of convening a Geneva peace conference (only three delegates, the United States, Israel, and Nicaragua had voted against it). The U.S.S.R. viewed China's position as giving "direct support to Israel's course of aggression." Beijing continuously spoke of the mythical "Soviet threat." By refering to a "nonexistent threat," they only "fanned a militaristic psychosis." The Soviet Union "was well acquainted with this charge, orginally made by the imperialists," having juggled with this bugaboo for several decades.

In *Pravda*, I. Aleksandrov referred to a Soviet Foreign Ministry memorandum of June 4, 1979, in which the U.S.S.R. also proposed that a Sino-Soviet agreement be reached "not to recognize anyone's claims to special right or hegemony in world affairs."(21) He criticized Beijing's claim to be the sole interpreter of "what hegemonism means." Some of the Western press was speculating that China intends "to play the /Soviet/ card," to pressure especially Vietnam. But the Soviet Union, the *Pravda* writer asserted, never sought cooperation with anyone at the price of renouncing its principles, "and to the detriment" of the interests of its friends and allies. Aleksandrov concluded that the improvement of relations between the U.S.S.R. and the C.P.R. can be the result only of mutual efforts. As the Chinese proverb says, "You can't clap with one hand."

Innovation under Deng and Continuation of Policy

After a brief overview of the C.P.R.'s evolution especially in the last decade, I. Aleksandrov concluded that Deng's position had recently been strengthened. Focussing on the close interrelationship of Beijing's domestic and foreign policy, he held that anti-Soviet Maoism lay at its root.(22) The 'not to make excessive demands.' 'Easing up,' that was evident in 1978 and 1979, had been consigned oblivion." The Confucian rule of feudal, imperial China — "the leaders are born to rule and the masses are born to obey unquestionably" — continues to operate. By ideologically and politically disorienting the party and broad massese of the working people, the Beijing leadership intended to link the path of China's development to the vigorous expansion of economic relations with the developed capitalist countries, first of all, the United States. The Soviets recalled that at the Communist Party Congresses in China in 1956 and 1958, Liu Shao-chi, prominent Party leader, but subsequently denounced as renegade and traitor, has championed a distinctively anti-imperialist course and had strongly supported the policy of the development of friendship and cooperation with the U.S.S.R. and other socialist countries.

During the Great Proletarian Cultural Revolution, the C.P.R. suffered "complete bankruptcy of Maoism as a theory and practice of the guidance of society." China's current leaders were forced to admit this by giving up some of Mao's postulates—his concept of the "great leap"—adjusting others to the new "modernization" course. Chinese contemporary leaders were doing all they could to "protect Mao and preserve the nationalistic and hegemonistic principles of Maoism." This hypocrisy was being passed off as "restoration of the true image of Mao's ideas!" "Maoism, as a theory and practice of great-power claims, hegemonism, and anti-Sovietism, remains the foundation of the C.P.R.'s domestic and foreign policy."

Is China "Going Capitalist"?

According to an article in *Kommunist* Maoism has created an atmosphere of intellectual terror in China when any criticism of "Mao's line is seen as a national betrayal, as an attempt to restore capitalism."(23) The Maoists' economic course is to create by 1980 an independent, relatively self-contained system of industry and within the next 20 years to put China "in the front rank of the world's countries." The Maoist course is an important reason why China's economy remains at a comparatively low level of development. The peasantry made up four fifths of China's population. The Maoists were trying to perpetuate the division of the peasantry. The Beijing leaders also continued to distrust the Chinese intelligentsia. The Maoists were not able to get active cooperation from the latter; compulsory assignment of educated young people to the countryside continued.

B. Barakhta raised in *Pravda* on July 31, 1982, the question whether China was "going capitalist."(24) For years China's "leftist excesses" were the favored target of the Soviets. In the post-Mao period, however, the Soviet Union aimed its criticism at the "bourgeois mentality" which "was corrupting China's moral principles." According to the Soviet view, now "the virus of private-ownership mentality and taste for ready cash and profits were spreading throughout Chinese society" and were affecting various strata of the population and especially the youth. There were 1.5 million so-called "personal businesses" in the area of trade and consumer service alone. The so-called "economic revival" in China included the restoration of a mixed economy in the country and encouragement of the Chinese and foreign bourgeoisie. According to a well-known Chinese economist, the semi-socialist and nonsocialist type private enterprises that employ more than ten hired workers have already appeared in a number of places in China.

On July 14, 1982, Commentator M. Yakovlev voiced in *Pravda* his concern about the recent Chinese National People's Congress(25) permitting foreign — chiefly West European and Japanese — companies and other economic organizations to form so-called "mixed enterprises" in the C.P.R.; the writer glossed over that Soviet Russia itself practiced this policy in numerous, especially East European countries. China, according to Yakovlev, had already made proposals to a number of capitalist countries to form joint working companies in China for deposits of coal, tungsten, tin, bauxite, copper, and oil. Beijing economically oriented itself increasingly toward capitalist states. The developed capitalist countries accounted already for more than two thirds of the C.P.R.'s total foreign turnover. Though China continually asserted that it would "follow a socialist path," Beijing's new economic policy, *Time* is quoted, "smacks suspiciously of capitalism."

Beijing retaliated with a criticism of Moscow's own economic policies. Moscow under Gorbachev, according to Wang Chongjie, commenting on his address "The Soviet Union's Economic Structure Under Reform,"(26) is applying itself to the overall reform of its economic structure founded more than 50 years ago in order to promote social productivity. The Soviet decision constituted "no surprise." The Soviet economic edifice set up in the 1930s has gradually evolved into an economic model which is clearly holding back the growth of the country's social productivity. The national economy has grown at the lowest rate since World War II. Despite this scathing reproof, it appears that the C.P.R., itself engaged in far-going economic and social reform, welcomes changes in the U.S.S.R. if for no other reason than to impress upon its own people that everywhere in the Communist world, change is planned and executed. It clearly disarms any real or potential opposition to the particular changes occurring in the C.P.R.

Mao's "New place in History" and Beijing's "Pragmatic Zigzag"

Neither of the two Communist rivals follows a consistent policy in its criticism of the adversary. As noticed, *Pravda* accused Beijing of embracing "capitalism" and thus betraying the Marxist legacy. In the next breath, it claimed that Beijing turned back to Mao and his ultra-leftist Maoism.(27) In recent times, China has shown a marked tendency toward a new glorification of the "ideas of Mao Zedong" and their creator. The basic thrusts of this sort of modernization of Maoism have already been set forth in a "decision on some questions of C.P.C. history, which was adopted by the 6th Plenary Session of the C.P.C.'s Central Committee in the summer of 1981. The campaign for a new glorification of Mao and his 'ideas' was gathering momentum. A drive to attribute all the victories of the revolutionary movement in China to Mao and his ideas, to absolve him of blame for defeats, to portray "sinicized Marxism" as the sole true course and to thereby theoretically, politically, and ideologically substantiate and reinforce the policy of the present C.P.C. leadership was really apparent. As for Mao's "mistakes," less and less was being written about them. Since the second half of 1981, the journal *Hong Ji*, the C.P.C. Central Committee's theoretical organ, has begun publicizing a special series of articles along the foregoing line.(28)

In the author's view, Mao, in unleashing the Cultural Revolution, was like "an honest doctor who has lost control of a serious illness. In short, anyone is to blame except Mao." Despite "all its costs," the Cultural Revolution, according to *Hong Ji*, provided the party with "valuable experience."

The Central Committee of the C.P.C. criticized the many years of "ultra-leftist" mistakes as well as the mistakes "that Mao. . .made in the last years of his life." It has restored "the true look of Mao's ideas" and has defined "Mao's place in history." Some erroneous theories advanced during the Cultural Revolution have, according to the Soviet press, been systematically debunked. The class struggle has ceased to be the main contradiction in the life of Chinese society, while the errors of Mao and some of his theories were now freely admitted, they are not considered part and parcel of genuine

Maoism. After shedding some of Mao's doctrines, Maoism has been restored to its greater purity!

Both China's domestic and foreign policy past and present are closely tied up with Mao's social and political thought. The Sixth Plenary Session of the C.P.C., adopted a decision on some questions of C.P.C. history from the foundation of the C.P.R.(29) This document reflected the sharp domestic political struggle that accompanied the drafting of its basic provisions. It criticized the "great leap" and "people's communes" and policies that Mao imposed during the Cultural Revolution that brought terrible misfortunes and upheavals to the country, such as the Maoist concept of "the continuation of the revolution under the dictatorship of the proletariat," which served to justify a campaign of mass repressions in all the Maoist campaigns.

Pravda took notice of the extent of de-Maoization — paralleling in some ways de-Stalinization in the U.S.S.R. — in the C.P.R. as well as the survival of basic Maoist thought in Communist China. The Plenary Session of the C.P.C. denounced Mao's personality cult and his characteristic features of "conceit," "divorce from reality and the masses," "subjectivism," and "putting himself above the party's C.C." This recognition comes "tardily." It actually repeated criticism of Maoist ideology by the C.P.S.U. and other Communist parties. In order "to camouflage Mao's mistakes and the tragic consequences to which they brought China, the authors alleged that Mao's merits were the most important thing, while his mistakes were secondary. Evidently the rival groupings in the Beijing leadership needed such a 'compromise' appraisal in order to use Mao's name and his 'ideas' to consolidate Chinese society."

Soviet experience with Stalin's personality cult, with de-Stalinization, and the subsequent "corrections" of the "errors" of "de-Stalinization" — which, Moscow claimed, went to extremes — made the citizens of the U.S.S.R. knowledgeable of the problems of the personality cult and its consequences, According to the Soviets, the C.P.R. clung after all ups and downs of Mao's thought since his death steadfastly to a Maoism purified from its mistakes; the expurgated Maoism they now called the "scientific system of Mao's ideas."

The Chinese draftsmen of the Plenum tried to "denigrate the Soviet union's attitude toward China, and were as hostile to the U.S.S.R. as Mao himself had been. The C.C. of the C.P.C. reiterated a number of anti-Soviet postulates in the foreign policy field. It continued to exploit the absurd anti-Soviet thesis about "social imperialism" and emphasized also Mao's services in the confrontation with the U.S.S.R. "The Beijing leaders are supporting the present United States administration's adventuristic line of escalating the arms race and aggravating international tension." Recently, Beijing criticized Hua Guofeng's "mistakes" in detail and contrasted them to Deng's line. All this presaged new purges and new clashes.

In the view of the Japanese newspaper, *Tokyo Shimbun*, which the Soviet press quoted,"unity of views" has been achieved in the C.P.R. by certain concessions made by Deng's very influential grouping. This has by no means dampened the intra-party struggle in Beijing and the provinces, According to *Renmin Ribao*, a "factional struggle" was continuing in China. Also, Chinese propaganda has begun to talk about the emergence of a so-called "right-wing deviation" towards "bourgeois democracy" and admiration of the West. All this is allegedly "a direct consequence of the Chinese leadership's pro-imperialist course in the international arena and of the so-called "open door" policy that is designed to help the hegemonistic "four-modernization progress." "Dissatisfaction and negative attitudes toward the authorities are allegedly spreading among young people and the intelligentsia. The latter is increasingly distrustful of the Beijing's bosses' pragmatic zig-zags in the sphere of culture and ideology.

Officially, the Soviets' sharp criticism of the Chinese leadership notwithstanding, the leaders of the C.P.S.U. have maintained, and still do, that as Communists and internationalists, they have no complaints to lodge against the Chinese but only against the C.P.R.'s leadership. Despite years and decades of unceasing but indecisive political battles with the C.P.C., the Soviets are compelled to display relentless optimism. Krushchev, too, ended his extensive discussion of China's problems in *Krushchev Remembers* with expressing the hope that some day "the deeds of friendship sown by the Soviet Union will be given a chance to grow and bear fruit."(31) The time will come "when China will return to a correct policy toward the U.S.S.R. and other socialist countries" and the C.P.C. will "overcome the sickness which has befallen it." This view is still occasionally voiced publicly by some of the Soviet politicians and analysts.

III

IN THE MIRROR
OF THE CHINESE PRESS

A. Changing Concepts of the Global Detente with the USSR

The Soviet Union—"The Main Threat" and "Normalization"

During most of the last decade, including the last days of Mao Zedong, the C.P.R. leadership has judged the Soviet Union its greatest potential enemy. While the Soviets themselves disavowed to pursue hegemony and aggression, in turn they accused Beijing of committing these very crimes.(1)

China's Foreign Policy Hit on all Fronts," sounded *Pravda*'s editorial of May 18, 1975, on occasion of a visit by leaders of the Socialist Party of Japan (S.P.J.)(2) who had been invited to the Chinese capital by the Sino-Japanese Friendship Association. The final joint communique produced by the two sides, the C.P.R. representatives and its Japanese counterparts, proclaimed an agreement of both parties on "the struggle against the hegemony of the two superpowers," but came out strongly against Soviet territorial claims and the Soviet concept of collective security in Asia. The metamorphosis on the part of the Chairman of the S.P.J. Central Committee who repudiated his party's foreign course was striking; the readers were reminded that the 38th Congress of the S.P.J. in December, 1974, had recognized the "Soviet Union's important contribution" to the making of a peaceful world.

At the U.N. General Assembly in an address of September 27, 1979, the Chairman of the Chinese Delegation Han Nianlong directed the main shaft of his criticism against the Soviet Union. He considered "particularly overbearing" "the late-coming /!/ superpower whose inclination to aggressive adventure is visibly growing. Waving slogans such as 'disarmament and detente,' it is engaged in frenzied arms expansion unprecedented in scale and speed." It is seeking to achieve "an overwhelming superiority in nuclear as well as conventional arms... It is pushing a global offensive strategy."(3)

"More and more frequently," the Chinese delegate continued, the Soviet Union was "using proxies and organizing mercenaries to launch unscrupulous armed invasions and military coups in other countries. With a view to encircling Western Europe, controlling strategic routes, seizing strategic resources and speeding up its expansion and strategic deployment for global hegemony, it has increasingly directed the spearheads of its aggression to Africa, the Middle East, the gulf area, and Southeast Asia. Facts prove that the late-coming superpower is "the main source of threat /!/ to world peace and security and is the most dangerous source of a new world war."

The Soviet policy of expansionism was double-edged. It had both an anti-Chinese thrust and was directed against the very interests of the Third World. "This very superpower" — Hua still named it sometimes only indirectly, though the Soviet target was unmistakable — is pushing its policy of hegemonism everywhere and has the effrontery to propose on this rostrum an item entitled, 'On the inadmissibility of a policy of hegemonism in international relations.'" Obviously, this is "the habitual clumsy tactics of a thief 'crying stop the thief' ... its aim is to pursue hegemonism even more."

After the years 1979-1980, the theme of hegemonism and especially of a country being the "main threat" to peace, though never completely disappearing from the Sino-Soviet polemics, abated somewhat, while such themes as the "normalization" of relations and of the policy of China's independence between the two superpowers were more frequently dealt with.

In a wide-ranging address in January 1984 to the Canadian Parliament, Premier Zhao stressed the themes of independence but also that of anti-hegemonism and hardly disguised anti-Sovietism. Touching not only on territorial and geopolitical problems but also on psychological and philosophical aspects of these questions, he assured the legislature and the Canadian people that he was bringing to them the friendship of a billion Chinese. "We do not attach ourselves to any big power and are not subject to any big power's will."(4) Beijing wished: 1) to develop relations with all countries on the basis of the Five Principles of Peaceful Coexistence, 2) to strengthen solidarity with other Third World nations and friendship with the people of all countries, and 3) to oppose hegemonism and safeguard world peace.

He placed China's striving for independence into the proper historical framework. "In modern history China was badly bullied and oppressed by brute force." "Having waged long and bitter struggles and ultimately won national independence, we are jealous therefore of our own independence and respect the independence of other countries." Back in the early 1950s, China had initiated five principles of mutual respect for territorial integrity and sovereignty, mutual non-aggression, non-interference in each other's internal affairs, equality and mutual benefit, and peaceful coexistence as norms guiding international relations. It is on these principles that we have handled our relations with other countries." It was also on the basis of these five principles that China was seeking to develop relations with the two superpowers: the United States and the Soviet Union. China also sincerely wished to see normalization of Sino-Soviet relations. Normalization of these relations, however, "requires the removal of the three obstacles" which China listed frequently, withdrawal from Afghanistan, cessation of aid to Vietnam in Kampuchea, and withdrawal of Soviet troops from along the Sino-Soviet border.

Although Sino-Soviet relations have "somewhat improved in recent years," greater efforts by the two sides are called for, if their relations are to be "really normalized." "China is a developing socialist country. We have similar historical experiences and face the same task of economic development with other Third World countries. We firmly support them in their just cause of safeguarding national independence and developing their national economies. We are in favor of increased Sino-Soviet cooperation, improving North-South relations, and establishing a new international economic order through global negotiations."

Anti-Hegemonism, the Policy of Independence, and the Third World

The theme of anti-hegemonism — primarily anti-Sovietism, but occasionally aimed against the U.S.A. — is by its nature complex and seldom clear-cut. The other theme, that of China pursuing the course of independence, has in recent years been more frequently stressed by Beijing. It implies less dependency on U.S. policy, equidistance from the policy course of both the U.S.S.R. and the U.S., and greater alignment, unquestionably in a leading role, with the nations of the Third World. This became also clear in a March, 1982 essay in *Beijing Review*, The Diplomacy of Zhou Enlai," which had first appeared in the *Journal of International Studies* (1981).(5) The article had focussed on Zhou Enlai to an extent not usual during Mao's lifetime. It averred that "China has all along been critical of the Soviet Union's chauvinistic tendencies and refused to dance to Moscow's tune." When the Soviet Union started in its bid for world hegemony, the basis of Sino-Soviet unity was destroyed. The Chinese people had no alternative but to resist Soviet hegemonism. Zhou Enlai had played a substantial role in this struggle. In 1969, after military clashes with China, the U.S.S.R. approached the U.S. to explore the possibility of a Soviet attack on China's nuclear bases and the likely U.S. reaction, but was decisively rebuffed by Washington.

Communist China had always, opposed "colonialism, imperialism, and hegemonism." It had opposed France's colonial wars in Vietnam: "when the Soviet Union superseded the U.S. as the main threat /!/ to world peace," the C.P.R. took a firm stand against Soviet hegemonism. Zhou had "many confrontations" with the Soviet leadership over this issue; at the time of the 1968 invasion of Czechoslovakia, he denounced the Soviet "social imperialists" and "social fascists." China had always "been true to its word." The debt it had incurred during the Korean War toward the U.S.S.R. had virtually been repaid by the end of 1964.

Hu Yaobang, since 1981 the C.P.C. General Secretary, in his report to the Twelfth National Congress of the Party in September, 1982, also emphasized the theme that China in its foreign policy had "never attached itself to any big power or group of powers" and would never yield to pressure from any big power.(6) The author stressed China's "close cooperation" with the "friendly socialist countries of North Korea, Rumania, and Yugoslavia," and other communist-ruled states which followed even a steady pro-Soviet line. Like the Soviet Union, the C.P.R. pursued the same goal of trying to improve relations with capitalist countries, notwithstanding their "different social systems." In the foregoing speech, Hu Yaobang levelled some minor criticisms at the policies of the U.S. and Japan, but directed the heaviest accusations against the Soviet Union. For the past 20 years, the latter has stationed "massive" armed forces along the Sino-Soviet and Sino-Mongolian borders. Subsequently the Vietnamese invasion and occupation of Kampuchea, supported by the U.S.S.R., and the attack against Afghanistan created "grave threats" to the peace of Asia and to China's security. Though Soviet leaders had more than once expressed the desire to improve relations with China, "deeds rather than words" were important. If the Soviet leaders would lift their threat to the security of China, Sino-Soviet relations could move towards normalization.

The superpowers that practiced hegemonism posed a new threat to all peoples and were the "main source of instability and turmoil" in the world. But people everywhere can "upset the strategic plans of the superpowers." China had always opposed their arms race and always firmly supported all victim countries and peoples in their struggle against aggression. China supported the case of the unification of Korea, the struggle of the Kampuchean people against Vietnamese aggression, that of the African people against South Africa's racism and expansionism, and strongly condemned Israel for heinous aggressive atrocities /!/ against the people of Palestine and Lebanon."

The anti-Zionism and anti-Semitism of the U.S.S.R. — the latter had deep historic roots in Russia — may explain discriminatory propaganda and practices against the Jews in general and those in the Soviet Union in particular. But in China there are virtually no Jews. The C.P.R.'s geographically distant anti-Zionism is of a purely opportunistic kind, designed only to woo Arab and Moslem peoples of the Third World and gain their gratitude. *Beijing Review* claims that anti-Semitism in China "never existed." Similar claims are, of course, not made in the U.S.S.R.

The emergence of the Third World on the international arena after World War II was, *Beijing Review* held, "a primary event of our time." It had changed the United Nations from a mere voting machine manipulated by certain big powers into a forum where imperialism, hegemonism, and expansionism were often justly condemned.

The common task confronting the Third World countries was, first and foremost, to defend their national independence and state sovereignty, develop their national economies so that they can back up the political independence they have already won with economic independence. The Chinese people had always spurned attitudes and actions which were based on despising the poor and currying favor with the rich, bullying the weak, and fearing the strong. "China was deeply disturbed" by the discords and even armed conflicts that have occurred between some Third World countries. They often cause heavy losses to both sides and allow only gains for the foe.

Though China disclaims any selfish interest in enlisting the support of Third World nations against both superpowers, it pursues, of course, its own national interests. In view of the widely disseminated "anti-Yankee" prejudice and the envy of American wealth and productivity, the propaganda value of a belligerent pro-Third World attitude is quite apparent to the C.P.R. Communist China's attitude varies frequently between condemnation of both superpowers and its increasing leaning toward sharper criticism of the U.S.S.R. as the "main enemy," as a "main threat" to international peace. Though the former stance grows out of propaganda needs, the latter position corresponds more closely to actual fears and immediate national interests of China, which geopolitically and strategically is located closer to the Soviet Union— "the threat from the north." Also, on the ideological front, the C.P.C. has come to be more hostile to the C.P.S.U. and vice versa than to the capitalist United States of America, which, just because of the deep ideological gulf between capitalism and Communism, represents no ideological threat to it.

The C.P.S.U., other Communist Parties, and the Italian Party
(ICP)

As far as relationships between the C.P.C. and the Communist parties of other countries are concerned, the C.P.C. holds that they ought to be developed in strict conformity with Marxism as well as the principles of independence in international affairs. The Communist parties of all Countries were equal. "Whether large or small, long or short in their history, in power or out of power, they cannot be divided into superior or inferior parties. Our Party has suffered from the attempt of a self-elevated paternal party to keep us under control." Only through resisting such control has the C.P.C.'s "independent external policy won its successes."(7)

The struggle of the C.P.C. against the "inferior" role of other Communist parties vis-à-vis the C.P.S.U. appealed of course to all Communist parties, those critical of Moscow as well as those, especially in the East European Communist bloc, having little practical choice but to accept Moscow's claim to preeminence and leadership.

According to Yaobang — and the C.P.C. point of view in general — all Communist parties should respect each other. Each fraternal party had its strong and weak points. Not all parties could be expected to hold completely identical views on the international situation and on their special tasks. The C.P.C. has maintained friendly relations with many other Communist parties and, according to Yaobang, "we wish to establish similar contacts with a greater number of progressive parties and organizations."(8) Its propaganda aims to reach also non-Communist parties and organizations.

In the article, "The C.P.C.'s Relations with Other Parties,"(9) the author Lian Yao refers to President Tito's visit to China in 1977, — calling the resumption of Sino-Yugoslav relations "the correction of a historic mistake" — and to new ties with the Communist Party of Italy — which, as is known, plays the role of a maverick in Europe. Since 1978, the C.P.C. has established party relations with "other progressive /!/ and friendly political parties and organizations in the Third World. This was followed by relations in 1981 with socialist parties, social democratic parties, and Workers Parties in

Europe and other regions." Many of their viewpoints coincide
with those of the C.P.C., though others are disparate. "So far
the C.P.C. has set up various types of relations with about 200
other Communist parties and progressive and friendly political
parties." Even if one of these parties makes a mistake, "the
only reliable way for it to draw a lesson from it and correct it"
is by itself, "through an autonomous and independent
process." The C.P.C. emphasized the independence of the
individual parties and opposed interference — with and control
of other parties. "The historic experience of the postwar
international communist movement has showm that a leading
center and a leading party are not needed. Nor should there be
any such center." No party, "no matter how old or powerful,"
was entitled to place itself above other parties. It was wrong to
impose one's view on others and seek artificial unanimity. As
the Twelfth National Party Congress has pointed out,
Communist Parties should help each other, "but it is absolutely
impermissible for any of them to issue orders or run things for
others from the outside."(10)

The C.P.C. was a "party of patriotism and internationalism," and it advocates the integration of the two. Today, the
Party's goals in its foreign relations are to serve China's socialist
modernization. This, of course, places primary emphasis on
China's domestic needs and subordinates "internationalism" to
"patriotism."/

The C.P.C. seemed especially pleased about the "polemics" between the Italian Communist Party (I.C.P.) and the
C.P.S.U., citing such incidents as the Soviet invasion of
Czechoslovakia and Afghanistan, and cautioned that it would
be a "suicidal" act, if the I.C.P. "adopted a position in line
with Soviet foreign policy."(11) In the past few years,
according to Beijing, more and more people in the world,
including many Communists, "have seen through and
condemned the aggressive and expansionist nature of Soviet
foreign policy" and Soviet behavior to forcibly impose its
politics on others. Finding itself in increasing isolation, the
Soviet Union declared that "the frantic movement against
realistic socialism /read Soviet hegemonism/" politically,
economically, and ideologically, was at a peak. Hence, the
Soviet decision, the C.P.C. concluded, to single out the Italian
Communist Party for attack. The accusation, according to

Beijing Review, demonstrated direct interference in the affairs of an independent Communist party. The C.P.S.U., without consulting anyone, tried to split other parties.

Though in the past Moscow had initiated a declaration that it was ready to dissolve the Warsaw alliance if only NATO would dissolve itself at the same time, it now castigated the I.C.P. for "rigorous maintenance of blocs." The C.P.S.U. "smeared" as "opportunistic" and "anti-Soviet" the efforts by the I.C.P. and other Communist parties to seek a socialist road in the light of the specific conditions of their respective countries and asserted that its own line was "of universal significance:" it was thus trying to impose its own model on others. The C.P.S.U. attacked the I.C.P. in particular for giving "moral and political support" to China.

In an article, "Moscow was more than rude,"(12) Yi Dong, along the same line, reported that the I.C.P. delegation head Giancarlo Pajeta had been denied the floor at the 26th Soviet Party Congress on the flimsiest of grounds. Only after a long delay was it arranged for him to speak before a smaller gathering unconnected with the Congress. This, according to *Beijing Review,* was the first time that something of this sort had happened, and to the biggest non-ruling Communist party in the worldÍ The Soviet put-down was illustrative of Moscow's "lordly attitude to other fraternal parties."

The I.C.P. repeatedly condemned the Soviet invasion of Afghanistan and had called for the immediate withdrawal of Soviet troops from that country. It has declared publicly that it was opposed to foreign interference in the internal affairs of Poland. The Italian Communist Party delegate Pajeta had later told the press that he had made it quite clear that differences had arisen between the C.P.S.U. and the I.C.P., including over the recent China visit and the restoration of relations between the C.P.I. and the C.P.C. The I.C.P. had insisted on its right to complete political autonomy." Enrico Berlinguer, General Secretary of the I.C.P., had previously declared publicly that the Party "will resolutely follow its own road" and maintain and foster "its unique character," and that leaders of other Parties had "no right to give lessons on the question of independence and autonomy."

The spirit of independence of Communist parties from Moscow has spread widely, not only among so-called

Eurocommunist parties, especially in the South of Europe, but also elsewhere, including the distant Japanese Communist Party. In 1981, the Soviet journals became increasingly critical of the attitude also of the Japanese Communist Party. *Partiinaya Zhizn*, referred to a letter from the C.C. of the C.P.S.U. to the Japanese C.P. Central Committee in which the latter's anti-Sovietism is hit: "We have noticed that the Japanese bourgeois press has approvingly characterized your letter as a detailed criticism of the U.S.S.R.'s foreign policy: you have been unilaterally waging war against our Party for nearly a year and a half now." "Your letter. . .lays a substantial part of the blame for the current world tension on the Soviet Union" and castigated the alleged Soviet violation of "rights of self-determination" in Afghanistan and Poland. Moscow's letter protested: "The U.S.S.R. does not aim at military superiority, only at an equilibrium:" this allegedly was not Reagan's policy.(13)

Against Appeasement and a "Fraudulent" Detente

On October 7, 1979, the C.P.R.'s Premier Hua Guofeng pointed out that China was not against detente: "But with the hegemonists engaged in expansion and aggression, it is impossible to have detente even if you desire it. There has been no detente in the world in the past year, particularly not in the Middle East, in Africa, in the Arab Sea and the Gulf area, in South Asia and in Indochina. While opposing hegemonism, we also want to caution people against following a policy of appeasement."(14) Beijing thus distinguished between detente and the policy of appeasement. A reduction of tension in the world was a desirable goal, but the hope of placating an aggressive and expansionist power was illusory, a method of approach which must be rejected.

Beyond this, the Soviet conception of detente, differing from that of other countries, including the C.P.R., was in Beijing's view, deceptive, if not outright fraudulent. At the turn of the 1970s, detente, according to *Beijing Review*, was the name given to the United States-Soviet Union relationship. With this policy, the Soviets thought to tip the balance of forces in the world in their own favor. Apart from trying to gain the edge on their adversary, the United States, they set

their sights on sowing dissension in the West, while pursuing a
southward thrust strategy and bringing about a strategic
encirclement of Western Europe. Their ultimate goal was to
seize worldwide hegemony from their North American rivals.
But the Soviet Union, according to Beijing, will find it more
difficult to press on with this policy in the 1980s.(15)

During the Krushchev era, the decisive factor in world
affairs was, according to *Beijing Review*, the imbalance of
forces between the two superpowers. While the United States
was stronger than the Soviet Union, the U.S.S.R. then aimed,
and still does, at transforming the era of United States world
hegemony into an era of Soviet world domination. As Soviet
leaders have repeatedly emphasized, "detente" was not an
"expedient measure," but played a special role in Moscow's
various tactics. In the thermonuclear epoch, Moscow has
repeatedly stressed that the only rational, the "wisest"
approach was to achieve relations between East and West and
to pursue "detente."(16) To do otherwise would mean the
destruction of mankind.

The substance and aim of Soviet "detente" can be summed
up mainly as follows: 1) Through detente between East and
West to create conditions for solving the remaining problems
in postwar Europe and consolidate the achievements of the
Soviet Union in Eastern Europe after the war. 2) To develop
Soviet economic relations and trade with the West, import
funds and technology from the West, to accelerate the growth
of its economic and military strength. 3) To use negotiations
and disarmament proposals to delay the expansion of Western
armaments, but at the same time to develop its war arsenal so
as to gain military superiority over the United States. 4) To lull
the West, especially Western Europe, into a false sense of
security and use economic bait and military deterrents to
encourage appeasement in the West, widen the rift between
the United States and Europe, and gradually get United States
forces out of Western Europe. 5) To use relaxation as a cover
so that the Soviet Union can bring its influence to bear and
expand toward its near neighbors, especially in the Third
World countries. In other words, "detente" is designed to split
the West, avoid a head-on conflict with the United States, and
realize the Soviets' strategic outflanking of Western Europe. It
is, finally, an attempt to defeat the United States, by war or

without it, in order to displace that country and seize world hegemony.

This hard-headed analysis of the Soviet Union's motivation in endorsing and pushing for detente differs radically from soft interpretations in some Western circles of the peace-loving character of the Soviet leadership's foreign policy. It practically is identical with the most pessimistic interpretations of the U.S.S.R.'s foreign policy intentions prevailing in the West.

Raising the question of what the Soviet Union has gained and lost in pushing detente over the past ten years, *Beijing Review*, quoting the Chinese *Journal of International Studies*, reiterated the latter's view that the U.S.S.R. "has won time to expand its economic and military strength. As regards the quantity and quality of strategic weapons it can claim parity with the United States. In the theatre of Europe, it has even a superior nuclear strike capability over the United States. It was partly due to Western financial aid and technology that the Soviet Union has improved the technical level of its industry, including its war industry. By pursuing the policy of detente, the U.S.S.R. has weakened its opponent and split the Atlantic alliance. By expanding its close trade and economic relations with Western Europe, it has not only won economic gains for itself, but has influenced Western Europe in such a way as to make it economically steadily dependent on itself. The West's recognition of the status quo of postwar Eastern Europe, as crystallized in the convocation of the European Security Conference and its resolutions, represents a Soviet gain. Finally, over the last ten years, the Soviet Union has speeded up its overseas expansion into several countries-Angola, Ethiopia, the three countries comprising Indochina, Vietnam, Laos and Kampuchea (Cambodia), and Afghanistan, where its control and influence has far surpassed what traditionally is known as spheres of influence.(17)

However, there was also a debit side to this account of the Soviet Union's gains. Strategically, the U.S.S.R., according to *Beijing Review*, has found itself increasingly isolated. On the reverse side of detente is a "sham relaxation:" taking advantage of the "breathing space," the Soviets "went all out to build up their strength and to reinforce their strategic positions in key areas of the world." But this has put the West on guard and has made the United States determined to turn the tide in its favor and to take a hard line towards the Soviet Union. The Second World countries, too, while pushing "detente plus defense" policy, have begun to pay attention to building up their military strength.

Third World countries have increased their understanding for "the need to drive the tiger away from the front door and resist the wolf at the back,"(18) and to close their ranks in the common struggle against hegemony. Therefore, the Soviet Union will find it more difficult to implement detente policy as time goes on. Just as Moscow is bent on driving a wedge into the United States-West European alliance, the West similarly is trying to split Soviet-East European relations. The United States in particular followed the principle of dealing with individual East European countries to promote political changes within them. The Polish crisis is, among other things, also an example of the West's infiltration into Eastern Europe.

East-West relaxation has provided an opportunity for the West to influence also life in the Soviet Union and to infiltrate it ideologically. The West exerts an influence on people, especially on the younger generation. "Many of them are obsessed with so-called Western democracy and dissatisfied with what they have to eat and wear, and go after creature comforts. They no longer respect Soviet reality and adopt a nihilist attitude." For all these reasons, it is unlikely that the world will see another "golden age of detente like the mid-1970s;" nor will it be threatened by a return to the "cold war period" of the 1950s. Under Reagan, the United States will increase its strength and will display the will to assume leadership; her alliance with Europe, recently weakened, will be recemented. While Western Europe wished to see the United States take a firm stance towards the Soviet Union, it nevertheless feared that too rigid a stance could introduce new tensions into a "peaceful and prosperous Europe."

This critical but objective assessment of the plusses and minuses of Soviet detente policy makes also abundantly clear why the Soviets pursued this policy in the past and why they would be interested in reviving it. Differently from unrealistic judgments of Soviet policy in the West, which stress the Soviet Union's selfless and humanitarian instincts and pacific inclinations, the writers of the foregoing article have correctly

judged Western Europe as "the major object"(19) of Moscow's
policy of detente. Since Western Europe cannot rid itself of
Soviet threats, it must depend on the United States.
Conversely, relaxation "makes it possible to erect a certain
restrictive influence on the Soviet Union." Western Europe
seeks "detente" with the Soviet Union in part to influence
Eastern Europe, hoping that some day the latter will become,
to a certain extent, a "buffer zone" between Western Europe
and the Soviet union. This, Western Europe holds, will
improve its own strategic position. "In brief, under the
present-day balance of international forces, reLaxation caters
to the needs of various quarters and thus provides the objective
possibility for the Soviet union to carry out its detente policy.
Of course, East and West have always differed in their
understanding of substance and aim of relaxation."

About two years later, on January 21 and January 28, 1985,
Beijing Review reached the same conclusion:(20) Military
superiority was out of reach for either side. "Neither side seems
to have the economic and technical strength to break the
balance." "The escalation of arms between the two countries
has caused both to squander a lot of financial and material
resources, but it has not helped make either country safe and
secure. It only aggravates international tensions and brings the
threat of war upon the whole world. The people of various
countries, including farsighted Soviet and American people,
are therefore demanding, with even greater urgency, that the
arms race be ended. They ask that both countries adopt a
serious attitude and negotiate nuclear reductions. It can be
seen that this is the only and sane alternative to the
uninterrupted arms race between the two superpowers. It is a
positive factor to safeguard world peace and coincides with the
fundamental interests of the Soviet and American people."

Despite Soviet expansionism, Beijing holds, the United
States has, especially since the beginning of the Reagan
Administration, economically and militarily gained ground in
relation with the U.S.S.R.

For the United Nations and the Third World. Against Both Superpowers

Though this apparently pleased the C.P.R., there was no complete lack of criticism of Reagan's policies. The Reagan Administration has used a carrot and stick approach to assume control over Third World countries and pit them against the Soviet Union. As self-proclaimed champion of the Third World, China obviously is highly critical of Reagan's policy toward underdeveloped nations. Jin Junhui thus criticized U.S. policy: The United States gave more bilateral than multilateral foreign aid and stressed military over economic assistance; "aid went first to countries that can best directly advance Washington's strategic interests." Jeanne Kirkpatrick, United States representative to the United Nations, had even threatened "economic reprisals" against countries voting against the United States by cutting aid to them. The United States had further adopted a rigid attitude towards North-South relations to protect its interests and has resolutely opposed the establishment of a new international economic order. It has also tried to reduce the moneys it contributes to the international monetary organization and had often taken "stubborn positions" in international organizations and conferences, "going against the will and interests of the majority of nations." To maintain the interests of Israel and South Africa, it has often exercised its veto power in the United Nations Security Council and also has threatened to withdraw from organizations which wanted to expel Israel and South Africa.

The U.S. has withdrawn from UNESCO, because it did not bend to its will. Another example was the Law of the Sea Treaty. These "extreme policies have also dealt the Reagan Administration some disappointments and given Moscow chances to increase its influence especially in the Middle East." United States policy in this region "has sent the United States up a blind alley." The U.S. was also beset with crises in Latin America: "Anti-United States feelings in Central America in general have deepened." The United States has maintained, however, a fairly strong position in the world economy, while most of the Third World countries were deep in economic trouble. Both American political parties, close on several important policies continued a stern attitude towards the Soviet Union, boosting military expenditures. Beijing, as might be expected, tends to overemphasize the importance of the negative Third World reaction to U.S. policy.

In an article by Chen Yicun, "U.N. Straitjacketed by Diluted Budget. Economic Difficulties threaten the very existence and viability of the U. N.," *Beijing Review* does not deny that the international body has "a lot of shortcomings, such as swollen and redundant organizations, inefficiency, and too much bureaucracy"—it had at present 11,600 employees. (21) It also had ambitious building projects for an Economic and Social Commission for Asia and a similar one for Africa, etc. However, the main thrust of criticism is aimed at the U.S. and a few other member nations which have cut their contributions, partly for political reasons. According to Chen Yicun, the U.S. has long been attempting to impose economic pressure on the U.N. and to sway the votes of Third World countries; it wanted "weighted voting"—voting power proportionate to its financial contributions. As a special pleader for the Third World, China's criticism of U.S. policy toward the U.N. hardly produces any surprise.

In discussing the relationship between China and the Third World, Shen Yicun, writing in *Beijing Review*, virtually identified the interests of China with those of the Third World.(22) He went to great length claiming that China "belongs forever" to the Third World. He also assured his readers that the C.P.R. will never, or at east not for a very long time to come, become an economically and technologically advanced country such as the United States, the Soviet Union, Japan, and West European states. This "modesty," and at the same time realism, of China's new leadership are characteristic of the post-Mao era. An African state leader, visiting recently China, had, according to Shen Yi, told his hosts that he had heard China was repudiating Chairman Mao and changing its foreign policy, and this had him worried. Actually, he had been misinformed. "If China were to totally repudiate Chairman Mao, which China is not, it would also include repudiating his correct foreign policy. Mao always /!/ opposed hegemonism" and supported the Third World people in their struggle against hegemonism and colonialism. "This was very much appreciated by the people of the Third World. But will post-Mao China continue to side with the peoples of the Third World? The answer is a definite yes."

First, Mao's strategic conception of the Third World is correct. Some Third World countries were asking whether the C.P.R. "will oppose only" Soviet hegemonism, but not imperialism and colonialism, as China develops its relations with the United States and other developed countries. "Waging a joint struggle together /!/ with some of the Western countries against hegemonism does not mean China has stopped supporting the struggle of the peoples of the Third World and no longer cares about the interests of the oppressed nations." It is a revealing denial that reaffirms China's deep interest in the Third World. Beijing's repeated calls for an anti-Soviet bloc, including the United States and the Western nations, has caused concern among traditionally anti-Western countries, mostly former colonies of the Western powers. While not necessarily pro-Soviet, to the contrary, beset by increasing doubts about Communist foreign policy, especially the Soviet invasion of Afghanistan, itself a Third World country and also an Islamic one, these former colonial countries were likely to be non-aligned and suspicious of, if not hostile, towards the West. China did not wish to relinquish whatever influence it wields and hold it has on the Third World. China, therefore, was anxious to give assurances to these nations and to eliminate the cloud of doubt hovering over some nations of the Third World.

According to *Beijing Review*, some Third World countries were "victims of Soviet hegemonistic expansion." Others regarded the United States and certain other countries as the "main danger" /!/, while some were primarily pitted against racist rule, Israeli "expansionism," or struggle for national independence and liberation. "As in the past, China will firmly stand side by side of the oppressed nations and oppressed peoples, oppose all acts of aggression and interference from outside against Third World countries, and firmly support their fight against imperialism, colonialism and hegemonism." The author of the foregoing and *Beijing Review* in particular placed main responsibility for the threat to world peace on "imperialism, colonialism and the superpower that practices hegemonism." This sounds neutral enough. Furthermore, the peoples of the Third World were given encouragement, since they allegedly could "upset the strategic plans of the superpowers."

The following makes clear that the C.P.R. opposes at times both superpowers, sometimes the United States, at other times the U.S.S.R. Developing relations with the United States "does not mean that China supports its erroneous policy towards some Third World countries. The United States, it charges, leans heavily on the side of Israel and the South African racist regime, supports South Korea while sabotaging the national reunification of Korea, and meddles with the internal affairs of some countries, China included. (The reference is obviously confined to Taiwan.) China is set against all such endeavors. It follows its own independent foreign policy.

There arises, of course, the question whether the rapprochement with the United States was more important to China than the "support" which it can count on in the United Nations and outside of it, from some African states, radical Arab countries, North Korea, and other Third World nations. If the Soviet Union is the main threat to world peace and to China in particular, neither the Arab nor African states are likely to be of tangible help to China against "the threat from the north." Then, the pious mouthings in behalf of the Third World have merely rhetorical significance.

Economic exchanges of China with some developed countries and importation of advanced technology and capital from abroad, *Beijing Review* admits, "helps in our socialist modernizations," "but China remains an underdeveloped country." Such modesty is not only realistic, but also becoming, and. likely to win friends among other Third World countries. China assures the latter that, like them, it wants to establish "a new international economic order," holding out to the underdeveloped countries the mirage of a quick economic upsurge and voicing the hope of closely working with them. At the same time, if China was properly perceived as one of the nations of the Third World, help expected from her to the latter will remain within narrow bounds, and not become an unbearable burden for the C.P.R.

Somewhat earlier *Beijing Review* had raised the question, "Why Moscow wants 'long-term cooperation' with developing countries?"(23) "In the course of exchanging machines from the developing countries for raw materials, the Soviet Union practiced extra-economic exploitation through exchange of unequal value. For instance, the Soviet Union exported to Egypt certain goods at prices 13% or even over 100% higher than those which it exported to West Germany. The machines and other commodities the Soviet Union exported to India were generally priced 20% to 30% higher than in international markets. On the other hand, many raw materials and other commodities the Soviet Union imported from the developing countries were usually priced lower than in the world markets.

The Soviets, Shen Yi hinted, fabricated rumor after rumor to foment discord and create trouble between China and other Third World countries.(24) Western states were not accused of such underhanded policies and dubious practices. The Soviet Union and Vietnam had invented the "China threat." The C.P.R., of course, was not a threat to her neighbors and to Southeast Asia in particular; it had not a single soldier in any other country. The Soviet Union, however, had "a million troops menacing China in the north;" the C.P.R. was also "constantly harassed by Vietnamese shellings and attacks along its southern boundary. It is China that is threatened." Soviet and Vietnamese hegemonists revealed a morbid fear of the new unity which had emerged between China and other Third World countries.

Ignoring its earlier revolutionary role and oratorical fireworks—when Beijing in domestic and foreign policy represented an ultra-leftist, more revolutionary stance than Moscow-Communist China, according to the author, did not import its revolution; nor would it ever export revolution. Whatever political road a country chooses was its own business and had nothing to do with China. China was an "implacable adversary of hegemonism. China advocates equality among all countries, big or small, and is against the strong bullying the weak." Even when it becomes strong and prosperous, it will never move against others, will never seek hegemonism. At present China was "still very poor." It would like to help other Third World countries more, but it was handicapped by its "limited strength." "As the Third World pins its hopes on China, so we place our hopes on the Third World of which we are a member." What was more or less freely admitted here was that the unwritten alliance between China and the Third World was not an alliance of strength but rather one of weakness; only in a more distant future will it become a camp of strength.

But the "link-up" between China and the Third World was the more imperative since "the Third World countries are increasingly threatened by Soviet hegemonism." While the contention for world domination between the superpowers was, in Beijing's view, ultimately and chiefly focussed on Europe, at the moment the Soviet Union is concentrating mainly on expanding its presence in several key areas of the Third World." Though the U.S.S.R. wanted to take over Western Europe, it could not do so at the present. So it was striking out to outflank Europe. It has launched sustained offensives against the Middle East, "the Persian Gulf region, Southwest and Southeast Asia, southern Africa and the Caribbean." "The Soviet Union can establish itself firmly in Afghanistan; it will push further, into Pakistan and Iran to seize control of the Indian Ocean and the Persian Gulf and to exploit the Middle East oilfields and cut the oil route to Western Europe. The Soviet Union will not stop with Kampuchea and Afghanistan in order to complete its global strategic deployment." If the Soviet expansionist drive will not be checked, more and more countries will fall victim to Soviet hegemony. As a member of the Third World, China will join other countries to oppose the aggression and expansion of Soviet hegemonism and defend peace in Asia and the world as a whole.

The article was most revealing both for what it said and for what it avoided to come to grips with. It proclaimed, at times it only hinted at, the community of interests with the United States and Western nations in stemming the Soviet hegemonic drive. It strongly appealed to the Third World to block, in alliance with China, a fellow Third World country, against Soviet aggression. It felt that it needed both the West and the Third World, and sought to win over to its point of view Third World countries which apparently did not quite share this philosophy. While the author realized that there were differences of outlook and interests between the United States, Western countries, and the Third World, he tried his best to paint the U.S.S.R. as a hegemonic power; not only Afghanistan and Kampuchea but the entire world was seen as a potential victim of Soviet imperialism; the primary importance of Europe in the global duel was always emphasized. The article was an attempt to align the United States, the Second World—the developed countries of Western Europe and Japan—and the Third World against the Soviet hegemonic drive. This most clearly paralleled U.S. policy!

Nonaligned Nations, the Soviets, and their "Mercenaries"

Again and again, the C.P.R. has warned the Third World nations of being wary of Soviet propaganda which pictured the U.S.S.R. as their loyal friend. In an editorial, reprinted by *Beijing Review* on September 14, 1979, the journal wrote: "The nonaligned movement continues to advance."(25) Commenting about the Sixth Conference of the Heads of State of Government in Havana, *Renmin Ribao* observed: "Soviet social imperialism, posing as the 'natural ally' of the nonaligned movement, has exploited certain differences among the nonaligned nations to provoke incidents, create conflicts, and divide these nations into two categories, the so-called progressives and the reactionaries."

Beijing approved wholeheartedly the stance of the Yugoslav President J. Tito, one of the founders of the nonaligned movement, who pointed out at the Havana Conference that he "had from the very outset been consistently opposed to bloc policies and foreign domination, and to all forces of political and economic hegemony." The Soviet Union had maligned China as the movement's "deadly enemy." In reality, China,"though not a member of the non-aligned movement, has always held it in high regard." In recent years, however, the Soviet Union, according to *Beijing Review*, by exploiting its ever-increasing military might, has been going in for more adventurism. "Acting as the string-puller, Moscow has been using the Vietnam and Cuban mercenaries to carry out expansion and aggression abroad, thus throwing Africa and the Middle East, Asia, and many important parts of Latin America into an intense and unstable condition. It is in these circumstances that Vietnam and Cuba, counting on the support of the Soviet Union, have had the audacity to sing a different tune within the nonaligned movement."

While Beijing criticized Moscow's "meddling" virtually everywhere, it prided itself on pursuing a strikingly different policy in the Third World, in Asia, Latin America, and Africa. In an article, "China and Africa are fated partners," Dafei, an advisor to the Chinese Foreign Ministry, underlined that China and the African countries had no conflict of interest.(26) The C.P.R. firmly supported their struggle to defend their independence and opposed racism; it regarded the African nations as equals and never meddled in their affairs. China and Africa have gone through many of the same historical encounters which have brought them closely together. With the further development of its national economy, China will give more aid to Africa. In dealing with the African countries, China was "careful not to show an arrogant attitude as a big country" and was even willing to "learn from their strong points," in accordance with the late Premier Zhou Enlai's example.

China is so immersed in the Third World, of which it hopes to become the undisputed leader, that it must take account of the widespread anti-American sentiments in the Third World and be wary to be perceived as their unrelenting champion also against the United States. Though geopolitically and practically, Beijing, in view of the openly discussed Soviet threat to China, should align herself with the United States, national pride and anger at U.S. unwillingness to yield sufficiently on the Taiwan issue — and Beijing's propagandistic interests in regard to the Third World and in being acclaimed by it as a bona fide member and leader — push China toward a "neutral" position as far as the East-West conflict is concerned.

B. Economic Problem. The Primary Soviet Focus: Europe or Asia?
The North-South Relationship

The C.P.R.'s leadership tried to exploit not only the political and economic suspicions in the Third World which are directed against the U.S.S.R., but also those aimed against the U.S. Its economic policy and propaganda aimed not only against the Soviet Union, but also was directed against the U.S. and the more developed countries. This manifested itself in the *Beijing Review* article of July 1, 1985, "North-South Cooperation for Mutual Prosperity."(1) Deng is quoted therein to the effect that the world today was confronted with two strategic issues, peace and economy. The first-named was an East-West problem, while economic development was a North-South question. The South is poor, while the North is rich, and the gap between them is skill widening. "For hundreds of years, colonialist and imperialist countries in the North forced their cruel designs on the South. The South's vast resources were laundered to lay the foundation for the modern edifice of the northern empires. The blood and sweat of the people of the South was the source of the North's capital accumulation." It was not practical, however, to blame the North for all of the South's troubles, though exploitation was truly a root cause of the situation.

Without mutual cooperation, neither South nor North will gain further development. Wile the North enjoyed an advantage in capital and technology, the South had superior resources and bigger markets. Independence movements and national-liberation movements have made gunboat diplomacy increasingly impossible and prevented the North from further plundering the resources of the South. On the other hand, in order to realize its modernization, the South must carry out effective economic cooperation with the North.

The Chinese authors made clear that they did not mean "cooperation" in the traditional sense. Trade historically has meant unequal exchanges. "The result of this is that the North, with only 20% of the world's population has taken 80% of its wealth." The gist of all this was quite clear. What China suggested to the Third World was a greater portion of the world's riches and what it suggested to the developed countries was a greater sharing of the global wealth! This would benefit the Third World, as well as the C.P.R., and raise the latter's international prestige and power.

Sino-Soviet Polemics in the UN

The main forum of the Third World was the United Nations which the C.P.R. herself had been able to join only after long delays and bitter frustration. The Sino-Soviet rivalry manifested itself also in its halls. In a sharp anti-Soviet address to the UN Assembly, the Chinese delegate, Vice-Foreign Minister Zhang Wen-jin, in September 1981, branded the

Soviet Union as "the major threat to world peace."(2)
Therefore, the struggle against hegemonism remained the
primary task for the maintenance of global peace. International realities did not bear out the view that the Soviet Union has
launched a "peace offensive" because it is on the defensive and
that its own difficulties are forcing it to consider a retreat.
Soviet aggression was not considered a response to allegedly
aggressive moves of the opponents in the West. It rather
sprang from the desire for world domination and, in
particular, was the result of the Soviet southward strategy
which aimed at enveloping Europe.

"Facts in the past year have shown that the Soviet Union
has not given up its bid for world hegemony, and the corollary
strategy of a southward drive remains unchanged. However,
because of repeated setbacks and its own vulnerabilities, the
U.S.S.R., while adhering to a policy of aggression and
expansion, has increasingly resorted to political tricks. The
Soviet Union has launched another so-called "peace offensive"
by putting forward political solutions and proposals for
disarmament, which are designed to confuse public opinion,
to disguise its hegemonism, and to deceive or lull the people of
the world.

The Soviet invasion of Afghanistan and its support for the
Vietnamese occupation of Kampuchea were not only aimed at
subjugating these two countries, but also at using them as
springboards for further expansion. "Many more countries will
come to grief," if the aggression against Afghanistan and
Kampuchea is not checked. China favors a political settlement
on both these issues; it considers, however, the withdrawal of
all foreign troops "the primary condition" for any political
settlement. Only when the aggressors have suffered "heavier
and heavier blows" on the battlefield and have been subjected
to mounting pressure from the international community, will
they be forced to consider pulling out their troops from the
occupied territories. Zhang Wen-jin referred to the resolutions
on Afghanistan and Kampuchea that were adopted by the
United Nations General Assembly, the declarations voted on
by the summit conference of the Islamic countries in January
1980, the foreign ministers' meeting of the nonaligned
countries in February of the same year, and the international

conference on Kampuchea in July 1980; all of them had urged that foreign troops be withdrawn from both areas.

The Minister further demanded Israel's withdrawal from the occupied Arab territories and South Africa's from Namibia and that the latter stop its attacks against the frontier states and abandon its apartheid system. "Crimes" committed by Israel and South Africa had provided the hegemonists with more opportunities and pretexts for infiltration. The defiance by both Israel and South Africa were attributable in a large measure to United States' support and shielding. The Chinese Minister thus appealed on so-called pragmatic grounds to the United States, which had repeatedly expressed its willingness to improve its relations with Third World countries, to consider that its policy only antagonized hundreds of millions of Arab and African peoples and a large number of other Third World countries. Placed, however, in its wider context and considering the major thrust of the speech, aimed, as it was, against Soviet hegemonism, the Chinese Vice-Foreign Minister wished an accommodation of the United States policies and those of the Third World on the two foregoing issues for the purpose of strengthening the joint anti-Soviet front. This became also evident in his remarks on the Caribbean region. After paying lip-service to the rights of Caribbean states to overcome the legacy of colonial exploitation and oppression, he, "on the other hand," noted that "another superpower and its proxies"—the U.S.S.R. and Cuba—had been "meddling in the internal affairs of those countries and are trying hard to infiltrate the region under the guise of supporting the progressive movements." According to Beijing, China was "opposed to all outside interferences, no matter where they came from." The people of the region should be "left alone to solve their own problems."

On the issue of economic help by developed countries to the developing nations—to achieve "economic independence" after having won political independence—the Chinese Minister criticized the developed nations for their refusal to go along with the irresistible worldwide trend and expressed the hope that the forthcoming Cancun meeting in Mexico could take practical measures to improve North-South relations.

The picture painted by the Chinese Foreign Minister Zhang Wen-jin of the U.S.S.R. could hardly have been bleaker. Her peace offensive was mere propaganda and every new territory under Soviet control was a mere jumping-off board for further extension of Soviet domination. Still, the United States, too, was criticized for some of its policies toward the Third World and there was a strong implication that these policies needlessly alienated "Third World countries." By implication, the C.P.R. regretted that the United States allegedly disregarded her own national interests. The U.S. was enlarging the area of disagreements and differences between herself and the Third World instead of narrowing it. The situation could be improved upon by furthering the economic means of the latter.

A greater than usual degree of objectivity was noticeable in the article authored by Lu Mingzhu, "Unesco. Steering Clear of the Storm."(3) When the United States pulled out of the United Nations Educational, Scientific and Cultural Organization (U.N.E.S.C.O.) early in 1985, reducing the organization in funding by one fourth in the process, things, according to the author, looked bleak for the international development group. Over the past several years, the United States had led a chorus of Western nations in complaining about UNESCO. It claimed that the agency was mismanaged and too politicized. Soon after the United States defection, Great Britain too, threatened to pull out. In the meantime, it did. Prior to the 1984-1985 budget discussion, China and 30 other countries, however, volunteered to make donations to help UNESCO overcome its current shortfall. These countries, the author recalled, were reiterating their support for the organization and expressed the "hope that the United States would rethink its decision and return to UNESCO as soon as possible." Despite this position of China—which paralleled that of many Third World nations, and even that of the U.S.S.R.—the C.P.R. has withheld any major criticism of the United States in particular over this issue and of the Western countries in general.

Referring to Soviet Foreign Minister Gromyko's address to the United Nations Assembly (36th session), *Beijing Review* contrasted the realities of Soviet policy with the Foreign Minister's claim that the Soviet union merely wished peace and security for its own people and for its allies and friends. *Beijing Review* recalled the Soviet Union's resort to the iron fist, her invasions of Czechoslovakia and of Afghanistan, Moscow's launching aggressive wars by "using surrogates, such as in the intervention in Angola, the penetration of the Horn of Africa, and the invasion of Zaire; more recently it has used Vietnamese troops to overrun Kampuchea."(4) The Soviet Union had stationed regular troops, military advisors, and other personnel, totalling nearly 900,000, in Eastern Europe and in some Asian, African, and Latin American countries. Bringing some countries under its control and penetrating key government departments of other states, the Soviet Union has established naval and air bases in southern Africa, the Middle East, Southeast Asia, and the Far East, such as Assab in Ethiopia, Aden and Sokotra Island in South Yemen, Cam Ranh Bay and Da Nang in Vietnam, and Port Kompong Som in Kampuchea, and turned Japan's northern islands into a military outpost. It has sped up the arms race with the other superpower in all fields, from conventional weapons to tactical and strategic nuclear weapons, on the ground, in sea, and in space. It has tried hard to win and retain superiority in armament, and in all regions. Moscow has developed and stockpiled bacteriological and chemical weapons and was using toxic chemicals against the people of Afghanistan and Kampuchea. It was sending large numbers of K.G.B. agents to infiltrate other countries, to carry out subversion and sabotage in order to collect intelligence. It has massed military troops around troubled Poland and issued menacing warnings, carrying out large-scale military exercises, one after the other, and was ready to send its tanks into Poland. It attempted to exploit the turbulent situation around Iran, as it bided its time waiting for the situation to ripen. While *Beijing Review* pointed to Soviet aggressiveness, it also focussed on the internal weaknesses of the Soviet Union and "the inherent contradictions and weaknesses within the Soviet Empire."

The Soviet Economic Policy and the Council for Mutual Economic Assistance (CMEA). Eastern Europe

"As the forms of cooperation between the member states of the Council for Mutual Economic Assistance (CMEA) diversify more and more, so the contradictions among them grow sharper."(5) This was particularly true of conflicts of economic

interests between the East European partners of CMEA and
the Soviet Union. Soviet "economic integration" plans were
being held back by these deepening conflicts. The East
European countries have run into shortages of funds and raw
materials for their sizeable industries. They wanted an assured
contracted supply of raw materials and fuel. The Soviets were
"exploiting" this, pointing out that "fuel bases" are moving out
towards Siberia—where transport is difficult and weather is
harsh; they wanted East European countries to contribute
manpower, funds, and equipment to "jointly developing" new
raw materials inside the U.S.S.R. Eastern European states
should chip in to help open up the oil and natural gas and
other energy resources. Since the East European countries on
the whole were rather resource-poor and got most of their fuel
and raw materials from the Soviet Union, the limited supply of
energy from the Soviet Union was exacerbating contradictions
with the CMEA. The Soviet Union was selling oil to its trading
partners at international market prices, and machine tools and
raw materials at even considerably higher prices. On the other
hand, the Soviet Union obtained produce from Hungary,
Bulgaria, and Poland at prices considerably lower than on the
international market, with Moscow thus reaping huge profits.

The Soviet Union has always demanded that CMEA
members first fulfill demands inside the bloc before developing
trade relations with the West and has fixed for each member
the proportion of exports to the Soviet Union out of their total
exports. Ever since the 1970's, however, all CMEA members,
the Soviet Union included, have been vying with each other to
expand trade with the West to earn hard currencies to pay for
advanced technological equipment from the West.

But the growing volume of Soviet exports to the West—the
turnover between the Soviet Union and the West European
nations has increased sevenfold between 1970 and 1980—
coupled with Soviet attempts to curtail exports to its CMEA
partners, has aroused strong feelings in East European
countries. They have not much to spare for export to the West
and are seeing their trade deficits growing. There are frequent
clashes inside the CMEA whenever the topic of East-West
trade is raised. For strategic goals and to enlarge its sphere of
influence, the Soviet Union has also brought three "poor
partners," Mongolia, Cuba, and Vietnam, into the CMEA

despite strong opposition from other CMEA nations. This put a heavier burden on the relatively more industrialized East European countries. The Soviet Union, again, was the only beneficiary.

China's New "Open Policy"

While Soviet economic policy in regard to East European socialist countries was sharply criticized in the Chinese press, the C.P.R.'s own economic policy, as might be expected, was discussed in favorable terms. In accordance with China's more modest claims concerning economic achievements, as compared to earlier years, *Beijing Review* freely admitted that the C.P.R. has been compelled to lower the extent of its economic aid to less developed nations. It has, however, increased its trade with East European socialist countries and has especially enlarged the import of technology, so important for Beijing's drive toward modernization.

China's open policy applies not only to developed countries, but also to South-South cooperation—meaning closer economic relations between underdeveloped countries— and to "socialist countries, even those with poor /!/ relations with China." "In the early days China paid more attention to economic aid to Third World countries. At the beginning of the 1970s more than 70 states received the C.P.R.'s aid. But China is a developing country and its wealth is limited." Thus, it has come to stress South-South cooperation. In early 1983, Premier Zhao Ziyang toured much of Africa and in May 1984, Vice Premier Li Peng visited five African nations; in December 1984, Vice Premier Tian Jiyun journeyed to Africa again. In the 1950s, China had had close ties with the socialist countries, but some of them were interrupted in the early 1960s. Over the past few years, however, the trade volume with the socialist countries in Eastern Europe had grown measurably. In the spring of 1984, a Chinese economic delegation visited Hungary, Poland, Czechoslovakia, the German Democratic Republic, and Bulgaria. Their governments agreed to take part in the technological transformation of 79 industrial enterprises in China.

China also hoped to improve Sino-Soviet relations and further expand contacts and exchanges with the Soviet Union in economic fields, trade, science and technology, culture, sports, and other fields. Bilateral trade is expected to reach í1,200,000 million this year, but it has not yet equalled the high level of the past.

The Main Soviet Thrust—Europe or Asia?

Is, in the Chinese mind, the focus of Soviet strategy Europe or Asia? The last few years have seen a mounting interest of the Soviet Union especially in preserving the political status quo in Poland and in preventing the deployment of intermediate United States missiles in Western Europe. But, at the same time, the Soviets have invaded Afghanistan and given vigorous support to Vietnam in Kampuchea and to creating a Southeast Federation in Indochina. There is no indication whatsoever of a lessening of Soviet interests and efforts in either Europe or Asia. To the Chinese, Soviet successes in either part of the world portend major problems, though Soviet victories in Asia forebode, perhaps, greater trouble. The international editor of *Beijing Review*, Mu Youlin, replied negatively to the question of whether the Soviet Union had shifted the focus of its strategy to Asia, despite the recent intensification of Soviet efforts in Asia. In his view, "the focus of Soviet strategy was still in Europe."(6) It was in Europe where the Soviets were "most capable of launching a large-scale surprise attack. Only by occupying Europe, which possesses greater economic, political, and military strength, can the Soviet Union achieve its ambition of dominating the world." True, the developments in Afghanistan and Kampuchea as well as the Soviets' "increased military pressure in the Western Pacific" menaced both China and Japan. But Soviet activities in those parts of the world did not represent a shifting of the focus of their strategy.

Still, the possibilities of a Soviet frontal attack on Europe were small. The U.S.S.R. "aims rather at outflanking Europe in the east by directing its spearhead against South Asia and the Persian Gulf area, which are strategically important, but weak in defense."

The Soviets were aware that a frontal attack on Europe would be "too costly." The U.S.S.R. "uses detente as a ploy," while maintaining a strong military presence in Europe and energetically pushing southward toward the continent's "soft belly." Kampuchea and Afghanistan were only staging posts for the Soviets in their southward thrust to the Persian Gulf, the Indian Ocean, and the Pacific to realize the fond dream of the old Tsars. Among past and more recent dreams, Europe continued to play the key role. According to some observers, the U.S.S.R.'s intent was to encircle China, and to push its own expansionism in Asia. China was uppermost in the Kremlin's mind. But its more important object was to enlarge its sphere of influence and eliminate the influence of its arch-rival, the United States, from Asia, and threaten the peace and security of Japan and other Asian nations, and that of Southeast Asian nations in particular. Soviet efforts, however, to reduce Vietnam to being its stooge for the pursuit of hegemony in Asia, were doomed to failure. Such endeavors "only promote the growth of an international united front against hegemonism."

According to *Beijing Review*, Moscow's "imperialist strategy in Asia" was merely the complement to its expansionist pursuits in Europe and the rest of the world. In its expansion overseas, Moscow was striving "to hook certain Asian and African nations up with the Warsaw Pact, the Council for Mutual Economic Assistance (CMEA), and to hold the socialist community under its thumb."(7) In turn, the Soviet Union has enlisted, or rather compelled, the assistance of its European satellites in its pursuit of selfish imperialist goals in Asia and Africa. Vietnam's admission to the CMEA, the Kremlin's pressure on member states of the Warsaw Pact to increase their military spending and pledge "solidarity" with Vietnam, and the use of military personnel of some Warsaw Pact countries in Soviet adventures in Africa — "all shows that Moscow is contemplating the extension of its military bloc and economic grouping to cover Asia and Africa. This is a new development in the Kremlin's pursuit of its global strategy." It felt acutely the need for its partners in the "community" to share the burden in manpower and resources imposed on it by its worldwide expansionism.

While the Soviet Union was noisily vilifying Communist China as being guilty of "hegemonism" and "expansionism," it was itself positioning its forces and "rattling its sabre in the Asia-Pacific region." Some people held that all this was intended to encircle China. But it rather aimed at enlarging its own sphere of influence at the expense of the U.S. Soviet social imperialism was "indulging in phantasies" when it thought that, "supported by a few hatchetmen, it can lord over the world." The Soviets forced other countries and peoples to mobilize, and, a consequence of its own drives, Moscow has found itself "besieged" by the peoples of the world.

Following World War II, both the U.S. and the Soviet Union had made Europe the focal point of their strategic rivalry. But in the past decade, the economic boom in Asia has helped to bring attention to the Asian-Pacific region; and the superpowers have begun to intensify their rivalry in the East.

Wang Baoqin, in the article, "Washington-Moscow, has the Strategic Focus Shifted?," referred to three different viewpoints on this issue. Baoqin himself held, and so apparently did *Beijing Review*, that, while Asia has been growing more important, the two superpowers would continue to focus on Europe as their principal arena for confrontation. (8)

It was undeniable, however, that U.S. economic expansion had begun to move from Europe to Asia, where at the same time the Soviet Union has sped up the exploitation of Siberia's resources and has established new eastern industrial bases. About 25% of the Soviet Union's fuel and energy resources were found in Siberia. Both superpowers needed to increase their military strength to safeguard their interests in Asia. Washington planned to concentrate its armed forces in Asia, especially in southern Korea and Japan; the U.S. regarded the Asian region as the Soviet Union's "weakest link."

Nevertheless, Baoqin continued, Europe was still the main stage for their global rivalry. By 1982, the gross volume of U.S. direct private investment in Europe was $99.8 billion, accounting for half of the total U.S. direct investment abroad.

From the strategic angle, Washington and Moscow were not preparing to launch a large-scale war in Asia; both continued to regard Europe as their major strategic battle-field. About 71% of the Soviet military forces and 73% of the Soviet continental and medium-range missiles were deployed in Eastern Europe and in the western part of the Soviet Union. Moscow thought it was better to use Eastern Europe as a springboard to thrust its influence into Western Europe, the Middle East, and North Africa, than to fight with the U.S. in

Asia, because these areas threatened the U.S. and West European countries most.

In conclusion, there has been no serious talk about a strategic shift to the east among Soviet leaders. Neither has the concept of weakening Europe for the sake of Asia prevailed in the U.S.

The Soviet Navy's Imperial Ambitions

For its global aspirations, no armed branch was more significant than the Soviet navy, showing its flag in distant waters. The naval build-up of the Soviets had taken on spectacular dimensions. In this context, *Beijing Review* discussed the writings of the Soviet naval commander-in-Chief, G. Gorshkov, in *Krasnaya Zvezda*(9). The Soviet fleet, he asserted, had 755 warships of various types totalling 1,300,000 million tons, 350 warplanes and altogether a 130,000 strong force; in number of warships, it exceeded the combined strength of the United States Seventh Fleet and Japan's naval force. Basing its article on Gorshkov's foregoing essay, *Beijing Review* held that the balance of United States and Soviet naval forces took "a turn for the worse" for the United States around 1981. The Soviet coastline was the longest in the world, but this did not much help the Soviet seaborne traffic, as most of it is on the Arctic Ocean. To enter the various oceans, Moscow's fleet would have to pass through straits controlled by other nations. And to overcome the handicap of the Pacific Fleet, whose outlets can be easily blocked, and to bring its naval strength into fuller play, the Soviet Union was expanding its naval port of Korsakov in the Sea of Okhotsk and strengthening its bases on Kunashiri and Etorofu with the aim of controlling the Sorga Strait and getting the port and the two islands to serve as transit stations between Vladivostok and other Soviet naval bases. The Soviet Union was also expanding existing naval bases and establishing new ones on the Kamtschatka Peninsula to keep an effective watch on United States missile-carrying submarines in the Northern Pacific and threaten the sea lanes and air routes from the United States to Japan through the Aleutian Islands. This will also give Soviet-guided missile submarines free access for attack on the United States proper.

The U.S.S.R. used two Vietnamese naval bases. Vietnam's ports have become halfway-stations for the Soviet Pacific Fleet in its entry into the Indian Ocean. This gravely threatened the United States strategic line of defense in the Western Pacific, Japan, and Australia, and other Oceanian nations dependent on Middle East oil, and West European countries with close ties to Southeastern Asia.

The Soviet Pacific Fleet's operations in the early 1960s were confined to areas close to the Sea of Japan and the Sea of Okhotsk. In the late 1960s, the operations were extended to the Indian Ocean, where a Soviet flotilla was stationed to confront the United States. In the 1970s, the Soviet Pacific Fleet had extended its operations to waters of the Hawaiian Islands in the Central Pacific and the west coast of the United States. In recent years, it has carried out activities in the Southern Pacific. It frequently holds large-scale maneuvers with the Soviet ground and air forces in the Far East. The maneuvers have been conducted from the Sea of Japan to the vast ocean expanses around Alaska, the Hawaiian Islands, and the Philippines, getting nearer and nearer to the main bases of the United States Pacific Fleet. These maneuvers are indications that Soviet strategy is to cut off the sea lanes and communication from the United States to Japan in time of war.

C. Regional Conflicts and the CPR

The C.P.R.'s Case against Vietnam: The Chinese Minority along the Border, Kampuchea, and the Soviet-Vietnamese Alliance

Referring to a Chinese-Vietnamese dialogue highlighting the divisive issues between the two Communist neighbors, *Renmin Ribao* on March 17, 1979, released a memorandum of China's Vice Premier Li Xiannian's talk with Premier Pham Van Dong on June 10, 1977.(1) The latter had then made the following points: "Owing to historical reasons there were more than one million Chinese residing in Vietnam. Acting on proletarian internationalist principles, we agreed in 1955 on gradually encouraging the Chinese residents to adopt the Vietnamese citizenship." This could only be done on a

voluntary basis, not by coercion. The problem was handled
fairly well through mutual cooperation. But since the
"liberation" of southern Vietnam, Chinese authorities had
accused the Vietnamese government of having "resorted to
coercion and treated Chinese in southern Vietnam, regardless
of their own wish, as being all Vietnamese citizens." Li
Xiannian charged: "You have imposed high taxes on Chinese
residents, prepared to deny them continued residence in
Vietnam. . .Every country has the duty to protect the
legitimate rights and interests of its nationals residing in other
countries." In contrast to Vietnam's practices, the Chinese
referred to about 5,000-6,000 Vietnamese residing in China
who were well treated. "For years Vietnam has propagandized
its opposition to invasion from the north." Tass has "made use
of your propaganda to foment discord and incite anti-Chinese
sentiments. We freely admit that China's feudal dynasties did
invade Vietnam, and we always condemn such aggression,"
but Chinese people themselves were then under feudal rulers.
Both countries should heed "the behests of Mao and President
Ho Chi Minh" and remain at peace.

Han Nianlong, head of the Chinese Government delegation, in a speech in Hanoi in 1981, put forward an eight-point
program of principles for handling Sino-Vietnamese relations.
(2) Neither side should seek hegemony in Indochina or any
other point of the world. The earlier Sino-French accords
should serve as the basis for a negotiated settlement of the
boundary question. They provided for the respect of the
12-nautical-mile territorial sea, respect by Vietnam of China's
sovereignty over Xisha and Nansha Islands, respect for the
rights of nationals of one country residing in the other. The
government of the country of residence shall guarantee their
rights and interests and personal safety, and the Vietnamese
government should take back the citizens it has driven into
China.

During the war against South Vietnam and the U.S.,
China, according to Beijing, had done "everything to support
Vietnam," but "Hanoi returns evil for good." It never occurred
to the Chinese people that the Vietnam authorities, "pursuing
expansionist goals they cannot disclose, would unscrupulously
and heartlessly antagonize their former friend and turn their
guns on China." Through their action from 1974 onwards,

disputes had occurred one after another and clashes had increased day by day on the once tranquil and friendly Sino-Vietnamese border. In 1974, there were 100 or so border incidents and they had increased in the following years. Incomplete statistics showed that the number of Chinese nationals and Vietnamese citizens driven into China has exceeded 200,000. "Moreover, it was reported that in southern Vietnam you /Vietnamese/ have driven hundreds of thousands of Vietnamese of Chinese descent and Vietnamese citizens across the open sea to Southeastern Asian countries and regions."

Concurrently with their large-scale anti-Chinese activities, the Vietnamese authorities had mobilized and stepped up their military build-up. In their directives to all lower-level organs, they openly referred to China "as the most immediate and dangerous enemy" and issued the slogan, "Do everything for the sake of defeating China and build many fortifications and other military facilities in the border areas." The border has been turned into "a springboard for invading China."

In 1978, the number of border incidents provoked by Vietnam had risen sharply to more than 1,100. Despite earlier recognition of Chinese claims, Vietnam had occupied some islands in China's Nansha group and even laid territorial claim to China's Xisha and all Nansha Islands. "Their bullying became simply intolerable." "Responsibility for all-around aggravation of Sino-Vietnamese relations in recent years. . .lies entirely with the Vietnamese side." "China's self-defensive counterattack was a just action."(3)

In an article of June 8, 1979, *Beijing Review* zeroed in again on Vietnam's expulsion of refugees. At a mid-May meeting in Djakarta, Hanoi's representatives had brazenly announced that Hanoi intended to export "10,000 refugees" each month.(4) *Beijing Review* raised the question why a million people had shown no enthusiasm for national reconstruction in "liberated" Vietnam and have fled their land at the risk of their lives. Hanoi's explanation and "most used excuse" was that people were "beguiled, incited, and organized by foreign reactionaries." Another explanation offered was that the "refugees" were "all capitalists," dead-set against socialist transformation. Furthermore, it was claimed that the mass exodus was "the consequence of war." *Beijing*

Review asked, "Which war?" Why should the "consequences of war" manifest themselves three years after the end of the war against the United States, and not during that war? Indeed, according to *Beijing Review*, the exodus was the "consequence" of war, that of Hanoi's "war of aggression" which was still going on. Today, destitution stalked Vietnam. The only way out was to escape Hanoi's clutches. "This is the real reason why a million people have chosen to quit their homeland, risking property and life."

Also, Hanoi has found the export of people "profitable." Of late, those who want to leave the country have been told to register in Hanoi and other places and to pay the sum of 2,500 dong per person. Large numbers of Vietnamese families have been broken up and their members scattered. The Vietnam authorities were not only warmongers, but "also traffickers in human beings."

On February 23, 1979, the Chinese delegate in the United Nations Security Council, Chen Chu, ridiculed Vietnam's and the Soviet Union's claims that there raged in Kampuchea (Cambodia) a so-called "civil war." This was a "pure invention" to cover up Vietnam's armed aggression against Kampuchea. The flagrant and large-scale bloody slaughter of Kampuchean soldiers and civilians by Vietnam constituted a gross violation of the United Nations charter.(5) "It has been the long-premeditated plans of the Vietnamese authorities to annex democratic Kampuchea" and to use the scheme of an "Indochina Federation" as a stepping stone for expansion towards other countries in Southeast Asia. The Soviet Union wants to control Southeast Asia through Vietnam." China's "counter-attack" /!/, however, is "a necessary action of self-defense taken by any sovereign state in accordance with article 51 of the United Nations Charter. . .Following the ending of the anti-United States war and the realization of unification, Vietnam had quickly embarked on the path of aggression and expansion abroad." The Vietnamese authorities have regarded China as the main obstacle to their pursuit of expansionism and have considered China their "No.1 enemy." "The greater and lesser hegemonists are working hand in glove."

"The Vietnam authorities think that as long as Vietnam claims to be a 'small nation,' sympathy will naturally go to it

irrespective of what evil it has done. Whether or not a nation
has ambitious designs, whether or not it is carrying out
aggression and expansion, depends not on its size but on its
political line and foreign policy. While history has seen
instances of a big power committing aggression, there is no
lack of instances of a big nation being the victim of aggression
and bullied by a small one. Is it not true that the small island
state Cuba, hiring itself out to Soviet social-imperialism, has
dispatched tens of thousands of mercenary troops across the
ocean to become the hatchet-man of the U.S.S.R.? Vietnam is
following its footsteps and even excelled it. In order to realize
its ambition of dominating Indochina and Southeast Asia,
Vietnam is bullying all its neighbors. . .The Soviet Union uses
Vietnam as a power and accomplice in establishing its sphere
of influence and carrying out aggression and expansion in
Southeast Asia and Asia as a whole."

The facts show that in dealing with the Vietnam
aggressors, conciliation and forbearance no longer worked.
"The Vietnam authorities have gone too far in bullying others.
Driven beyond forbearance, Chinese frontier troops have been
forced to rise in limited counter-attack in defense of our own
border." China did not want to resort to armed force. "We do
not want a single inch of Vietnam territory but neither will we
tolerate wanton incursions into Chinese territory. . .After
counter-attacking the Vietnam aggressor, as he deserves, the
Chinese frontier troops will return and strictly keep to
defending the border of their country."

"The Vietnamese-Kampuchean Treaty" was a "hoax."
Signed on February 18, 1979 by Pham Yan Dong during his
hurried visit to Phnom Penh, it was nothing but a clumsy trick
to deceive world-public opinion and legalize Vietnam's
annexation of Kampuchea, enabling the Vietnamese authorities to formally incorporate Kampuchea into their "Indochina
Federation." The "treaty" also revealed the Vietnam authorities' regional hegemonist ambitions. In 1977, the Vietnamese
government had compelled Laos to sign a so-called "friendship
and cooperation treaty" with them, which established a
"special relationship," allowing them to have the right of
stationing thousands of troops in Laos and actually to control
that country.

Chinese writers had pointed out long ago the growing hegemonistic and ambitious Vietnam and the Soviet Union's lending support to this client state. On occasion, on the other hand, of Nguyen Giap's report to the Vietnam National Assembly, the Assembly designated China as a "dangerous enemy" of Vietnam and claimed that Vietnam's moves against Kampuchea, its close link with Laos, and the setting up of an Indochina Federation were within its "legitimate rights." The Soviet Union was praised as "the strong bulwark of world peace and revolution." Giap "showered abuse" on China from the Qin dynasty up to the present time. During the 30 years since coming into existence, Communist China has been helping Vietnam, but only for the purpose of "controlling" it.(6)

The C.P.R.'s "Self-Defensive Counterattack" against Vietnam. The Kampuchean Issue

In a 1979 editorial, "The Crux of the Sino-Vietnamese Dispute," *Renmin Ribao* asserted that the Chinese frontier troops were engaged in "launching a self-defensive counterattack. . .a just action to safeguard China's sovereignty and territorial integrity."(7) They had captured important Vietnamese cities and towns, "thereby deflating the Vietnam aggressors' wild arrogance and exploding the myth of their invincibility. China did not want "an inch" of Vietnam territory. All we want is a boundary of peace and tranquility." The boundary between the two states has been "demarcated long ago." "No serious disputes" existed over these boundaries which could not be resolved. The "drastic deterioration" of Chinese-Vietnamese relations was "entirely the result of the policies of national expansionism and of hostility towards China and Chinese residents implemented by Vietnamese authorities with the backing of Soviet social-imperialism." Even while Chinese troops were withdrawing from the Vietnamese border regions, they were incessantly harassed, Chinese border areas were shelled, and anti-Chinese sentiments "fanned up." Soviet and Vietnamese authorities, "big and small hegemonists," were slandering the so-called Chinese "aggression."

Beijing Review raised the question, "what led up to the Sino-Vietnam border conflict?"(8) Soon after the war against

the United States had come to an end, the Hanoi leadership
started to regard the establishment of hegemony in Southeastern Asia as its state policy. The swell-headed authorities in
Hanoi described Vietnam as the "third military power in the
world" and carried out frontier expansion abroad as early as
1975. Vietnam had dispatched troops to Kampuchea's Way
Island, stationed armed forces in Laos and occupied six isles of
China's Nausha Islands. In recent years, Vietnam had raised
the question of so-called "disputed border sections," created
troubles in the border areas and instigated large-scale
incidents of bloodshed by opening fire on Chinese frontier
guards and inhabitants. In December 1978, it launched a
massive invasion of Kampuchea. The Vietnamese authorities
have regarded China as the biggest obstacle to their pursuit of
regional hegemonism. They were clamoring that China was
"the number one enemy" of Vietnam.

The border conflict provoked by Vietnam with China
would have been inconceivable without Soviet support and
instigation. In fact, it was only after Vietnam formally joined
the Council of Mutual Economic Assistance in 1978 and then
signed a treaty of a military nature with the Soviet Union that
Hanoi became more and more unscrupulous. "The Soviet
Union has a pawn for its expansion into the Asian and Pacific
region. It is precisely under the pretext of the Sino-Vietnamese
border conflict that the Soviet union has dispatched naval
vessels to the ports of Da Nang and Cam Ranh and to the
South China Sea, thus constituting a direct menace to the
Southeastern Asian countries, aggravating its threat to Japan's
oil supply route, and strengthening its stance of contention
with the United States in the Asian-Pacific and Indian Ocean
regions. Secondly, the Soviet Union needs Vietnam to
spearhead its anti-China campaign. . ." Furthermore, on its
way to seeking "world domination," the U.S.S.R. needs to
upset China's advance towards modernization. If China
"remains poor and backward, it can only make limited
contributions to the people of the world and play a limited role
in "checking the Kremlin's strategy for world hegemony." The
U.S.S.R., therefore, needs a "Cuba of the East" to make
trouble around China's borders. The Vietnamese have gone in
for a full-scale "clearing-up" action also on their side of the
border.

While carrying on aggression and expansion abroad, Hua Guo Feng charged, Vietnam had practiced a policy of genocide at home and created the world-shocking tragedy of Indochinese refugees. Under President Ho Chi Minh, the Vietnamese people had fought heroically over long years to win national liberation and defend national independence. But, after his demise, "the Vietnam authorities betrayed his political line step by step and feverishly pushed a policy of expansionism," which had Soviet backing. The invasion of Kampuchea by Vietnam was "by no means a local issue, but an important component of Soviet attempts to establish an "Asian collective system" in furtherance of their strategy of seeking world hegemony.

Soviet social imperialism was indulging in phantasies when it thought that, militarily equipped as it was and supported by a few nations playing the role of hatchetmen, it could lord over the world.(9) It "cannot hope to check the historical trend against hegemonism." This global Soviet expansion, directed against "its arch-rival, the U.S., was to deny its opponent the possibility of hegemony in the world. The purpose of this propaganda line was apparent: to arouse interest in the U.S. for a global alliance, which would include the C.P.R. and was aimed against the Soviet Union.

During the year 1985, if not earlier, there has been a noticeable decline in the number of anti-Soviet Chinese articles and commentaries and the shrillness of the criticisms, but no complete turnabout. That the C.P.R. feels as strongly as ever about basic divisive issues separating Beijing and Moscow is manifested by the article, "All Talk, no action," by Tang Tiauri.(10) Referring to a recent article in *Pravda* and to the utterances of Soviet Vice-Foreign Minister M. S. Kapitsa to a Moscow press conference that if a political solution was found to the Kampuchean problem, the Vietnamese troops would possibly withdraw from Kampuchea in 1987, the Chinese commentator in *Beijing Review* questioned whether "this rhetoric" really represented a new Soviet policy on the Kampuchean issue. Kapitsa asked the Democratic Kampuchea President S. N. Sihanouk to negotiate with the Phnom Penh regime, but on condition that they first cut all ties with the Democratic Kampuchean Army. This was "clearly a ploy" to disrupt the unity of the three resistance forces of the

Democratic Kampuchean people. Such elections as he held out would be under Soviet control and would only legitimize the Heng Samrin puppet regime and lead to the establishment of an "Indochina Federation" which was backed by the Kremlin and controlled by Hanoi. Moscow merely wanted the international community to recognize Vietnam's occupation of Kampuchea and Soviet hegemony in Indochina. The fact that in 1985 the Soviet Union had doubled its annual economic and military aid to Vietnam to 4 billion U.S. dollars clearly revealed Soviet ultimate goals in the region. "Moscow's attempts to rely on its economic and military superiority and use of its power politics to conquer a weak country directly or indirectly should not be allowed."

On Soviet Goals in Northern and Western Europe

While the Soviet Union was threatening Asiatic countries and was pursuing a "southward strategy in both Europe and Asia, it represented a special threat to Northern ad Western Europe.

According to *Beijing Review*, of November 23, 1981, "Soviet Military Threat to Northern Europe," We Yingchun asserted that the Soviet Union "has built up massive forces and deployed a great number of guided missiles around Northern Europe."(11) Its military bases on the Kola Peninsula are the largest in the world. Its Northern Fleet, the Soviet Union's largest, operates out of Murmansk. Murmansk is ringed by Backfire bomber bases and SS-20 missiles that can hit all the North European countries and Western Europe as well. There are 170 submarines and about 700 attack planes in the coastal areas of the Baltic Sea, a sea the Soviet Union has been advocating to turn into a "sea of peace." The Soviets were turning the Barents and Norwegian Seas into Soviet "inland seas" and the Baltic Sea into a "Russian lake." A British newspaper has pointed out that, once war breaks out, the Soviet Northern Fleet would join the Soviet Baltic Fleet to seize control of Norwegian ports through a two-pronged attack. The Soviet forces would also move through the three passages between Greenland, the Faroes, and the Shetlands to dominate the eastern Atlantic to thwart United States endeavors to reinforce Europe by sea.

An estimated 150 sorties were flown by Soviet aircraft over the air defense area of Iceland in 1979. Soviet military planes also overfly the Baltic region westward in practice runs close to Copenhagen, the capital of Denmark. Northern European countries have often discovered unidentified submarines in their waters; Sweden alone discovered 17 submarines last year. Soviet military exercises with Northern European countries as the imagined enemy grow in frequency and in scale. The Soviet Union also infiltrates large numbers of agents into North European countries to collect military intelligence and carry out subversion and sabotage. The U.S.S.R. obdurately lays claim to 150,000 square kilometers of the continental shelf of the Barents Sea—which Norway challenges. In negotiations with Sweden, the Soviet Union has tried to push its continental shelf right up to the coast of Gotland. It has tried to annex the Spitzbergen Islands of Norway. The Soviet Union for many years and in many ways has tried to make itself out to be the defender of European peace, repeatedly declaring that it is concerned about the "peace" and the "security" of Northern Europe and that it wants to develop "good relations" with these countries. Not long ago, the U.S.S.R. has expressed its willingness to "guarantee" the security of these non-nuclear countries in the capacity of a nuclear power.

China is greatly interested in the unity and strength of Western Europe as a counterweight to the U.S.S.R. There is clearly a natural identity of interest between the two regions of China and Western Europe, both "neighbors" and targets of the Soviet Union. An article in *Beijing Review* of August 4, 1986, "Western Europe's role in U.S.-Soviet Rivalry(12), points to similarities between China's and West Europe's policies. West European governments, though allies of the U.S. government, try to restrain the superpowers' arms race, while "retaining for themselves a positive and independent role." Without exception, they are "seeking to develop in a relaxed international environment" and are, therefore, promoting dialogue between the U.S. and the Soviet union and "detente between Eastern and Western Europe."

Western Europe's contradictions with the U.S. are something the Soviets can make use of. But Western Europe's fear of the Soviet military threat is a guarantee for U.S.-Western European partnership. The Soviet Union sees

Western Europe as one of "three centers of capitalist force" and tries to isolate it from the U.S. It also engages in maneuvers aimed at undermining the unity among West European states. The U.S., in turn, hopes Western Europe's united forces were capable of resisting Soviet expansion into Europe and some parts of the Third World. West European friendliness to Eastern Europe "poses a threat" to the Soviet Union. The Soviets aim at "scuttling" the West European-American alliance. But Western Europe is a force for world peace and stability.

Soviet Imperialism, the Third World, and the C.P.R.

On occasion of Deng's visit to Washington, he was quoted as having referred to the U.S.A's and China's hostility toward each other for the past 30 years and having welcomed that "this abnormal state of affairs" was "over at last."(13) "Our two countries have different social systems and ideologies," but our "interests require that we view our bilateral relations in the context of the overall international situation and with a long-term strategic perspective." Both countries had committed themselves "that neither should seek hegemony and that each was opposed to efforts by any other country or groups of countries to establish hegemony." According to Deng, "the world today was far from tranquil. . .We do not wish to fight a war unless it is forced upon us." Firmly set against a new world war, Deng continued, "one of the objects of China's foreign policy is to delay /!/ its outbreak." The outlook of official China could hardly have been more defeatist. Still, the only chance for all concerned—this was the very gist of Deng's appeal to the United States—was a grand alliance against the Soviet Union. At the same time, any lingering fear that China might ever become the aggressor was completely dismissed.

Deng refuted the allegations that China was "warlike" and that it was "a potential source" of global conflagration. Throughout modern history, China has been a victim of aggression, and "even today it is under the threat of aggression. There is no reason for us to start a world war, nor are we qualified to do so." "The 'danger' of war comes precisely from the warmongers who are daily propagating an illusion of peace and detente... It is gratifying to note that a growing number of people of insight in the United States are coming to recognize this danger."

At a luncheon with American journalists, Deng focussed on three agreements concluded between the United States and the U.S.S.R., in 1963, 1972, and 1974 respectively. As a result, in 1974 even American public opinion acknowledged that the military strength of the two countries was on a par. While China was not opposed to American-Soviet agreements to limit strategic arms, Deng warned against illusions that the Soviet build-up could be restrained or reduced through mere negotiations and agreements. "We /Chinese/ are of the view that the danger of war comes from the Soviet Union... So the thing that we can all do is that we should try to hamper and undermine whatever they do and frustrate what they try to do in any part of the world."(14)

Japan, according to Deng, while a friend of the C.P.R., was a special target of Soviet threats.(15) In reply to a question by Walter Cronkite, referring to Deng's suggestion by a *Time* reporter, of concluding a pact between Japan, the United States, and China, Deng came close to confirm it, though he subsequently disavowed it: "In order to oppose hegemonism and to safeguard world peace, security, and stability, the United States, Europe, Japan, and China, and other Third World /!/ countries (the latter was going beyond Deng's statement to the *Time* reporter) should unite and earnestly deal with the challenge of the danger of war. We do not need any kind of pact or an alliance. What we need is a common understanding of the situation and common efforts." To a further question of Cronkite why Deng felt that he had a better understanding of the real nature of the Soviet threat "than the United States leadership," he answered evasively that the Chinese government hoped "that the United States will adopt more effective measures," and stronger ones, to deal with the challenges posed by hegemonism. There were also strong clues of China's impending military action against Vietnam, against "local hegemonism," supported though it was by the Soviet Union.

On occasion of the 5th anniversary of the conclusion of the Sino-Japanese Treaty of Peace and Friendship in 1979, the General Secretary of the C.P.C. Hu Yaobang visited Japan. Editor Mu Youlin voiced then the hope that the visit would provide "a new impetus for Sino-Japanese friendship which has been improving steadily, since the establishment of diplomatic relations between the two countries."(16) In the ongoing socialist modernization drive, the Chinese people are working with the single idea of overcoming backwardness in the nation's economy and technology. There are many ways in which the two nations can learn from and complement each other. . .The Sino-Japanese Treaty. . .solemnly proclaims that both sides will not seek hegemony and will oppose the attempt by any other country to establish hegemony." The only country which, in China's view, pursued hegemonistic goals in that part of the Pacific region was, of course, the U.S.S.R.

The U.S.S.R. and the Role of Cuba

The U.S.S.R. made use not only of Vietnam, as seen, but also of Cuba in the pursuit of her imperialistic global interests. "With Cuba and Vietnam as its falcon and hound, the Soviet Union has started a southward offensive, from Africa and the Middle East to Southeastern Asia, to seek strategic war materials, to occupy strategic military bases, and to control transportation lines. It is trying as best it can to complete its global deployment to attain world supremacy."(17) "The Soviet hegemonists are insatiable. Their ambition is to dominate the whole world. Compromises or concessions will not get the Soviet hegemonists to call a halt to their expansionism, much less to put away their murderous knives and become a Buddha. On the contrary, they will only become even more arrogant and greedy."

In an article of September 21, 1979, *Beijing Review* wrote on "Cuba-Moscow's advance post in the Western hemisphere:"(18) "For years the Soviets had wanted to turn Cuba into an unsinkable aircraft carrier, only 90 miles from U.S. soil; and make this island its bridgehead for expansion into the Western hemisphere." This assessment hardly differs from the official American assessment. Even the liberal American judgment, though pointing to the indigenous economic sources of social unrest in Central America and the Caribbean as roots of persistent trouble, had few illusions about its propagandistic exploitation by the Soviet Union. The presence of even a small number of Soviet troops has worried the world public and is "seen as a move to bring the United States within easy striking distance of strategic weapons." Moscow was trying to wrest spheres of influence from the United States into its own "backyard" to serve its own global strategy.

As American public opinion sees it, the Soviet Union has posed right outside the United States front door a "new challenge." Exposing Soviet global strategy, Latin American commentaries stress that the Soviet drive to turn Cuba into a forward post and to continue its military build-up was not only directed against the United States, but also against Latin American countries, or even far-away states in Asia and Africa.

Back in 1975, when the Soviet Union had dispatched Cuban mercenaries to intervene in newly independent Angola and plunged the country into war and suffering, no effective measures were taken internationally to check Moscow's criminal actions. After attaining its goal in Angola, the Soviet Union sent more and more Cuban mercenaries to more and more African countries. It provoked a large-scale armed conflict in the Horn of Africa. Now, Soviet military advisors and Cuban mercenaries are found even as far as the southern tip of the Arabian peninsula at the entrance to the Red Sea. The whole Arab world was uneasy. "Its appetite whetted by having met with no obstruction in using Cuba to rampage and wreak havoc in Africa, the Soviet Union is now fostering a 'Cuba of the East'—Vietnam." In the East, Vietnam had dispatched 100,000 soldiers into Kampuchea, and occupied that country in "a blitzkrieg of the Hitlerian type."

Cuba—the "Sixteenth" Soviet Republic

Long ago Castro's Cuba had shown strong sympathies for the C.P.R. Its radical revolutionary stance appealed to the expansionist and missionary drive of the new Cuba. But after the Sino-Soviet split deepened, Cuba, economically and militarily dependent on the Soviet Union, was forced to align herself more closely with the U.S.S.R. against China.(19) Subsequently, Sino-Cuban relations cooled off and even grew hostile. Though Cuba has a population of less than ten million, the number of Soviet "advisory" experts, diplomats, military personnel, engineers, teachers, etc., totals 150,000.

Moreover, Soviet businessmen, cultural workers, and intelligence officers stream in and out of Havana and other Cuban cities on temporary missions. In 1964, after his visit to the U.S.S.R., Castro announced Cuba's relations with the Soviet Union had "entered the highest stage." In 1972, he declared that Cuba had "spiritually and economically" achieved integration with the community headed by the Soviet Union. "Integration" actually meant "Sovietization." Clearly, Cuba was no longer nonaligned. "Reality shows Cuba is the 'armed fist' of the Kremlin in Africa today and will be so in other continents later." "The Soviet Union has not only equipped and reorganized Cuba's armed forces but also has sent its military personnel into Cuba. Today in place of Cuban pilots who have been sent to Africa on combat missions, Soviet pilots are flying patrol over Cuba; Soviet warships and submarines are cruising in Cuban waters, and Soviet tanks, army vehicles and self-propelled tanks rumble over Cuban soil.

The Soviet Union placed such a huge stake on Cuba "not to protect the 'island of freedom' but to promote Soviet global strategy." This goal, apparently, is facilitated if Cuba is fully "integrated" or "Sovietized," if it becomes a sort of 16th Republic of the U.S.S.R. According to *Beijing Review*, Cuba was now considered "a Soviet military stronghold in Latin America."(20) Though a small country, Cuba's military strength has approached or surpassed that of Brazil. Since the 1960s, Moscow has provided several billion U.S. dollars worth of weapons to Cuba, which has approximately 200,000 soldiers and nearly one million troops in its reserves. Cuba has become one "huge barrack" and has been, and is, using its military superiority in Latin American countries. In the mid-seventies, Cuba has dispatched more than 52,000 troops or military personnel stationed in 17 Asian, African, and Latin American countries, and sent an especially large number of troops to Angola and Ethiopia. Flaunting the banner of supporting the national-liberation movement, "it has made use of the turbulent situation in the region to foster pro-Soviet and pro-Cuban indigenous forces." Her "expansion and infiltration" of Central America and the Caribbean region had been carried out with the full backing of the Soviet Union. President Reagan, feeling that "the traditional interests" of the United States in this area were seriously challenged, has made "countermoves" by increasing military and economic assistance to dictatorships in some Central American countries such as El Salvador. Thus Beijing, while not acquitting either superpower, leans, as fas as Central America is concerned, more heavily toward criticism of the Soviet Union's Latin American policy than that of the U.S.A. The same may be said of Beijing's judgment on Soviet and American Mideast policy.

China on Soviet Mideast Policy

An early account in *Beijing Review* of the Egyptian-Israeli peace treaty of 1979 was remarkably objective and detached, compared to usual Chinese observations on the Mideast, and showed no opposition to it. Avoiding taking sides for either Sadat or the P.L.O., it was, however, critical of Soviet policy, which had consistently been opposed to direct Egyptian-Israeli contacts. When Sadat journeyed to Israel, the Soviet press had raised a hue and cry, attacking him for "currying favor with imperialism" and "betraying" the Arab people. Sharply refuting these Soviet attacks, the Chinese author concluded: "The Russians never play a constructive role."(21) The Soviet media have unleashed a torrent of wild criticism on the progress achieved by Carter's visit to Egypt and Israel. *Tass* had claimed "that the treaty might ignite new flames of war." This shows how rankled the Soviet Union was at being left out of the Mideast peace talks and how it was doing its "utmost to disrupt United States activities on the Mideast question."

Chinese comments on Mideast problems, even if they occasionally approached standards of objectivity, were colored by wishful thinking or pious recommendations. Describing the Arab-Israeli situation, the reporters and analysts always pointed to the need for Arab unity. They regretted again and again the hostility of Arabs toward each other, their being split along religious and sectarian lines, and rent by differences of power, resources, politics, and individual rivalries. Beijing was quite hostile to the Soviet Union and had few illusions about the Soviet "threat from the North," but made a point to take a stance critical both of the Soviet and American policy in the Mideast and, in general, to preserve the appearance of neutrality and evenhandedness, though it obviously wished U.S. military presence in the region as an essential counterpoise to the U.S.S.R. Referring to the Iran-Iraqi war, the Beijing journal admitted that it had split the Arab and Islamic countries. It tendered advice to the effect that complicated questions can be solved only "by peaceful consultations" and also that the Gulf region should be "guarded against superpowers' intervention."(22)

Beijing Review also displayed some objectivity in its discussion of the Iranian situation.(23) In their contention for world domination, "both superpowers have scrambled for Iran because of its strategic importance and its rich oil resources. . .both sides have, in fact, poked their noses in the country. In this test of strength, Washington has been on the defensive, Moscow on the offensive."

Discussing the Iranian-American dispute, heated up in consequence of the hostage situation, the Chinese press was reluctant to take the side of the U.S., but it singled out the U.S.S.R. for criticism. *Beijing Review* wrote: "Throughout the crisis, the Soviet propaganda machine has continuously churned out material to exacerbate Iran-U.S. relations."

Even before the invasion of Afghanistan proper in December 1979, Chinese journals and dailies had observed strong political tremors in the Mideast, especially in Afghanistan, Iran, and Turkey, all of which "share common boundaries with the Soviet Union" and have experienced "increasing pressure from the North." Since February 1981, "the Soviet Union has been. . .sowing discord between Iran's minority nationalities and the central government. It has instigated unrest among the Kurds, Turkomans and Baluchis from the north to the south in an attempt to dismantle Iran." In Turkey, the Soviet Union has caused turmoil by taking advantage of the Kurdish problem in the areas adjacent to the borders and smuggling larger quantities of weapons there. The Kurdish Turkish Senator Kamuram Inan has charged that the Soviet Union was trying to "build a pro-Moslem state" there. It has been reported that the "independent state" would include the Kurdish areas in Iran, Iraq, and Syria, and be linked with the Kurdish areas within the Soviet Union. The attempt, in Beijing's view, was obviously an important step in the Soviet drive southward to the Persian Gulf.

Repeatedly the C.P.R. pledged "unswerving support for the just struggle of the Arab and Palestinian people. We strongly condemn the expansion and rivalry of the superpowers /!/ in the Middle East and are firmly opposed to the sinister superpower attempt to sow discord among the Arab countries and to Israel's peremptory attitude of obstructing an overall settlement of the Middle East question."(24) The superpowers, *Beijing Review* claimed, had no sincere desire for disarmament. In view of the geographic remoteness of the C.P.R. from the Mideast and the disunity among Third World nations — some of which wage bitter and prolonged war against each other — all declarations for the "united struggle" of these states, were, however, mere expressions of pious hopes.

In South Yemen, Soviet deployment, according to Beijing, aimed at closing in on the Persian Gulf from behind. Soviet naval and air missiles and logistic and satellite tracking stations have been built there, and installations for accommodating ten submarines at a time are under construction. The Soviet Union had stepped up its offensive against Saudi Arabia. It had interfered in the armored conflict between South and North Yemen by sending big shipments of arms and Cuban troops to South Yemen. The United States in turn had rushed large numbers of the latest planes and armed weapons to North Yemen. Despite the superpower confrontation also in the Mid-East, the Chinese voices of alerting and warning the Arab world were primarily directed "against Soviet expansionism" in this region.

Ghaddafi's Libya's support of terrorism and U.S. retaliation in an attack on Libya itself in 1986, revealed that Beijing was far from genuinely neutral. It resorted to sharp criticism, "condemnation," of the U.S. military strike against Libya. It claimed that the attack against the territory of the Socialist People's Libyan Jamahiriya by U.S. military forces "drastically worsened" the situation in the Mediterranean and caused "deep concern and anxiety" to the Chinese government. Though Beijing asserted that it had "always opposed and condemned all forms of terrorism and opposed the use of terrorist means" in carrying out a political struggle, it completely ignored here the use and support of terrorism by Lybia!

On April 16, 1986, *Renmin Ribao*, China's official newspaper, declared that "terrorist activities" which injure and kill innocent people are undoubtedly always offensive and,

disgust most of the world's nations and peoples.(25) The
Chinese government opposed and condemned all forms of
terrorism and disapproved of political struggles by terrorist
means. "But at the same time we hold that no country has the
right to launch military attacks on other countries to violate
their territorial integrity, under the pretext /!/ of anti-
terrorism." Beijing would "call on both the US and Libya to
exercise restraint and halt in their hostilities and seek a proper
settlement through dialogue and other peaceful means." It is
quite obvious that propagandistic considerations, lining up in
this case with Libya, the Arab and Moslem states and
remaining in a competitive relationship with the anti-
American position of the Soviet Union and the East European
bloc, heavily outweighed the need of keeping on good terms
with the U.S. The C.P.R. leaders may also have figured that a
mere oral "condemnation," without tangible deeds to follow,
would be understood and "forgiven" by Washington and
would not seriously affect the latter's relations with Beijing.
(26)

India and Nonalignment

India is a leading state among the nonaligned nations of
the Third World. Democratic at home, it was after World
War II, engaged in military conflicts with Communist China,
and is the rival of Pakistan on the Indian subcontinent.
Belying the importance of the impact of ideology upon the
making of alliances, India has established a friendly
relationship with the Soviet Union, while its dictatorial
neighbors in Asia, China and Pakistan, have developed a good
relationship with the United States.

In a report on Prime Minister Rajiv Gandhi and his
journey to Moscow, the authors Tang Ziushan and Xi
Shuguang noted both the agreement reached between India
and the Soviet Union as well as their apparent continuing
disagreements.(27) The Soviet Union had received Gandhi's
firm support "on a wide range of foreign policy issues,"
including criticism of the United States' Star Wars program
and its trade embargo on Nicaragua. Moscow, in turn, lauded
India' leading role in the nonaligned movement and reiterated
its support for a peace zone in the Indian Ocean. However, the

two countries apparently agreed to disagree on several key issues, including Afghanistan. While refusing to criticize the U.S.S.R. openly, Gandhi told the Moscow press conference that India was against any country intervening in the internal affairs of another. Later, when asked how he reacted to Gorbachev's proposal for an "all-Asia forum," he declined twice to give a direct answer. Gandhi also appeared cautious on questions concerning India's relations with the United States. He said that Indo-American relations had been good, bilateral trade had increased, and that "today the United States is our largest trading partner." Just before Gandhi set off on his visit to Moscow, United States Commerce Secretary Malcolm Baldridge had rushed to New Delhi to sign a major agreement on transfers of high technology, including computers, electronics, and telecommunications equipment. The authors concluded that, while both superpowers showed great interest in better relations with India—a situation which no doubt will benefit that country—it still "remains to be seen which of the two countries will get the upperhand." They gave no clear indication of whether the C.P.R. would prefer the one over the other.

China, Korea, and Japan

Following the end of World War II, Soviet troops, disarming Japanese military units, occupied the northern half of Korea and American troops the southern half of the peninsula. The attempt of Communist North Korea to invade South Korea generated war between the two Koreas and, ultimately, caused war between the U.S., the U.N., and Communist China.

Since the end of the Korean War, North Korea has often veered between her two neighbors, China and the Soviet Union, though it has tried to maintain relations with both.(28) Especially since 1969, with China's foreign relations conducted by Zhou Enlai, North Korea—ruled dictatorially by Kim In-song, a fierce nationalist and totalitarian Communist,— remained intent on unifying both Koreas and on extending his power into the South. In foreign affairs, he has resisted Soviet pressure to join in the encirclement of the C.P.R. North Korea seems to pursue the policy of keeping equidistance vis-à-vis

Beijing and Moscow. Recently, an American observer concluded that North Korea "in reality is in neither camp and probably never will be."(29)

The difference between Chinese rhetorics and the C.P.R.'s actual policy frequently becomes apparent also in Beijing's endorsing the peaceful reunification of Korea. Yet, while China talks, it is unable to act. According to Hua Guo Feng, the C.P.R. has opposed the perpetuation of Korea's division. A reunification resolution adopted by the United Nations General Assembly at its 30th session asked for the United States to withdraw all its troops and armaments and to stop its military aid to South Korea. The United Nations Command in South Korea must be disbanded. In Hua's opinion, the proposal of the Democratic People's Republic of Korea on holding United States-Korean talks and replacing the armistice with a peace agreement was reasonable and should meet with a positive response. As for the discussion of the reunification issue through a north-south dialogue, it is purely the Korean people's own business, which brooks no foreign interference.

While many of the Asiatic countries are underdeveloped and also nonaligned states, Japan is a highly developed capitalist nation as well as a democratic country and aligned with the United States. It has become increasingly friendly disposed to Communist China and vice versa. In 1979, Deng had referred to the Soviets' recent military build-up on Japan's four northern islands that have been occupied by the U.S.S.R. since the close of World War II. Since May 1978, Soviet military strength on these four islands had quadrupled. Barracks had been built and 5,000-6,000 Soviet troops, heavily armed, were stationed there. The Hokkaido coast was now within range of Soviet guns. "This build-up is a danger pointed at Japan's throat." The Japanese government, in a note of protest of February 5, had demanded that these bases be immediately dismantled. The Soviets, however, countered that Japan interfered in Soviet internal affairs, since the Kurile Islands were allegedly Soviet territory. The U.S.S.R. was also clearly annoyed at Japan's critical attitude toward the Vietnamese invasion of Kampuchea, and at Japan's close coordination of policy with the U.S. and ASEAN nations on this issue.

Exaggerating or Minimizing the Soviet "Threat."
The Situation in 1986.

The Chinese authorities and the Chinese press have made
no attempt to minimize the growing threat to China's security
as a result of the Soviet invasion of Afghanistan, the support
given to Vietnam in Kampuchea and Indochina as a whole,
the consequence of the concentration of troops along the
Sino-Soviet frontier, and of the tremendous Soviet naval
build-up during the last decades. On one hand, the C.P.R.
alerts its population, on the other, it does not wish unduly to
alarm it. It tries to explain to the Chinese the Soviet military
escalation primarily in terms of the pervading Soviet-
American competitive rivalry, and attempts at times to
soft-pedal China's concern over developments having adverse
geopolitical and military implications. After having deliberately exaggerated the long-term Soviet threat, the Chinese
leadership has apparently gained greater self-confidence: its
conviction that the Soviet Union will not venture to unleash
war against China and will avoid getting stuck in the morass of
a conflict with China's one-billion population, has apparently
grown stronger.

All this becomes also evident in an article by Shan Cheng,
"Second Siberian provides vital Link,"(30) where he discussed
the new Baikal-Amur Mainline (BAM) railroad which
stretches from Ust Kut to Komsomolsk-on-Amur, near the east
coast. In contradistinction to previous articles stressing the
Soviet threat to China, the article is virtually free of anti-Soviet
gibes. After stating that BAM is economically crucial to the
Soviet Union, since its planners hoped to develop Siberia—
"about half of the Soviet Union's total area"—with all its rich
resources as an independent industrial area, the author
conceded that BAM will also help the Soviet military to
improve its strategic situation in the east. With two rail links to
the Far East—and BAM following the route 200 to 500
kilometers north of the Trans-Siberian and three branches
connecting them together—"Soviet troops could be mobilized
quickly if the need arose." Transportation survivability during
wartime will be increased. All this will allow the Soviet Union
also to expand its influence in the Pacific region. What is
striking in this article is the absence of patent conclusions

regarding the mounting Soviet threat to China, which is posed by the new Soviet railroad. The greater distance of the new railroad from Chinese territory enhances Soviet security and would make any interference in Soviet traffic by Chinese wartime actions less likely.

The same appearance of detachment and seeming disinterestedness in major Soviet achievements and future development plans in Asia, close to the C.P.R.'s borders, is displayed in the article "The Soviet Union: Bringing Prosperity to Siberia" on November 19, 1985, when *Beijing Review* simply stated that "the Soviet government is forging ahead with the development of Siberia and the Far East region in order to set straight the unbalanced distribution of its industries and get ready for its take-off in the 21st century.(31) "Although Siberia and the Far Eastern Soviet region accounted for 57% of the entire Soviet territory, only 10% of the Soviet population was located there. Special reference was made to funds, technology, equipment, and loans provided by West European countries in the building of the Soviet natural gas pipeline and the progress in the building of the BAM railroad. But the complete omission of coming to grips with the strategic and geopolitical significance of these Soviet development plans in Asia for China's security is both startling and suspect. The C.P.R. clearly suppresses what must be its genuine concern!

The C.P.R.'s Peace Policy and the Soviets

The propagandistic appeal of a foreign policy which seems to be based upon striving for peace and shunning war is of such power that many a state is anxious to wrap itself into the mantle of pacifism.(32) In the words of *Beijing Review*, China has commanded increasing recognition as a major force behind peace and development in a world where "peace-loving forces have outstripped the growth of those bent on war." According to Foreign Minister Wu Xuequian's report to the fourteenth session of the Sixth National People's Congress Standing Committee, held in Beijing on January 16, 1986, international tension had been "eased in the past year." The superpowers had switched from a state of "stubborn confrontation to at least a blend of confrontation and dialogue." This "praiseworthy" policy had led to a measure of relaxation.

Still, it was not enough to pay lip-service to "ever popular" themes of shunning "military superiority," and "prevention of the outbreak of war;" what was needed were "drastic slashes of nuclear arsenals and halting the arms race from entering outer space—both of which are preconditions for a total ban and complete destruction of all nuclear weapons." The latter course would strengthen the C.P.R.'s position vis-à-vis the Soviet Union.

The Chinese Foreign Minister reeled off a number of "hot spots" in the world. Regarding Afghanistan, the Soviet Union had "shown no sincerity" or given any indications that it will "pull its troops out of the neighboring Muslim country." Concerning Kampuchea, the Vietnamese occupation troops have undertaken a dry-season offensive last year, but have failed to subdue the patriotic forces of Democratic Kampuchea led by Prince Nordon Sihanouk. A latent crisis prevailed in the Mideast "because of the stand of the U.S. and Israel and the meddling of the Soviet Union." (Israel's position is more sharply criticized than that of the U.S.) Though the dialogue between North and South Korea seemed to achieve "some tangible results last year, some ceasing of the tension along the boundary," military confrontation remained the norm. he situation in South Africa had definitely worsened. A current deadlock on the North-South dialogue, coupled with East-West confrontation, complicated world relations in 1985. The Chinese Foreign Minister called China's independent foreign policy of peace "sound and the most effective" in the C.P.R.'s history. China wished to develop friendly ties with all countries on the basis of the five Principles of Peaceful Coexistence. During the past year, 1985, the Chinese leadership had visited more than 40 countries and received leading representatives from as many states. The total number of nations having diplomatic relations with China had reached 134.

Special progress had been made in regard to Sino-Japanese relations. With the exchange of visits by the leaders of the C.P.R. and West European countries, China and Western Europe "now had more in common;" economic ties and trade between them had increased. "Heartening progress," according to Wu, had also been achieved in relations between China and the socialist countries in Eastern Europe. "China has furthered its unity and trade relations" with Rumania and Yugoslavia, and improved its relations with the German Democratic Republic, Poland, Hungary, Czechoslovakia, and Bulgaria. Sino-U.S. relations had been stable. While progress had been made in "bilateral cooperation" in the fields of economics, trade, science, and technology, the issue of Taiwan remained "the main barrier to better ties." Sino-Soviet relations had "improved to some extent" during the past 12 months, particularly in their economic relations and trade. But "no fundamental improvement has ever been in sight in the political relations between the two nations. The U.S.S.R. should not shun removing the political obstacles." The first thing to do, according to Wu, was for the Kremlin to stop supporting Vietnam in its aggression against Kampuchea. In this context, Wu did not list the other "obstacles," regularly cited, namely withdrawal of Soviet troops from the Sino-Soviet border, from the Mongolian People's Republic, and from Afghanistan, and the growing naval "encirclement."

Relations between the U.S.S.R. and Japan had deteriorated after the Soviet invasion of Afghanistan and Tokyo's joining in economic sanctions against Moscow in 1979.(33) At the funeral of K. Chernenko, Gorbachev and Nakasone had met, the first such meeting between the two countries' top leaders after twelve long and meager years. Tokyo, a staunch ally of Washington, was not only concerned about Afghanistan, but also, undoubtedly more so, by the number of Soviet missiles deployed in the Far East.

The first five-day Tokyo visit by the Soviet Foreign Minister Eduard Shevardnadze, resulted in new efforts to resume diplomatic ties after an eight-year impasse, but their long-disputed territorial problems remain unsolved. The last official visit of a former Japanese Prime Minister was undertaken in 1973. The joint final communique referred to cultural, trade, and tax agreements reached by the two sides and also to an agreement about the development of Siberia and about negotiations concerning the conclusion of a Japanese-Soviet peace treaty; but there were no definite agreements on the four northern islands, seized by the Soviet troops at the end of World War II.(34) Moscow still disputes that there exists a territorial dispute at all. At a press conference on January 19, 1986, Shevardnad emphasized that the Soviet Union had not changed its policy on the northern territories. No mention was made at the meeting in Tokyo of an Asian Security Conference, upheld by Gorbachev, but ignored by Tokyo. *Beijing Review* was not overly optimistic regarding "significant improvements" in Soviet-Japanese relations in the foreseeable future.(35)

While the number of anti-Soviet articles in the Chinese press has diminished especially since 1985 and hostility between Japan and the Soviet Union has also somewhat declined, the Chinese have persisted in sharp criticism of Vietnam, the Soviet ally.(36) *Beijing Review* cited Vo Dong Giang, a senior Vietnamese Foreign Ministry official, who recently called for the "peaceful coexistence" of South-East Asia, while his government continued to escalate aggression in Kampuchea and to ignore all UN resolutions to the contrary. In the view of Beijing, Hanoi tried to "legitimize the Heng Samrin regime and the Vietnamese presence in Kampuchea" by appealing to all factions in Kampuchea to enter into talks with the Heng Samrin government. The Vietnamese authorities had currently 180,000-200,000 troops in that country, trampling upon the sovereignty and territorial integrity of Kampuchea and had no intention of removing its troops until they completely controlled it.

IV

THROUGH THE SOVIET PRISM

A. The Soviet Case against Chinese Communism

A glance back: *The Sino-Soviet Honeymoon*: *1949-1950*

Sino-Soviet relations have had a long history. A revealing glance on these relations in the early 1950s was offered by the anonymous author of the article, "Eight Years in the Foreign Ministry"; he had been appointed Director of the Department of Soviet and East European Affairs in the Chinese Foreign Ministry, and on January 10, 1950, he accompanied Zhou Enlai to Moscow. His account and impressions published first as an essay and later as a book under his name, Wu Xiuquan, in Beijing, 1985, constitute an important contemporary source.(1)

According to his account, confirmed by many other sources, Stalin conceded that he had administered bad advice to the leaders of the C.P.C., warning them against continuing the civil war. In Moscow, while Mao had given general instructions to Premier Zhou Enlai, he had left it to him to write the details of the Sino-Soviet treaty for the C.P.R. Thus, the new treaty, signed on February 14, 1950, bore the marks of the careful revisions by Premier Zhou. Stalin himself, who was then "fairly modest and amiable" and "respectful and polite to the Chinese leaders," was also "obviously weak and old;" still, the Kremlin atmosphere was marked by an all-pervading personality cult. The Yugoslav defection had "infuriated" Stalin; and he was plainly worried that China might also follow the road of Yugoslavia and become independent of him. The Chinese delegation, the author disclosed, was most unfavorably impressed by the Soviets having shipped entire factories and machinery they had seized from Japan in Northeast China to Russia, all "in pursuit of self-interest."

While in Moscow, most of the Chinese guests did not attend the performance of the Russian ballet in honor of the

Chinese Revolution, since, in their view, the performance was based upon a distortion of history. In the words of the author, "it was no accident that the Soviet Union became later a superpower, bent on pursuing worldwide expansionism and hegemonism." All the symptoms of Soviet ambitions were already there in the era of Stalin; unpleasant things already happened in the early 1950s. Despite the grand display of the unbreakable friendship between China and the Soviet Union, the seeds of dissension had already been sown, and they were to grow and eventually drive the two countries apart. "The friendship of the two states at that time was marked by /significant/ contradictions."

These "contradictions" grew deeper in the late 1950s and early 1960s, and by leaps and bounds during the "Great Proletarian Cultural Revolution" and the last years of Mao's life.

Sino-Soviet Relations Since the 1970s

With the beginning of the Cultural Revolution in 1966, the mutual hostility of China and the U.S.S.R. intensified; it found expression both in the Chinese and Soviet press and publications. In both countries, the attention paid to developments in the other and to its foreign policy increased to a large extent. In November 1971, for instance, the Institutes of Oriental Studies and of the Far East jointly sponsored an all-union conference to discuss "The Problems of Soviet Sinology," published two years later.(2) In 1972, the Institute of the Far East commenced the publication of the journal *Problemy dalnego vostoka*. The declared purposes of this journal were, among others, to promote "normalization" between the two Communist powers, to illuminate China's contemporary civilization, and to "expose the struggle against the Maoists and Great Han nationalism."(3) The task of Soviet sinologists was "to help our Party" in its tireless struggle for the "purity of Marxism-Leninism" and to expose "any attempts at nationalist and Great Han distortions of the history of China."(4)

The Soviets described the C.P.R. as a "bourgeois-bureaucratic dictatorship." Its origins lay with the policies of Mao and his following and in the prevailing of bourgeois ideology among the masses.(5) Some Soviet analysts voiced the opinion that the P.R.C. was in an early stage of the transition to socialism; others implied or maintained that a retrogression to capitalism was a possibility in China. Several works, for example *Critique of Mao Tse-Tung*'s Theoretical Conceptions (Moscow, 1972), stressed the "militarization" of China's towns and countryside and asserted that Mao did not understand Marxism-Leninism. His concepts were to be subjective and idealistic and based on Confucianism rather than Marxism. He was adopting the policy of self-sufficiency because of his chauvinistic leanings. He also overemphasized the role of violence and adventurism in securing and maintaining power. Other Soviet sinologists stressed that the Chinese realized only a fraction of their aid commitments; in Africa, for instance, 30%. The C.P.R. also tried to pitch rich nations against poor ones. The common denominator of many of China's policies was, plainly, hostility to the Soviet Union. Though many Soviet experts on China agreed on fundamentals, there were clearly some disagreements among them.

Lin Piao's fall in 1971 produced several Soviet commentaries which indicated that he had represented pro-Soviet elements in the C.P.R. His name was linked with Kao Kang, the late Manchurian Party boss, and with Peng-Teh-huai and Liu Shao-chi, who were also considered pro-Soviet. Still, *Izvestia* and *Pravda* offered different assessments of the position of Liu Shao-chi toward the U.S.S.R.

In general, the Soviets did not question that China was a socialist state, but were puzzled about its anti-Soviet and anti-socialist policies. They pointed to the weakness of China's material base to explain apparent contradictions in the C.P.R. and outright retrogressions. Most Soviet analysts were appalled at China's apparent collusion with the U.S. Some, however, held that this cooperation would in the end prove only temporary and tactical.

With the Cultural Revolution losing steam, *Kommunist*, welcomed the apparent restoration of the role of the Chinese Party and its seeming return to the road of friendship with the U.S.S.R. and to the struggle against imperialism.(6-7) With Mao's end approaching, Sino-Soviet mutual relations would be nil, unless Beijing repudiated Maoism in an unmistakable manner.

In 1976, there appeared in Moscow a book on the China problem for Party workers.(8) According to it, Mao, conversing with foreigners, said that in the event of a Soviet-American conflagration, China's sympathies would be on the American side. Beijing had tried to push Washington toward hard positions vis-à-vis the U.S.S.R. and, in case of a deterioration of the Beijing-Moscow relationship, Beijing would like to obtain a guarantee at least of benevolent neutrality from the U.S.

Following the death of Mao, the Soviets stopped polemicizing with the P.R.C. for about seven months. Their broadcasts to China offered the resumption of good relations and the return of the glorious days of close cooperation and alliance. From the rostrum of the UN, Foreign Minister A. Gromyko held out the olive branch of "normalization," and a few weeks later, Brezhnev made similar conciliatory gestures. But when China did not respond, Moscow resumed its anti-Maoist propaganda.

After the purge of the "Gang of Four," including Mao's widow, Chiang Ching, and the emergence of Hua Kuo-feng as the C.P.C. Party Chairman, the Soviet KGB agent Victor Louis, writing in *France-Soir* (Oct. 1976) welcomed it that through the purge the "most anti-Soviet of Chinese leaders" had been eliminated.(9) As long as Mao's widow had been at the helm, there was "no chance of reconciliation between China and Russia." According to Louis, Moscow had set its hopes on some Chinese military leaders of the older generation, with whom the U.S.S.R. thought it could strike a deal.

Both sides took the initiative to move toward mutual negotiations. A Chinese reply to the Soviet initiative in February 1978 stated, however, that real deeds and not hollow statements(10) were required. For instance, a withdrawal of Soviet troops from the border area and from Mongolia were the prerequisite for any successful negotiations. After Mao's death, talks were resumed in 1977, but broke down again. Both sides seemed alarmed when the other improved relations with the U.S.

According to Soviet analysts, discontent was growing among all classes of the Chinese populace, workers, peasants, and intellectuals. The protest took the form of mass

demonstrations and big character posters.(11) The Beijing
leadership was moving to the right. The Chinese army was the
most influential force in the country. Maoism was still the core
of contemporary Chinese ideology. The P.R.C.'s minority
nationalities continued to be discontented and constituted
another major source of the protest movement.(12)

Semyonov in *International Affairs*, 1978, showed the
progression of Chinese hostility to the U.S.S.R. between 1969
and 1977.(13) Turning his attention to various Party
Congresses of the C.P.C. in 1969, 1973, and 1977, he stressed
that the Ninth Congress still came out in support of seeking
friendship with the socialist states, while attempting to defeat
their revisionist philosophy. But in 1973, the Chinese claimed
that the "socialist camp had ceased to exist," denouncing the
U.S.S.R. as an imperialist power. At the 1977 Congress, the
Soviet Union was even held to be a greater threat than Western
imperialism. Semyonov had earlier judged that the P.R.C.
acted as "an accomplice to imperialism."(14) While some
writers considered China a threat to all nations,(15) others
were especially concerned that the Chinese, as their maps
indicated, looked upon all of Southeast Asia as "lost Chinese
territories."

Considering the critical Soviet tone in the early post-Mao
period, an article by F. Burlatskii in the widely read *Novyi
Mir*, 1978, was an exception. Burlatskii distinguished between
the "leftists," who dominated during the Cultural Revolution,
and the "pragmatists." According to Burlatskii, the current
leaders of Beijing must claim to be following in Mao's
footsteps; to do otherwise would rob them of their legitimacy.
The article was of special interest since, by implication, it
contained some criticism of past Soviet policy toward the
C.P.R. On the whole, however, the Soviets looked upon the
Chinese leadership in the post-Mao period as being "even more
anti-Soviet and pro-imperialist than Mao" was.(17)

The C.P.R.'s Anti-Sovietism and Mao's Expansionism

"Blinded by anti-Sovietism," *Pravda* charged in an
editorial in May, 1975,(18) "Beijing's leaders are ready to put
any of their principles up for a bid and to waive the interests of
the Taiwanese and the Chinese people." Thus, Moscow leaders

seem to have been more impatient about the return of Taiwan to Beijing's untrammeled sovereignty than the Beijing government itself. They criticized Deng because he allegedly had stated that China "can wait until the United States is ready to change its Taiwan policy."

The unique theoretical basis for the Beijing expansionists' territorial claims were utterances by Mao that were widely known in China, but hardly known beyond its borders, such as, "We must secure Southeast Asia for ourselves, including South Vietnam, Thailand, Burma, Malaysia, Singapore, etc." Mao continued that China "must become the world's leading country." These aggressive aspirations of Mao and the Maoists only "duplicate the doctrines of Chinese nationalism of old..." *Pravda* excoriated the "traitorous essence of Maoism."(19) Beijing, it charged, supported "the imperialist alliance of NATO, SEATO, and CENTO—it approves of the U.S. military presence in Europe, Asia, the Mediterranean Sea, and the Indian Ocean."

It was hardly surprising that Soviet security interests in Europe and Asia were closely linked.(20) The Maoists were making territorial claims on their neighbors in Asia, something that was demonstrated by articles published in *Jenmin Jihpao* and *Kuongming Jihpao* in November 1975. There existed conspiracies against Asian states, which cannot be covered by the Maoists' screen of anti-Sovietism or by their mask of friendliness for Third World countries. The Soviets considered Beijing, therefore, a "threat to world peace"—a plain reversal of the charge hurled by Beijing against Moscow, But contrary to Beijing's phantasies, what has come to prevail in international relations is an "easing of tension."

The Helsinki Conference was a "great success," though imperialist reaction and accomplices have not laid down their arms. The imperialists have only regrouped their forces. "Having betrayed the revolutionary principles on which the C.P.R. was created, proven unfaithful as far as friendship and cooperation with the Soviet Union and other socialist countries are concerned, and having violated its international duty to the world revolutionary movement, the chauvinist Mao . . . grouping has taken a path of class betrayal of the cause of socialism and is making common cause with the most reactionary circles of imperialism." Recently, the Beijing leaders have stepped up their political and propagandistic attacks on the Soviet Union.(21) Despite its apparent successes in Europe, the Soviet Union cannot rest at peace due to Beijing's sinister plots and machinations.

Moscow on Historical and Territorial Disputes with Beijing

Strife over territorial possessions and claims has always been accompanied by historical disputes. This is also true of territorial disputes over the long Sino-Soviet border.

Sino-centrism, largely responsible for Chinese territorial claims, was, according to the editor of *World Marxist Review*, resurrected by the right wing of the Kuomintang, the party of the Chinese bourgeoisie that ruled the nation until 1949. It found expression in the book entitled, *China's Frontiers*, by Hua Qiyun, published in Shanghai in 1932. In a map of this book are listed so-called "lost territories;" they embraced Korea, the Ryukyu Islands, Taiwan (then occupied by Japan), Annam (Vietnam), Burma, Bhutan, Nepal, part of India, "and vast territories in the Soviet Union (part of Kazakhistan and Central Asia) the Amur region, Primorye (Maritime Territory), and Sakhalin." The whole of the Mongolian People's Republic was delineated as belonging to China, though in the mid-1920's Mongolia had become an independent nation. In 1939, Mao, in *The Chinese Revolution and the Communist Party of China*, had specifically listed territories seized by Japan, Great Britain, France, and even Portugal. His list coincided "almost entirely" with Hua Qiyun's foregoing list of lost territories. In September 1959, Mao had told the C.P.C. Central Committee: "Our object is the entire globe."(22)

Chinese historians, according to *World Marxist Review*, have overestimated China's historic, military, and political influence in northwest Central Asia, the area they call the "Western Region," and have idealized relations between the Chinese rulers and neighboring peoples. At the same time, they have underestimated Russia's impact on the history of the Kazakhs, Kirgiz', and other Central Asian peoples. Chinese historians, speaking of "China's historical rights" in northwestern Central Asia, hold that these "stem from the presence of Chinese conquerors in these areas at various times." "But if territorial rights are to be based on the remote past, it is possible to prove anything." China herself was once conquered by the Mongol descendents of Genghis Khan. The Chinese version of Central Asian history is a "crude distortion of reality.

The Soviet historian Gurevich has taken issue with the Maoist claim to 1.5 million square kilometers of which 500,000 square kilometers were in Kazakhistan and Central Asia, which is part of the U.S.S.R.(23) He disputed the C.P.R.'s leading history journal *Lishiu Yenchiu*, which dared to write of "our lake Balkash," "our lake Temurtu (Issyk-Kul)," "our lake Zaisan," and "our Chu river," and had questioned "the reality" of the construction of the towns that are today Alma-Ata, Frunze, and Tokmak."

The C.P.R.'s territorial claims, slightly downplayed after Mao's demise, were still critically discussed in *World Marxist Review* in August 1981.(24) According to its board of editors, bourgeois mass media have recently written of "positive changes" in China's foreign policy and of China's peaceableness in particular. They asserted that, since Mao's death, China has ceased pursuing a policy of imperilling peace and stability and was only showing legitimate concern for its national security. This assertion was based on "pronouncements of high-ranking Chinese political leaders seeking to soften Mao's theory that war is inevitable." Beijing was maneuvering in an effort to adjust to public opinion, with declarations that another world war can be avoided. However, according to *World Marxist Review*, "some new elements in Beijing policy do not, regrettably, give grounds for expecting Mao's successors to renounce China's hegemonistic ambitions," its territorial claims on neighboring states, and his bellicose bid for world supremacy.

Deng for "curbing the polar bear"

Concerning Deng's speech while visiting the U.S. in February 1979, Petrov observed in *Pravda* that it was "permeated with dyed-in-the-wool anti-Sovietism and hostility."(25) Deng agreed with the opinion of 70 retired American military officers who had demonstrated a hostile attitude toward the idea of any accord with the Soviet Union in the field of disarmament. He held that even after the signing of an agreement, the arms race would continue.

It was also evident from Deng's interview that Peking was revamping the Maoist "theory of the three worlds" in such a way that imperialism disappeared altogether, and the U.S. was even assigned the role of China's ally. Beijing found no room now for even verbal assurances about the continuing "leading role" of the states and peoples of the "Third World" or about the significance of the nonaligned movement and other international forces, two ideas to which the Beijing leaders ardently swore allegiance not very long ago.

The following day, *Pravda* was aroused that Deng, while in Washington, had declared the U.S.S.R. to be the "main hotbed of fear" and had called for "unity and firm joint action against the Soviet Union."(26) According to the *Washington Post*, Deng wanted to "put Washington on the anti-Soviet team." He abandoned the policy of easing the tension, condemned all efforts to curb the arms race, and appealed for the creation of a united front against the Soviet Union. The Peking leadership, *Pravda* claimed, was "oriented toward war, hegemonism, the suppression of the national liberation movement and the struggle against the socialist countries.(27) Deng's visit signified "a week of inflammatory speeches and statements," unleashed against the Soviet Union. In the interview with *Time* reporters, Deng spoke of "placing curbs on the polar bear." At the same time, the Carter administration, in which "the demon of anti-Sovietism" was rampant, was anxious to press "the China lever" to wrest one-sided concessions from Moscow.

On February 10, *Izvestia* followed suit with an article, "Dangerous course."(28) Subsequently, Deng's aggressive tone, while in Tokyo, had caused serious concern in Japan, which feared the repercussions in Moscow. In his meeting with Japan's Prime Minister, M. Ohira, Deng demanded that Japan apply sanctions against Vietnam for its invasion of Kampuchea.

The C.P.R.'s Aggression against Vietnam and the Sino-American Collusion

According to Aleksandrov, "Concerning China's Provocations against the socialist republic of Vietnam," in *Pravda* in February 1979,(29) the Chinese leaders were trying to shroud their military preparations in a dense smoke screen of misinformation and slander against the S.R.V. and the U.S.S.R. "The brazen armed incursions into the territory of socialist Vietnam and other hostile actions of the Peking expansionists are a logical result of the policy of provocations that China's current leaders who inherited Mao's great power course have pursued for many years with respect to Southeast Asia in general and Vietnam in particular. They reveal still more of the true face of the hegemonists, who have had their eyes on other people's lands for a long time. The Chinese military's bandit raids against the S.R.V. are further evidence that Peking regards Southeast Asia as a zone in which China's supremacy should ultimately be established as a staging ground for eventual seizure of all Asia." The Soviet press thus magnified China's aggressive intentions and moves beyond measure.

According to Aleksandrov, Beijing did not want to see the creation of a united socialist Vietnam. It had previously seized the Paracel Islands, allegedly staged border incidents with Vietnam, had begun reductions in food and other deliveries, and carried on "subversive activity among ethnic Chinese living in Vietnam." The liberation of South Vietnam undermined the plans of the Chinese leadership to bring all of Indochina under its control. Vietnam actually became "a major obstacle" in the way of Peking's expansion in Southeast Asia. As their weapon, the Chinese authorities "selected the antipopular Pol Pot-Ieng Sary clique in Kampuchea and used it to wage an undeclared border war against the S.R.V."

China had unleashed a war of aggression against Vietnam, "a modern war involving aircraft, tanks and artillery." This is what Deng was talking about in Washington when he promised to "punish" Hanoi for insubordination to Beijing's dictatorship.(30) Beijing's ruling clique was more and more openly closing ranks with imperialism. *Pravda* belittled China's value as a U.S. partner.(31) The author of the article,

S. Vishnevski, held that there was hatched a "plot" in Washington between the U.S. and Communist China. The Beijing delegation, while in the state of Washington, was "attracted most of all by such 'sights' as the weapons-making Lockheed, Boeing, and McDonnell Corporations." But every cloud has a silver lining. The *Pravda* commentator pointed to many American voices and journals which, like the *Christian Science Monitor*, warned that a further rapprochement with Beijing was fraught with big risks for the U.S. Prominent politicians warned of the futility for the U.S. to play the "China card."

At the same time, A. Petrov in "Aggressor in the Pillory" claimed that China had great-power aspirations in Southeast Asia.(32) Having concentrated several divisions and hundreds of tanks and airplanes against the S.R.V.—just as Beijing adventurists had done against India in 1962—Beijing based its interference in the internal affairs of Burma, Thailand, and Malaysia on territorial and other claims. The prospect of the appearance of a group of independent states, apparently under the leadership of the S.R.V., was "a barrier on the path of Beijing's aggressive plans." When the C.P.R. showed its displeasure with the reunification of the Vietnamese people in a single state and Vietnam objected to China's claims to hegemony in the region, Beijing began to threaten the latter indirectly. The author did not rule out that Deng's "American friends" would approve of China's "teaching the Vietnamese a lesson" and of belatedly punishing them for the ignominious defeat that the American military had suffered in Vietnam." It was no accident that, at the moment Chinese troops invaded Vietnam, the presence of U.S. naval forces in the South China Sea was made known. On February 21, *Pravda*'s Yar Kabharov was appalled that the Yugoslav newspaper *Vjesnik* took the side of the Chinese "aggressor" while Albania castigated the C.P.R.'s attitude.(33) "Chinese social imperialism, the most zealous ally of American imperialism, had treacherously attacked heroic Vietnam." It noticed that Romania has observed with "profound distress and concern the exacerbation of combat operatives" on the Chinese-Vietnamese border and had taken an "evenhanded stance."(34)

Beijing's Refusal to renew the 1950 Sino-Soviet Alliance

In May 1979, the Beijing Government announced that it would not extend the 30-year Treaty of Friendship, Alliance, and Mutual Assistance, signed in 1950 by the Soviet Union and the C.P.R., beyond April 1980.(35) In order to justify this hostile action, the Chinese side, the Soviet statement charged, was "resorting to crude fabrications." "Faithful to its internationalist duty and consistently fulfilling the commitments stemming from the treaty, the U.S.S.R. from the very start firmly and consistently defended the interests of the C.P.R. in the world arena and effectively helped the young People's Republic to rebuff attempts by imperialist forces to interfere in its affairs. . .The existence of the Soviet-Chinese treaty of 1950 also played a decisive role in preventing direct imperialist aggression against the C.P.R. during the 1950-53 war in Korea," and also during the Taiwan crisis of 1958.

In turning down the Soviet Union's 1971 proposal for the conclusion of a treaty on the nonuse of forces and its 1973 Chinese government had alleged that these treaties were not necessary, since the 1950 agreement between the two countries was then still in existence. With the latter treaty being "terminated, there is a clear indication that the Chinese leadership is systematically pursuing a line aimed at the further exacerbation and undermining of Soviet-Chinese relations. The treaty's termination is closely linked with the degeneration of the Chinese leaders' political course, which has gradually come to be defined more and more by great-power, hegemonistic aspirations, a scornful attitude toward other countries and peoples, hostility toward everything that leads to the strengthening of peace and international security, and runs counter to their plans for establishing world domination. China's shameful aggression against the S.R.V. shows how they have fallen, betraying the interests of socialism."

People of the Soviet Union invariably retain deep respect for the Chinese people and for their history and culture. "There are no objective reasons for alienation, and certainly none for antagonism, between the peoples of our two countries."

The unwillingness of Beijing to renew the 30-year treaty with the U.S.S.R. had incensed the Soviet leadership. In August 1979, Chernenko, visiting France, emphasized that the "Chinese leadership's policy of heightening tension must be rebutted."(36) "Going one step further," Suslov in Bryansk stressed on September 18, 1979, "We resolutely condemn the Maoist ideology and policy."(37) Several articles in Soviet publications went so far as to urge China to "split with Maoism." Soviet journals insisted that the very issue of withdrawing Soviet troops from the border area should not be a topic of discussion with Beijing. The Soviet Central T.V. Station screened on September 4, 1979, an anti-Chinese film entitled, *Instigations from the Celestial Empire,* to whip up anti-Chinese sentiment among the Soviet people. A correspondent of the *Corriere della Sera* (Milano) reported from Moscow on September 9, 1979: "In the past few days the Soviet press almost daily made continuous harsh attacks on China and the Chinese people . . . in preparation of the eventuality that the Sino-Soviet negotiations would flop."(38)

Warming of Sino-SoViet Relations.
Brezhnev in Tashkent.

During the summer of 1979, Aleksandrov, discussing in *Pravda* the recently completed session of the National People's Congress of the P.R.C., concluded that, judging by Chinese sources, the P.R.C. for the last two decades had been on the "wrong road."(39) An effort was made to convince the Chinese people that Lin Piao and the "Gang of Four" were solely to blame for all the shortcomings, mistakes, and crimes which had been committed especially during the Cultural Revolution. But he noticed a greater caution in foreign affairs and thought about war and peace. "As far as the Beijing leadership's approach to international affairs was concerned, there was no repetition of its previous thesis, justifying war as a commonplace phenomenon that has not only a dark side but also a bright one."

A decline of open hostility and desire to improve mutual relations is reflected in an *Izvestia* review, "In the name of good neighborliness," in which Academician A. Rumyanstev discussed a book about Sino-Russian economic relations by H.

M. Gladkovsky, corresponding member of the U.S.S.R. Academy of Sciences. Rumyantsev concluded that good neighborliness between the two peoples was a historic necessity."(40) Gladkovsky's present and earlier works "convincingly show good neighborliness, mutually advantageous relations with China developed at various stages of history," especially during the years 1917-27, 1945-49, and 1973-75, and thereafter. His work was "suffused with the idea of proletarian internationalism and historic optimism and a deep regard for the Chinese people." In two previous works about China's relations with Japan and Great Britain, the author had "shown the fundamentally different nature of the policies applied to China by Japan, Britain, and the other capitalist countries that were pursuing imperialist goals—including aggressive wars of conquest against China.

Occasionally, the Soviets were responsive to Beijing's toning down of major criticisms.(41) On October 14, 1983, Academician Tikhinsky in *Izvestia*, "A Mission of Friendship,"(42) reported: "After an interruption of almost 20 years, a specialized tourist group of activists of the Union of Socialist Societies for Friendship with Foreign Countries and the Central Board of Soviet-Chinese Friendship Society have recently visited the C.P.R. They were impressed that the Chinese people retained kindly feelings about the Soviet Union." "As is known, during the so-called Cultural Revolution the main blow fell on that part of China's party and state cadres and intelligentsia that advocated scientific socialism and the creative utilization of the experience. . .of socialist construction in the U.S.S.R. and other countries." The achievements of the Chinese working people since the end of the Cultural Revolution made a "big impression on our group." "Unfortunately, familiarization with the Chinese press, radio and T.V. during our stay in the C.P.R. convinced us that the peace-threatening policies of the imperialist powers—the United States and Japan first of all—are, as a rule, presented to the Chinese public as a counterbalance to the policies of the Soviet Union and fail to receive proper condemnation." The Chinese press continued to deliberately distance itself from the struggle for peace that is being waged by the fraternal socialist countries and the world's progressive public."

Though the Soviet press castigated Chinese treatment of the people of the U.S.S.R. and its life, and the policies of its government, especially its anti-Soviet course, it noticed, on the other hand, some alleged "warming" of the Sino-Soviet relationship; this might originate with some conciliatory remarks made by Brezhnev during his trip to Tashkent, capital of Uzbekistan, in which he touched on relations with Beijing.(43) Brezhnev, referring to the decisions of the 25th and 26th C.P.S.U. Congresses, stated: "First, despite the fact that we have openly criticized and continue to criticize many aspects of the Chinese leadership's policy (especially its foreign policy) we have never tried to interfere in the internal life of the C.P.R. We have not denied, and do not now deny, the existence of a socialist social system in China—although Beijing's fusion with the imperialists' policy in the world arena is, of course, at variance with the interests of socialism." (Brezhnev was correct that Soviet leaders, despite the escalation of the polemics, had not disputed the "socialist" character of the C.P.R. This contrasted with Beijing's claim that the U.S.S.R. had abandoned socialism and was restoring "capitalism." In the ideological polemics, Beijing was, indeed, more extreme than Moscow, though the latter had become no longer reluctant to accuse Beijing occasionally of "restoring" capitalism, under the influence of its Western allies and the U.S. in particular.)

Secondly, Brezhnev assured Beijing that Moscow fully recognized the C.P.R.'s sovereignty over Taiwan. In contrast, Beijing has repeatedly and loudly accused the United States of reverting to the "two Chinas concept." Thirdly, Brezhnev disavowed the existence of any Soviet threat to the C.P.R. and pledged that the Soviet Union had no "territorial claim against the C.P.R." (This assurance, however, sidestepped the real issue of Chinese territorial claims against the U.S.S.R., which is the root cause of all territorial disputes.) Fourth, Brezhnev continued, the Soviet Union recalled the time when both countries were united by bonds of friendship and comradely cooperation: "We have never considered the state of hostility and alienation between our countries to be a normal phenomenon." The Soviet Union was prepared to reach an agreement with the P.R.C. "on the basis of mutual respect for each other's interests, non-interference in each other's affairs and mutual benefit and, needless to say, not to the detriment of any third countries."

On March 24, 1983, I. Aleksandrov wrote the following commentary on Brezhnev's foregoing address in Tashkent which expressed the views of the Politburo.(44) In a historical overview of Sino-Soviet relations since 1949, Aleksandrov claimed that Soviet-Chinese relations became the most important of the favorable foreign-policy factors that the C.P.R. needed to accomplish the task of social, political, and economic progress! "Even today when the wave of anti-Sovietism in China has not abated," the Chinese have been forced to acknowledge that this initial period of C.P.R.'s existence "was the most fruitful period in the country's progress along the path of socialist transformations." During the last two decades, however, a "drastic alienation" between the two states has taken place. But the U.S.S.R. has "never" been "the initiator in the deterioration of mutual relations."

There still existed numerous ties linking the two states. Embassies continued to function in both states. Trade was conducted between them, though its volume was modest. Regular railroad traffic, aviation, postal and telegraph communications were maintained between the U.S.S.R. and the C.P.R. The Mixed Commission of Navigation on Border Rivers had its annual conference, and the Mixed Border Railroad Commission was in operation. There existed other contacts between certain departments of the two states. The participation of representatives of the two sides in various international forums, conferences, symposiums and sports competitions, held in both the U.S.S.R. and China, has expanded. Unofficial trips by scientists and specialists from the Soviet Union to the C.P.R. and vice versa were becoming commonplaces. The U.S.S.R. had recently proposed to China that contacts be established in the scientific and technical fields and that student exchange be intensified.

However, according to Moscow, the C.P.R. leaders were advancing a whole series of preliminary demands that the U.S.S.R. was supposed to fulfill before any significant Soviet-Chinese talks could begin. The list included three main points: 1. renouncing support and assistance to the Mongol People's Republic, the Indochinese countries, and Afghanistan. 2. the unilateral withdrawal of the armed forces of the

Soviet Union from the C.P.R.'s border and 3. recognition of China's "rights" to sizeable areas of the U.S.S.R.

This piling up of preliminary conditions, "verging on ultimatums," did not, in the Soviet view, indicate a desire on the Chinese side to seek a way out of the impasse that Soviet-Chinese relations have gotten into. The Soviets, in contrast, did not insist on any preliminary conditions. Also, the Beijing leaders and the C.P.R. press put out publications that were hostile to the Soviet Union and spoke of the U.S.S.R. as the "main enemy" and "the main source of the danger of war." It was difficult to get rid of the impression that the Beijing leaders were moved by "shortsighted calculations stemming from China-centered and hegemonistic ambitions." China, "in return for the promissory note of anti-Sovietism," received increased investment from capitalist countries speeding the modernization and militarization of China. As a matter of fact, "the Beijing hawks were pushing the imperialists in every way toward a confrontation with the U.S.S.R."

"It seems to us /the Soviet Union/ that, in conditions of detente and lasting peace China could devote far more of its energies to domestic construction and to overcoming the heavy Maoist legacy and the consequences of the Cultural Revolution." While the U.S.S.R. has never interfered and is not now interfering in China's internal life, "at the same time, we criticize a number of aspects of the Chinese leadership's policy, primarily foreign policy, since it does not correspond to socialist principles and was detrimental to the U.S.S.R. Above all, we criticize the closing of ranks between the Chinese leadership's course and the policy of imperialism." "The U.S.S.R. has wanted and still wants to see China as a good neighbor." This statement, of course, placed the burden of improving the relationship between the two countries plainly upon the shoulders of the Beijing government.

Beijing's Imperialist Allies and Taiwan

Both Beijing and Moscow, while attempting to negotiate outstanding issues, remained inherently skeptical about prospects for improving their relationship. On September 26, 1979 the Soviets complained that the arrival of a C.P.R.

delegation in Moscow was being accompanied in China not by a lessening of anti-Soviet propaganda, but, in fact, even by a certain increase,(45) pointing to as many as ten recent hostile articles in *Jenmin Jihpao*. In its September 24 issue, Moscow remonstrated that the Chinese press carried articles misrepresenting the U.S.S.R.'s policy toward Iran, Turkey, Nepal, Burma, the Central African Republic, Norway, and the U.S.(46)

On July 16, 1979, an incident took place along the Sino-Soviet border, 44 kilometers southeast of Khabar Sasu pass. It became promptly the object of an exchange of notes, involving on July 24th the C.P.R. Ministry of Foreign Affairs. According to the Soviet version of the incident, four armed Chinese soldiers had intruded into Soviet territory for a distance of one kilometer; one of the Chinese was killed, another wounded. The Soviets maintained that the Chinese had distorted the circumstances under which the clashes occurred.(47)

Early in 1980, Aleksandrov charged in *Pravda* that Beijing was teaming up with the most reactionary and adventuristic forces in the international arena.(48) Under Mao, Beijing's foreign policy line was characterized by extreme anti-Sovietism and by hostility toward the friends of the U.S.S.R.; it was still so today. The Beijing leaders were making a maximum effort to form the "broadest possible international united front," "egg on and support those who are inclined to rattle the saber and are fond of adventures and uncompromising confrontation under the false slogan of opposing Soviet hegemonism." Beijing hoped thus to enhance its reputation in the eyes of the ruling classes of the United States and other capitalist countries and to get expanded material support from the West to build up its military potential and implement the "four modernizations" program. It opposed proposals for stabilizing the world situation. The inflammatory nature of Beijing's propaganda was also shown in its obvious attempt to create clashes between the U.S.S.R. and the United States. A seemingly endless flow of appeals and "warnings" was pouring forth from the C.P.R. to cause a confrontation between East and West, such as: "One can never trust agreements with the Soviet Union." Beijing recommended that the United States take urgent steps to prepare for the use of force. It even suggested that Japan become a "major military power" and to wage together with the United States and Western Europe "a struggle against Soviet hegemonism."

The Chinese leaders would like to use the West to help pave the way to the realization of hegemonistic schemes that Beijing was hatching above all with respect to the Asian peoples. The countries neighboring China were worried. Beijing was giving its support to the pro-Chinese "fifth columns" in South Eastern and South Asia in the form of Beijing-inspired "insurgent" and separatist movements and associations of persons of Chinese nationality. While whitewashing the aggressive N.A.T.O. bloc and provoking it into a further arms buildup, the Maoists at the same time turned the facts upside down, stating that the Warsaw Treaty Organization was "a principal instrument of the policy of aggression and war."

Having previously failed in its attempts to create a unique pro-Maoist International and to implant Maoist groups and groupings in the revolutionary movement, the Chinese leadership has switched to a no less insidious tactic, of instilling its ideas and policies in the world Communist movement.

The Soviet Union, according to Beijing, was jubilant over the growing rift between China and the United States over Taiwan. The Beijing leaders had suddenly "discovered" that the Americans, while formally recognizing Taiwan as part of China, were in effect continuing to treat Taiwan as an independent state. A. Bovin quoted the *Washington Post*: "The up-to-now inactive volcano known as Beijing is beginning to rumble." The U.S. is now declared a "superpower on the decline," and Washington is experiencing a "bitter sense of weakness," Beijing caustically remarks. Chinese newspapers, according to Bovin,(49-50) were also informing their readers that America was "slighting small countries and violating Third World countries' sovereignty." But all this did not mean that China had decided to support these countries to oppose the U.S. expansionist, hegemonist policy. The aim of Chinese leadership was rather to convince the Americans that the U.S. by itself cannot stand up to the Soviet Union. The C.P.R. was imploring the Americans to finally realize that it was to their "strategic advantage" to turn away from Taiwan and thereby secure the constant help and support of China—"in order to step up pressure on the Soviet Union, needless to say." According to Moscow, Beijing's hopes to secure further concessions from Washington concerning Taiwan, were based on illlusions. At the same time, the C.P.R. disregarded her real interests in close relations, including economic and strategic ones, with the Soviet Union. Beijing and Washington will one day grasp the illusory nature of their attempts to "squeeze" the Soviet Union.

Breakup of the Soviet Union or of the Chinese Empire?

Any discussion of Soviet foreign policy,, its tactics and strategy, remains buried in the archives of the Politburo, rarely reaching the outside world. The policy is challenged openly only by dissenters, whose means of making public their criticism or divergent views are, of course, sharply circumscribed in a totalitarian society like the U.S.S.R. Many dissenters, however, true patriots, side, as far as the Sino-Soviet dispute is concerned, with the government and, as they believe, with their people, against the Chinese "enemy." After the clashes on the Ussuri river in 1969, the poet Yevtushenko, "On the Ussuri Snow,"(51) promptly demonstrated his patriotism and anti-Chinese sentiments, lamenting that "even a sacred idea" can be abused "in the hands of a scoundrel" (Beijing's rulers). But Andrei Amalrik, playwright, historian, and prophet, in his best-known work, *Will the Soviet Union Survive in 1984?*, indicted the Soviet regime for being mediocre, fearful, backward, and inflexible.(52) He also accused the Soviet Union of applying an oppressive nationality policy and, in the foreign policy field, including its China policy, of being imperialistic and militaristic. He was sentenced to five years in a severe-regimentation concentration camp. Some Soviet critics have charged Amalrik with "Russophobia," but he has proven to be objective and has countered by emphasizing that Russia ought to overcome "its national and social inferiority complex." Actually, neither of the two sides, according to Amalrik, is a political innocent, but the Chinese character emerges in the book more favorably than the Russian one, and the author is sharply critical of Soviet policy.

The last full third of the foregoing book deals with the question of China and her relations with the U.S.S.R. Amalrik holds that the Chinese Revolution, like the Russian Revolution before, passes through three major stages. The last of these is a nationalist and imperialist stage, and Marxist doctrine is a mere camouflage.(53)

China has already reached the stage of "external expansionism," as demonstrated by her "aggressive tendencies toward countries where she did not expect to encounter strong resistance, for example India." She has not been able to achieve her aims by pitting the Soviet Union and the U.S.A. against each other. "The relentless logic of revolution is propelling China toward a war which the Chinese leaders hope will solve the country's difficult economic and social problems and secure for China a leading place in the modern world."

According to Amalrik, it is not likely that China or the U.S. will become involved in war with each other. China is not interested in expanding her influence and territory on the North American continent, but primarily in Asia. Across the Sino-Soviet border lie "the vast and sparsely populated territories of Siberia and the Soviet Far East." It is essential for China somehow to eliminate or neutralize this rival, if she is to play a dominant role in Asia and the world at large; moreover, the Soviet Union is "a much more dangerous rival which, as a totalitarian state with expansionist tendencies, may in one form or another strike the first blow."(54) Already the Soviet Union has tried to play on the nationalism of the smaller nations within China's borders." Amalrik holds that China in a war with the Soviet Union will "enjoy advantages"—a view not seriously entertained by others, including present-day military experts. Although Amalrik admits that the Soviet Union, everything considered, was more powerful than China, the U.S.S.R. fears the latter. He believed that war between the Soviet Union and China might begin between 1975 and 1980, and end between 1980 and 1985—not a very good prophet in this respect.

Soviet leaders, considering China a potential nuclear rival and aggressor, may decide in favor of a preventive nuclear strike against China's nuclear centers before China is ready. In this event, they will present China to the Soviet people and world public opinion "as the aggressor." But while China's main rocket bases would be destroyed, China herself will not succumb. The ensuing guerrilla war would be "equally terrible" for both states. Amalrik holds an attempt to eliminate China's might, by a controversial invasion and occupation of all or part of the country, unlikely. A Soviet decision to aim at "total destruction" of China by nuclear weapons may be an "apocalyptic picture," but is entirely conceivable, since it is "fear" which drives people to take the most desperate actions.

Since China may foresee the possibility of a Soviet strike, she will follow "a more cautious policy over the next five years and even flirt with the Soviet Union." Meaningless contacts and ambiguous declarations might be made and the tone of attacks might be softened. However, anti-Soviet propaganda within China would not be let up to keep the Chinese people "constantly on the alert." China might also seek closer contacts with the U.S.

China may well test her strength toward some neutral country which was once in her sphere of influence and which has a Chinese minority. Though the Soviet Union presumably has long drawn up plans for the eventuality of a war with China, it is allegedly not prepared, either technically or psychologically, for guerrilla and semi-guerrilla warfare. The Soviet Union would have to cope with enormously extended lines of communication and face a patriotically inspired Chinese soldiery; the war would be waged in an area sparsely populated by non-Russians.

Much will depend on the attitude of the U.S. toward a Sino-Soviet war and especially on the possibility of a rapprochement between the U.S. and the Soviet Union. But the latter would make sense only after serious steps toward democracy were taken in the U.S.S.R.(55) Cooperation between the superpowers presupposes "mutual reliance," "but how can one rely on a country that has been capable of no other aim over the centuries than distending itself and sprawling in all directions like sour dough?"

One can hear nowadays in Russia remarks like, "The U.S. will help us because we are white and the Chinese are yellow." But it would be very sad if the U.S. adopted such a "racist attitude." Everything considered, Amalrik does not believe it likely that the U.S. will side with Russia against China. By pursuing the Stalinist policy of territorial expansion and the deliberate fostering of international tension, the Soviet Union has created a danger for itself. A Soviet concentration of its energies on the war against China would result in considerable changes in Central and Eastern Europe, including the emergence of a reunited Germany. This will "coincide with a process of de-Sovietization in the East European countries. These de-Sovietized nations will present to Russia "territorial claims" that have not been forgotten, namely, Polish, German, Hungarian, and Rumanian lands wrested from them during the last phases of World War II and thereafter. Japan, too, will revive her claims to lost territories and even to a portion of the Far East.

The beginning of a war against China will cause "a flare up of Russian nationalism," but, as war progresses, Russian nationalism will "decline, while non-Russian nationalism will rise." These nationalist tendencies will "intensify sharply," first in the Baltic area, the Caucasus, and the Ukraine, then in Central Asia and along the Volga,(56) and the Soviet Union will "disintegrate" into anarchy, violence, and intense national hatred. "The boundaries of the new state which will then begin to emerge on the territories of the former Soviet Union will be extremely hard to determine." The resulting military clashes will be exploited by the neighbors of the Soviet Union, above all by China. It is also possible that the Russian "middle-class" —Amalrik's definition of it is somewhat unique—will prove strong enough to keep control in its own hands. In that case, the granting of independence to the various Soviet nationalities will come about "peacefully" and some sort of federation will emerge, similar to the British Commonwealth. Peace will be concluded with China, which will also have been weakened by the war. But Amalrik concedes that none of these things may actually happen.

Everything considered, Amalrik casts a long shadow not only on Russia's past and present, but also on her future as a mighty state. De-Sovietization of Eastern Europe, the rise of secessionist non-Russian nationalism within the Soviet Union, territorial claims by her European and Asiatic neighbors, including China, and the likelihood of a breakup of the Soviet empire are cataclysmic phenomena. No wonder that Amalrik's book never saw the light of day in the Soviet Union, but only abroad.

While a Russian dissident anticipated the destruction of the Soviet Empire—with its unavoidable gains for China—Soviet planners and strategists, as a book by a KGB operative, the well-known Soviet journalist Victor Louis, *The Coming Decline of the Chinese Empire* (1979), demonstrates, are expecting the disintegration of the Chinese Empire, the loss of its largely non-Han border regions, and the thrust of the Soviet Union into this vast area.(57)

In his introduction to Victor Louis's book, *The Coming Decline of the Chinese Empire*, Harrison E. Salisbury calls it, justifiably, a "book of spurious content, dubious logic and flagrant untruth." But it is read, he writes, somewhat exaggeratedly, "like Hitler's *Mein Kampf*," "not because we trust the author," but because, as a well-known KGB agent, he is presenting a "rationale" for a Soviet war of liberation against the C.P.R.(58) At the least, Victor Louis apparently wishes to make China and the West think that the Soviet Union would contemplate heeding a call from the "oppressed minorities" of China and militarily assist them. Victor Louis, son of a French father, Soviet citizen, married an English woman and, having numerous links with the West and the Western press, has played a unique role as a Russian journalist who, in the course of time, was entrusted by the Russians with some strange missions. In the autumn of 1969, after the clashes along the Ussuri river and other places along the Sino-Soviet border, he wrote several exclusive articles concerning the threat of war between the two neighbors. He has since concentrated on Sino-Soviet relations and is considered a mouthpiece of the all-powerful Soviet secret police. While his views may not be shared in their entirety by the Soviet leadership past and present, his book is revealing at least of the goals of some influential circles within the U.S.S.R.

Lenin had called Russia "a prison house of peoples." The C.P.R., however, according to Victor Louis, is worse and more dangerous to national justice and peace than tsarist Russia ever was. The Soviet dissenter Andrei Amalrik, had, as noticed, developed the thesis that in the event of a catastrophe befalling the Soviet Union, it might break apart. Alexander Solzhenitsyn(59) similarly came out in favor of the separation of the Baltic peoples, the Caucasian nationalities, and the Central Asiatic peoples from the Slavic nationalities. It was in

the national aspirations of the many non-Han peoples, who
"today are incorporated territorially in China, can become
reality."(62)

B. Persistence of Regional Conflicts after Brezhnev

Continuing Soviet Concerns about China. Western Europe.

After the death of Brezhnev, Chinese leaders in a number
of conciliatory speeches gave credit to his important role in
Soviet policy. Overlooking the worsening of Sino-Soviet
relations during his stewardship and Mao's Cultural Revolution, Brezhnev was now credited for having been "an
outstanding statesman," and his death was considered "a great
loss for the Soviet people and state." In the early 1950s,
Sino-Soviet relations had gradually worsened, and after the
late 1960s, this deterioration became more serious. Shortly
before his death, Chairman Brezhnev had more than once
expressed a readiness to make an effort to improve relations
between the Soviet Union and the C.P.R. *Pravda* wondered
then whether the "softer tone" was in response to "a Chinese
bid for better relations with the U.S.S.R."(1)

The Sino-Soviet dispute centers not only on the two parties
directly concerned, the U.S.S.R. and the C.P.R., but also on
other nations of the world. Both countries are closely involved
in U.S. policies, and the U.S. plays thus a crucial role in this
triangular relationship. But the Second and even Third
World, not to mention Communist Parties, ruling and
non-ruling, are also important factors in international
policies, all greatly influencing the Sino-Soviet relationship.

Let us at present focus on the Second World, and primarily
on the West European states. Their postwar history was
marked by economic and political recovery and attempts at
reassertion of their former decisive role in European and world
affairs. While after 1945, the U.S.S.R. began to build up its
East European empire, the West European states, after having
suffered in the war destruction and social and economic chaos,
were helped along by the U.S., economically, diplomatically,
and through military alliances, and made a spectacular
recovery. Soon Europe was divided between East and West
with neither side capable of breaking down the separating wall
in the Germanies or elsewhere along the Iron Curtain. This

created a sort of uneasy stability across Europe, while the spheres of influence between the two superpowers elsewhere in Asia and the world were more flexible and frequently shifted.

The development of the Sino-Soviet dispute has given an opportunity to the United Kingdom, France, West Germany, and Italy, U.S. allies in N.A.T.O., to assert new influence in world affairs and a measure of independence from the U.S., and the opportunity of dealing with the Soviet Union on more favorable terms. In the 1960s already De Gaulle's diplomatic overtures to China and the Soviet Union had shown France's desire for independence in her foreign policy, if not for "glory." The same goal was pursued, as mentioned, by the initiation of a policy of East-West detente by the leaders of the Bonn government and De Gaulle; the latter was anxious to establish a "third force," besides those of the two superpowers. France under De Gaulle, defying the U.S., recognized the Chinese Communist government and also moved diplomatically closer toward the U.S.S.R.(2) He wanted a limited rapprochement with Moscow rather than playing the "China card" against it, though he realized that the Chinese defection from the Soviet bloc was a blow to the U.S.S.R. Both French moves in the direction of Moscow and Beijing were aimed at reducing U.S. influence over French policy. The policy of Paris toward Beijing did not constitute an anti-Soviet move.

The Sino-West European rapprochement was by no means undisturbed. The Soviets strongly protested against the projected British sale to China of Harrier jump jets. In 1978 and 1979, Brezhnev himself wrote several times personal letters to the leaders of the four largest West European countries, France, the United Kingdom, West Germany, and Italy, voicing serious misgivings about the delivery of U.S. cruise and Pershing II missiles and threatening severe countermeasures. When Hua Guofeng journeyed to Western Europe in October 1979, the Soviets repeated their threats. Western political leaders, wary of arousing Soviet ire and of aligning themselves too closely to the Soviet enemy, urged Hua privately to tone down his criticism of the Soviet Union, while on their soil.

The "third force" notion to be played by De Gaulle's France and continued under Pompidou and Giscard d'Estaing found imitators in other West European nations. This notion, underlining independence from both superpowers and repre-

sovereignty of the C.P.R. China felt that her own situation and
that of the Germanies had strong similarities and that it was
only consistent to champion the unification of Germany also in
view of her own national interests, to end the separation of
Taiwan from the mainland—aside from China's strategic
interest, as mentioned, in establishing a West European
counterbalance to the Soviet Union, including a unified
Germany. Since the early 1970s, the C.P.R. gave increasingly
its support also to the military strengthening of N.A.T.O., and
has continued to do so.

The C.P.S.U., the C.P.C., and Other Communist Parties

Some students of Communist affairs, while focussing on the
major adversaries tn the Sino-Soviet dispute, have neglected
minor protagonists, though they at times have played an
important role in the confrontation. This is especially true of
the Italian Communist Party (P.C.I.). According to Kevin
Devlin, "The Challenge of the 'New Internationalism,'" in the
post-Mao period, other independent Communist parties,
especially the Yugoslav, Rumanian, and Spanish parties,
having established relations with the C.P.R., have disavowed
Moscow's "proletarian internationalism."(6)

The "rebellion" of the P.C.I. against Moscow's leadership
commenced in the early 1960's, especially in 1963, when
Togliatti, leader of P.C.I., cast off the "method of
excommunication," contemplated by the C.P.S.U. against the
C.P.C. In October 1962, the P.C.I. adopted the slogan "unity
in diversity and autonomy."(7) While the P.C.I. criticized
Beijing's policies, it insisted on its own right to criticize the
shortcomings of all existing socialist regimes, including the
C.P.S.U., and on establishing new rules of interparty
relations, of what was to become, years later, the "new
internationalism." This was followed by Krushchev's postpone-
ment of a conference project designed to isolate the Chinese
Party and by a visit of Togliatti in January 1964 to Tito.
Again, while holding the Chinese stance on many problems
mistaken,(8) the Italian and Yugoslav Communist Parties'
joint communique warned against "anathemas" directed
against the C.P.R. Actually, at that time, only half of the
fourteen existing communist regimes followed the Soviet

lead,(9) out of loyalty to the U.S.S.R. or because of complete dependence on her. Some, as China and Albania, were definitely anti-Soviet, while others, such as Yugoslavia, Rumania, Cuba, and China's Asiatic neighbors, North Korea and North Vietnam, were "independent-neutralist."

A major role in the C.P.I.'s attitude was played by its leader, Togliatti, author of a paper written in preparation for a meeting with Krushchev only a few hours before he was felled by a stroke in the Crimea in August 1974. This document, known as the Yalta Testament, was subsequently published by the Secretary General of the C.P.I., Luigi Longo, in L'Unita and Rinascità, September 4, 1964. On September 10, Pravda published it without a commentary.(10) Krushchev, undeterred by Togliatti's posthumous publication, was resolved to continue along the road against Beijing, when he was suddenly ousted from his leading post.

After the outbreak in August 1966, of the Cultural Revolution, marred as it was by fanatic excesses, the projected conference was postponed, largely due to the skilled maneuvers of the C.P.I. The invasion of Czechoslovakia and the Sino-Soviet clashes on the Ussuri river in 1969 undermined both the Soviet case against China and the Soviet endorsement of monolithic Communism.

On the whole, the C.P.S.U. and the C.P.C. have sharply competed with each other for the support of individual Communist parties and for the leadership in world Communism: ideological fanaticism on both sides was extreme. According to K. Devlin, "occasional approaches or gestures of rapprochement" by independent Western Communist parties received little or no encouragement from Beijing during Mao's stewardship.(11) This was true of the C.P.C.'s attitude toward the Italian and Spanish Communist parties. The representatives of these Parties made it rather clear that, while their stance differed from that of Moscow, they did not consider "passing from being under the guidance of the C.P.S.U. to the guidance of the C.P.C."(12)

What emerged in the post-Mao era was a sort of alliance of independents. Yugoslavia, Rumania, and the non-ruling parties of Italy, Spain, Great Britain, Sweden, and, occasionally, the French party. They all emphasized increasing independence, respectively autonomy, rejected the Soviet and

dangerous to the preservation of peace.(15) The talks in Beijing, in his opinion, were marked by hostility on the part of Beijing and Washington toward Moscow and the cause of peace throughout the world. The efforts to coordinate the two states' parallel operations on the basis of "common strategic interests" had begun during the visit of the former United States Secretary of Defense, Harold Brown, to Beijing in January 1980. A linkage between the intelligence services of the United States and China had occurred even before "full normalization" of relations between the two states. An additional impetus was provided by the overthrow of the antipopulist monarchist regime in Iran, which deprived the C.I.A. of electronic intelligence stations on the Soviet Union's borders. On the basis of a secret accord between Washington and Beijing, "two tracking stations have been built in North-West China that use American equipment operated by Chinese personnel under the guidance of instructions from the C.I.A."

"Those who put weapons into the hands of the Chinese hegemonists obviously think that they will gain an opportunity to influence Beijing's policy and channel its expansionism mainly toward the north. That's a grave error!" The danger of China's growing military power consisted in the fact that American weapons in Chinese hands will be directed primarily against comparatively small neighboring states, some of which, incidentally, were American allies. China, as it were, was being urged to realize her territorial claims in South-East and South Asia. Washington's persistent demands that the country of Hiroshima and Nagasaki rid itself of its nuclear allergy and set about transforming itself into a military power were receiving increasingly vigorous support from Beijing.

From the Invasion of Afghanistan to the Death of Brezhnev

The Soviet invasion of Afghanistan in December 1979 stalled ongoing talks between Moscow and Beijing. On January 20, 1980, the Chinese declared that, in view of this Soviet act of aggression, further Sino-Soviet negotiations were no longer appropriate. The following year, on March 7, 1981, Moscow proposed a conference on Korean affairs between the U.S., the C.P.R., Japan, and North Korea conspicuously omitting

South Korea.(16) Beijing, however, considered this too unacceptable.

Though the high pitch of Sino-Soviet polemics has somewhat declined in 1981 and athletic events bringing Soviet and Chinese athletes together have multiplied, relations between the two countries, on the whole, remained strained. At times Moscow, at other times Beijing, has made a gesture to resume serious discussions. Among such gestures figured a visit of Mikhail Kapitsa, Chief of the Far Eastern Department of the Soviet Foreign Ministry, to Peking in early 1981, and some proposals to resume talks were made by Moscow in September and December 1981. The rejoinder made by Peking in December 1981 and especially on January 8, 1982, the latter by Li Xiannian,(17) a high-placed Chinese official, made clear that Sino-Soviet differences were no longer about ideological differences; Beijing thus removed the latter from the agenda because both sides, apparently, considered them insoluble. Li Xiannian insisted, however, that the Afghan and Indochinese issues would have to be discussed, though apparently Moscow was not likely to yield.

The contacts established between Beijing and the Italian and Spanish Eurocommunist Parties, often critical of the C.P.S.U., were also no move toward reconciliation or even mere abatement of the differences with Moscow. The visit to Beijing of the French Communist Maxime Gremetz in March 1982 and later in the year by the French head of the P.C.F., Georges Marchais, falls under the same category, being an attempt to give these Communist Parties some elbow room vis-à-vis Moscow. Brezhnev, in his address at Tashkent on March 24, 1982,(18) proposed border negotiations to the C.P.R., shoving ideological divergencies aside; these latter played no longer, he asserted, a vital role in their mutual relations. In any case, Moscow did not dispute that China was socialist. Brezhnev made clear, however, that the U.S.S.R. would not retreat on the issues of Mongolia, Afghanistan, and Indochina. In September 1981 and again in his last major address to a group of military officials, Brezhnev voiced his desire for Sino-Soviet normalization. He had perceived some minor positive changes in China's policy, thus offering some hope.

Neighborliness and Cooperation.(23) After the Soviet invasion, Amin was executed, and denounced as "that bloodthirsty
spy of American imperialism, oppressor, and dictator."

The Declaration of late May 1979 that Afghanistan was
now a "member of the Socialist family of nations" was a clear
warning to the West that the Soviet move into Afghanistan was
irreversible. The American government issued five warnings
during the last weeks of 1979 against any Soviet plan to invade
the country—of which only the last communication was made
public on December 22; it came definitely too late. The
judgment that the U.S.S.R. may have reached military parity
with the U.S. unquestionably emboldened the Soviets and
sharpened their aggressiveness.

"Afghanistan in Turmoil" by Xin Changlin, was one of
several articles which showed Chinese perspicacy in regard to
threatening developments in Afghanistan before the Soviet
invasion of the country.(24) While armed clashes between
Moslem forces and government troops in Afghanistan have
been growing, "Soviet efforts to jump at the chance to step up
control and interference have aroused strong opposition
among the people." There were reports that anti-government
forces in at least 15 of the 29 provinces were fighting the army.
In the so-called "April Revolution" of 1978, the Daoud regime
was toppled and a new government formed with the leader of
the Peoples Democratic Party, Taraki, as President and Prime
Minister, but the new party had never been able to establish
effective control. The Taraki government had repeatedly
declared its intention to pursue a foreign policy of independence and nonalignment.

But in less than a year, it had signed no less than 40
agreements with the Soviet Union, and large numbers of Soviet
specialists and advisers had been rushed to Afghanistan.
During his visit to Moscow in December 1978, Taraki had
signed a treaty of friendship and cooperation with the Soviet
Union and declared that he stood with it on many important
international issues. But the Afghan leader opposed the
Soviet-sponsored "Asian Security System." According to an
Afghan Moslem leader's public statement, the Soviet Union
had taken Afghan natural gas, copper, uranium, wool, and
other resources, at very low prices; it had actually plundered
the country. Moscow had long coveted Afghanistan "as a

strategic goal, as a land route southward to the Indian
Ocean." The officers of the 100,000-man Afghan army were
Soviet military men. But Moscow was shouting itself hoarse
about "interference" of the West in Afghanistan.

On December 31, *Pravda*'s A. Petrov, a pseudonym for the
daily's editorial board, tried to justify the Soviets' invasion of
Afghanistan as a mere response to alleged American plans of
staging a revolt in that country to use it as a glacis for the
invasion of the Soviet Union.(25) Petrov charged that there
was an obvious connection between trips to Pakistan by
American emissaries and the outbreak of the Afghan revolt.
Calls for help to Moscow had been made by the government of
Afghanistan, and repeatedly so during 1978-1979. The Soviet
government had made "no secret of the fact that it would not
allow Afghanistan to be transformed into a staging ground for
the preparation of imperialist aggression against the Soviet
Union. The U.S.S.R., therefore, had decided to satisfy the
most recent request from Kabul and to send to Afghanistan "a
limited Soviet military contingent, which will be used
exclusively to help repel armed interferences from the
outside." Moscow, quoting especially article 4 of the
Soviet-Afghan treaty and article 51 of the United Nations
Charter, rejected the "fabrication" of imperialist propaganda
relating to the alleged occupation of Afghanistan by Soviet
troops!(26) In mid-January, Brezhnev, responding to international criticism of Soviet actions in Afghanistan, attacked in
turn "imperialist and Beijing propaganda" which "deliberately
and shamelessly" was distorting the Soviet Union's role in
Afghanistan's affairs.(27)

A few weeks later, V. Kobysh in *Literaturnaya gazeta*,
March 12, 1980, rejected Washington's plea for a "neutraliza-
tion" of Afghanistan.(28) The journal again seemed puzzled
that a mere contingent of Soviet troops in Afghanistan was
arousing "such a rage" in Washington, Beijing, and certain
other capitals.

About half a year after the start of the invasion, on June
25, 1980, A. Petrov in *Pravda* held out the promise of reducing
the Soviet military in Afghanistan, but charged that the United
States, China, Pakistan, and Iran were continuing to train and
supply "counterrevolutionary bands."(29) China, in particular, was allegedly shipping anti-aircraft and anti-tank guns

proponent of American policy whose goal was to involve the
C.P.R., in one form or another, in the imperialist strategy of
"deterring" the Soviet Union.(35) As far as Japan's economic
assistance to China was concerned, it was supposed to be a
lever to back up the strategy plans of Washington and Tokyo
with respect to the C.P.R. It was no accident, therefore, that
before flying to Beijing, the Japanese Prime Minister
emphasized that his visit would take place right before
Reagan's trip to China and thus would prepare the ground for
a successful continuation of the American-Chinese dialogue.

Observers have also noted the fact that for some time
Beijing has toned down criticisms of many aspects of
Nakasone's governmental policy. The Chinese press no longer
raised questions of distortions in Japanese history textbooks of
the events connected with militaristic Japan's aggressions in
China and Asia in general during World War II. In the Words
of Deng, the problem of ownership of the Senkaku Islands "has
been left to our descendants to decide." Beijing has stopped
criticizing Tokyo's course aimed at the renewal of militarism
and strengthening of the military alliance with the United
States. Recently, the newspaper *Asahi* wrote that everything
has been done to avoid touching upon subjects that might have
a negative impact on bilateral relations. Contrary to obvious
facts, at the Beijing talks the Chinese Premier declared that, at
present, "the Nakasone government is not pursuing a policy of
militarism." Participants in the talks had indulged in crude
distortions of the Soviet Union's foreign policy.

On May 30, 1984, *Pravda* observed: Reagan and his
administration with an eye to the unfolding election campaign
in the United States, wanted to make the utmost use of the
"China factor." They wished to play the "China card" in the
context of confrontation with the Soviet Union in the Asian
and Pacific regions, to expand the areas, as Reagan stated it,
"of coinciding and harmonizing interests with China," and to
continue the coordination of actions with the C.P.R. on a
number of questions in the international arena.(36-37)

McFarlane, Assistant to the President for National Security
Affairs, confirmed that Beijing "unequivocally supported steps
aimed at the restoration of American might," with the aim of
checking "Soviet expansionism." "As one can judge from the
outcome of the talks, the Chinese side raised no objections to

the stepped-up encouragement of the militarization of Japanese and other United States allies or to the steps to knock together a Washington-Tokyo bloc." In view of Reagan's known proclamation of a "crusade" against communism, "the very fact of emphasizing during the American-Chinese talks the common nature of the two-sides' viewpoints on a number of fundamental questions of international politics was highly indicative."

In these talks, Beijing and Washington, in the Soviet view, called for the continuation of all-round support to the Afghan and Khmer counterrevolutionaries. During the discussion of the situation of Korea, the C.P.R. State Council, according to press reports, did not demand the withdrawal of American troops from South Korea—which, in the Soviet view, was the key problem for the resolution of the Korean question. Referring to the situation in Central America, the head of the Chinese government limited himself to the statement that "China does not approve of certain United States actions in this region," without mentioning American imperialism's aggression against Grenada and Nicaragua and the escalation of Washington's threats against socialist Cuba. Reagan's visit to the C.P.R. coincided with Beijing's exacerbation of tension on the Chinese-Vietnam border. The Beijing leadership reported its demand that it was necessary for the Soviet Unicn to remove the so-called "three big obstacles," which, as is known, concern the interests of the U.S.S.R.'s security and the Soviet Union's cooperation with Afghanistan, Vietnam, and Mongolia. Beijing was thus emphasizing that it would continue to hold to these well-known positions, which impeded the normalization of Chinese-Soviet relations. The Taiwan question, according to Western news agencies' reports, took less than five minutes to dispose of at the Beijing meeting. Both sides "obviously desire" not to accent, in Reagan's words, the "spheres where interests differ."

After his return from China, the President voiced his pleasure over the "introduction of the spirit of the free market in China's economy and expressed an optimistic view of prospects for American-Chinese economic cooperation." The Reagan Administration's openly hegemonistic power politics gave rise to a certain wariness even in official circles in Beijing. The world press cited this as the reason that the most offensive

and even being guided by a "grand design." Beijing fears encirclement and Moscow is persuaded of China's part in the encirclement plotted foremost by the U.S. It is, of course, difficult to establish with certainty to which extent this notion is based on genuine conviction and to which degree it rests on propagandistic needs to cast an unfavorable light upon the opponent. The past history of both China and the U.S.S.R. has, undoubtedly, bred suspicion and fear of penetration and invasion and has thus contributed to the phobia of conspiracies gripping their leaders and their peoples.

The C.P.R., Vietnam, Chinese Refugees, and the Indian Ocean

Vietnam, Kampuchea, and Indochina in general, and their relationship to the C.P.R. are in Soviet perception as significant as they are to China. According to M. Nikitin in *Pravda,* July 15, 1979, Beijing was "shouting that the Indochinese refugee problem might bring "destabilization" in Southeast China and blamed Hanoi "for the disastrous plight of the refugees from the Indochinese countries."(41) It accused the S.R.V. of violating human rights. The formation of a sizeable army of refugees from the Indochinese countries has taken place in several waves, each of them being directly connected with a certain stage in the policy of imperialist interference as well as with Chinese expansion in Indochina. Chinese propaganda and Beijing's agents are declared to have played a "provocative role by inciting Vietnamese citizens of Chinese descent" to leave the country by whatever means they could! Beijing was allegedly responsible for organizing a "wide-scale illegal emigration" and for "blackmailing and intimidating people to force /!/ them to leave Vietnam," and for smuggling of refugees aboard ships unfit for long voyages/!/; this has led to the death of passengers on the open sea.

The subversive anti-Vietnamese nature of this kind of activity can be seen in Beijing's special services to stimulate the departure from Vietnam, "above all of technical specialists, physicians, and other representatives of the intelligentsia." This "sabotage," according to Moscow, does maximum damage to socialist Vietnam and to its economy and culture.

It is evident that the Soviet press engaged thus in every untruth, to try to turn evil into good and good into evil.

In the competitive struggle for influence in the Third World in general and the so-called nonaligned movement, Moscow was anxious to align the latter—an apparent contradiction—with the Soviet camp and against China, prior to and during the Havana Conference of September 1979. A. Petrov charged that Beijing intrigued against the nonaligned movement and was essentially acting in concert with the imperialists.(42) The Politbureau of the C.P.C. envisioned imposing on the nonaligned countries Beijing's version of "anti-hegemonism." Beijing was steering a course aimed at creating a pro-Maoist nucleus consisting of Pol Pot's Kampuchea, Sadat's Egypt, and certain other states, at undermining the positions of Cuba and Vietnam, going so far as trying to expel them from the movement. It aimed at delaying and finally torpedoing the 6th Conference of Heads of State and Government of the Nonaligned Countries, slated to be held in Havana in September 1979. China is anxious to knock together an alliance hostile to the Soviet Union.

Some time ago, Beijing propagandists began to declare that it was possible to "postpone a war" (which they had earlier proclaimed to be "inevitable")—but only if all forces united to rebuff the "main threat" to peace which, the Chinese leadership asserted, was the Soviet Union. Chinese propaganda was sending out a torrent of insinuations and slander against Cuba, Vietnam, Laos, and Afghanistan, but primarily the U.S.S.R. The Soviet government in turn denounced the "perfidy" of China's current rulers and China's threat to the independence and sovereignty of all states in Southeast Asia.(43)

In the article, "Give Peking's Aggression a Resolute Rebuff," I. Aleksandrov held that this was the more imperative since the C.P.R. tried to create the impression that it was fighting "Vietnam aggressors" and to "regain" territory "supposedly seized from China at some unspecified time. It also claims to have entered Vietnam only in pursuit of the enemy.(44) Once again, the Maoist ruling clique was "misleading the Chinese population with fabrications and slander concerning the neighboring states" and was stirring up chauvinistic sentiments in order "to conceal its true expansion-

acting against democratic Afghanistan. As the people's revolution unfolded in Iran, Beijing also stood by the Shah to the end. Hardly anyone in Iran would be favorably impressed by Beijing's latest 180-degree turn, executed just the other day, when it belatedly announced its "support" for the new Iranian government and offered an "apology for its previous hostile position toward the revolution."

The Soviets blamed China also for Kampuchea's distress. (48) Vietnam had "not occupied Kampuchea, but extended a reliable hand of fraternal assistance, friendship and solidarity to that country's people."

The United States was assailed for balking at Indian Ocean Arms Talks.(49) Maintaining peace in the vast Indian Ocean was not only a problem of ensuring the security of several dozens littoral states in Asia and Africa whose peoples make up one-fourth of mankind. The question of a tranquil peaceful solution had also a direct bearing on the security of the Soviet Union. "The waters of the Indian Ocean, its shores and its island territories are comparatively close /!/ to our country, if one bears in mind the range of modern means of strategic attack. Futhermore, the only sea route linking the European part of U.S.S.R. and the Soviet Far East that is opean the year-round runs through the Indian Ocean." "Of course, the Soviet Union cannot remain indifferent to the rapid build-up of the United States military presence and its military activity in the Indian Ocean."

Andropov and Chernenko; Dispute Over the Sino-Soviet Border, Afghanistan, Indochina, and Outer Mongolia

Long after Brezhnev's first overtures to the C.P.R. in 1964 to improve mutual relations, China appeared little responsive. (50) Following the border clashes of 1969, the Soviet Union withdrew its troops from all islands in the Ussuri river along the Manchurian-Soviet border except one island across Khabarovsk. But ever since these clashes, the Chinese have insisted that this island and some land in the Pamirs were among the "disputed territories." In 1980 Beijing even refused to renew the 1950 Sino-Soviet treaty of alliance.

Prominent Soviet leaders, though unwilling to make major concessions to the C.P.R., were prepared to tone down the bellicose tone of their controversy. On November 22, 1982, Y. V. Andropov, General Secretary of the Central Committee, came out for establishing "prompt solutions" everywhere.(51) "This also refers to our great neighbor, the C.P.R." Brezhnev himself had earlier placed emphasis on common sense and on the need to overcome the inertia of prejudices: "We are paying great attention to every positive response from the Chinese side."

Under Chernenko, Andropov's successor, Foreign Minister Gromyko, repeating a hard line on the U.S., did, however, while referring to Afghanistan and Indochina, not mention China by name.(52) *Pravda* wrote then: "Provocative intrigues against sovereign, nonaligned Afghanistan are continuing. The foes of the Afghan people are not giving up their hopes of returning to medieval darkness. To this end, armed incursions from outside are being organized."(53) It was necessary and possible to "stop the formation, arming and infiltration into this country from the outside of anti-government bands of marauders and saboteurs and not to interfere in Afghanistan's internal affairs. The policy of external forces is complicating the situation in South-East Asia. Provocations against Vietnam, Laos, and Kampuchea are continuing. An attempt is being made to bring these countries into conflict with their neighbors — states that belong to the Association of South-East Asian Nations."

On occasion of a visit of Mongolia's new leader, Zh. Batmunkh to Moscow in November 1984, Chernenko struck a solemn tone, while not closing the door to the possibility of improving Sino-Soviet relations: "Putting its stakes in a policy of force, the United States is declaring more and more parts of the planet, including the Far East, Southeast Asia and the Pacific and Indian Oceans, to be zones of 'vital interests.' The build-up of U.S. military strategic means in the region near the U.S.S.R.'s Far Eastern border continues. The military cooperation of the United States, Japan, and South Korea, aimed at the creation of a kind of eastern branch of NATO, is expanding. . .a tense situation remains in other parts of Asia as well."(54) The Soviet proposal of confidence — building measures in the Far East and in the Pacific and Indian Oceans remains in force." Normalization of the situation on the Asian continent was a Soviet goal. This was especially important at

policy parallels U.S. policy, while it is diametrically opposed to
that of the Soviet Union. After the Vietnamese war, the
C.P.R. did no longer fear a return of the U.S. to the mainland
of Asia; it sees no threat from the U.S. comparable to that
from the Soviet Union. But the Beijing tactics of "independence" of its foreign policy dictates a propaganda line which keeps
equal distance from Moscow and Washington, though Beijing
entertains little doubt that such propaganda, dictated by
opportunism, distorts reality.

Ideology, "Normalization," and Detente with the C.P.R.

Since Mao's demise, both Beijing and Moscow may well
have concluded that they exaggerated the differences between
themselves and that a realistically interpreted national
self-interest demanded the reduction of these divergencies to a
more rational level. Ideological, territorial, and geopolitical
differences, and those relating to national rivalry between the
two Communist giants in regard to other Communist parties
and the Third World are all too real. The likelihood of either
of the two powers surrendering vital national interests and
basic points of view to the opponent, without receiving
tangible compensation in return, was always non-existent. But
nationalist and ideological truculence and fierce power rivalry
have often inflamed passions on both sides and complicated
reasonable solution of the conflict.

There was, however, at times, little room for diplomatic
maneuver. Chinese demands for Soviet concessions in Asia,
which are of major concern to the C.P.R. — in Afghanistan,
Kampuchea, Mongolia, and regarding Soviet troop deploy-
ments along the lengthy Sino-Soviet border — were unlikely to
be met in a substantive manner. But these were the very
demands most regularly posed by Beijing. The Soviets could
not be expected to surrender hard-won gains. While mutual
Sino-Soviet criticism has continued during the last decade, it
has somewhat abated. Both sides, having acquired an
immunity against the accusations hurled against each other,
have grown tired. Thus, the dispute has lost some of its
sharpest edges. Neither side dwells any more on ideological,
the "theological," aspects of the dispute, as they did in earlier
years.

Communist ideology as a divisive factor, however, is by no means dead and will never completely disappear. Marxism-Leninism will not totally vanish from the intellectual, political, and economic life of either the U.S.S.R. or the C.P.R. But, at the moment, both sides keep Marxism-Leninism, and in Beijing also Maoism, under wraps and refuse ideology and the interpretation of the Marxist holy scriptures to dominate their mutual relationship. Repeatedly, both sides, when talking about "normalization" of relations, limit it to state rather than Party relationsí State relations may have improved since the end of the Cultural Revolution and the death of Mao, but, in the opinion of both parties, they have not reached the level of "normal" state relations. The relations of China with the capitalist and economically and socially developed states of Western Europe and Japan are more pacific and friendly than Sino-Soviet relations.

"Normalization"—whatever the meaning of the term—is not only in China's but in the Soviet Union's national interests. The military build-up of the U.S.S.R. along the China frontier has given the Soviet Union a greater degree of security. On the whole, the Soviet Union has somewhat lessened its propaganda war against the C.P.R. Its earlier attempt to discredit the C.P.R. and to isolate it as a "heretic" has failed. It has been unable to curtail the contacts of the C.P.C. with the Eurocommunist Parties and others. Even the pro-Soviet French Communist Party has sent its leading spokesman, G. Marchais, to Beijing. The C.P.R., in turn, after starting to run the gamut of a Deng-inspired policy of a global alliance against the U.S.S.R., has reverted to a less provocative and dangerous policy of criticizing both superpowers and maintaining an uneasy balance between both.

Under Gorbachev's leadership, the Soviet Union seems to be increasing its contacts with the U.S. and is also bent on improving its relations with the C.P.R. The Soviet Union's policy is based upon the recognition that it cannot control the entire range and intensity of Sino-American relations. Moscow has ridiculed China's fears of encirclement, but, though controlling a much larger territory, it fears encirclement itself, or claims to do so. In any case, the Soviet support for Vietnam in Kampuchea and Indochina in its entirety and the Soviet invasion of Afghanistan have actually resulted in "encircling"

China in a vast pincers movement. Such encirclement may not
have been Soviet intention from the beginning, but it has been
the inevitable result of its policies. The huge Soviet naval
build-up in the Western Pacific merely completes the actual
Soviet encirclement of the C.P.R. Despite the Soviets'
undisputed military superiority, as compared to Beijing's
military stance, they fear strategic encirclement themselves,
especially by the U.S., the Second World—Western Europe
and Japan—and China.

At present, and for the foreseeable future, China remains
the weakest power in the triangular relationship between the
U.S.S.R., the U.S.A., and the C.P.R., due to its economic,
technological, and military backwardness. Its potentialities,
however, in the long run, are striking, not the least for reasons
of its population being larger than that of the U.S.S.R. and
the U.S.A. together, and the abilities of its people. While the
latter two states are able to project their power almost to every
part of the globe, China will remain for some time to come a
regional, Asiatic power, a Third World nation, rather than
one of global outreach.

Hu Yaobang and Gorbachev

On June 11, 1986, Hu Yaobang, General Secretary of the
C.P.C., spoke at the British Royal Institute of International
Affairs in London. He admitted that China may appear to be
an "inscrutable country" "to some of our friends in the
Western world."(55) After citing historical and geographic
causes for this sentiment, he conceded that since the founding
of New China more than three decades ago, there has been
great progress but there have been "many twists and turns." In
the past few years, the reform in the C.P.R. and its opening to
the outside world, while scoring successes, have not been
favored by all people abroad. While their first reaction was
that our policies were "nothing but heresies"—apparently the
reaction of Soviet critics—these suspicions have tapered off in
recent years. Others still believed that the new Chinese policies
will "lean to and eventually merge with the model of Western
society." But Yaobang confirmed that China's policy of
socialism, which has enabled China to solve the problems of
food and clothing, has found to be the "correct road for

building socialism with Chinese characteristics." Reform in China will not lead people "astray," but will rather help perfect China's socialist system.

Peking will not enter into alliance with either East or West, but firmly side with Third World countries. China, "not having completely lifted itself from poverty and backwardness," it will be impossible to bridge the historical gap between herself and the developed countries "without decades or even a century /!/ of peaceful economic development." China is "determined to remain independent in our foreign relations vis-à-vis certain big powers and maintain friendly ties with Third World countries, in accordance with the Five Principles of Peaceful Coexistence. China's foreign relations will not "hinge on the similarity or differences in social systems and ideologies." Clearly, Peking's stance for peace and furtherance of her national interests takes unquestioned primacy over ideology, including the interests of the Soviet Union and the Socialist bloc.

Similarly, the C.P.R.'s placing emphasis on economic development takes priority over "expansion" of military strength. Nor will China be able even "in the next several decades" "to spend heavily on expanding its military forces."(56) China will never become a party to the arms race. After careful consideration, "we have reached the conclusion that the right thing for us to do is to concentrate on economic development and gradually improve the people's livelihood, and, on that basis, to strengthen our defense capabilities step by step."

However, since the C.P.R. must be prepared against any surprise attacks, it will be necessary to maintain an adequate defense capability and to import some advanced military technologies. But China, with a vast territory which gives her much room for maneuvering, and also being a populous nation, has her own ways of defense. She will not be intimidated if war is imposed upon her. The current policies, based on collective wisdom, having the support of the overwhelming majority of the people, will not be changed.

Addressing in 1986 the Soviet Party Congress, Gorbachev made a few remarks on China which were remarkable for the absence of any criticism(57) of the C.P.R. and her policies, and his cautious approach, while admitting differences between the two communist countries, particularly differences in regard to a number of international problems: "One can speak with satisfaction," he claimed, "about a certain amount of improvement in the Soviet Union's relations with its great neighbor-socialist China (Applause)." While other differences "remain," "we also note something else — the possibility in many cases of working jointly and of cooperating on an equal and principled basis, without detriment to third countries." (Actually, on the latter ground the Soviets have rejected numerous Chinese proposals regarding the settling of the divisive issues of Outer Mongolia, Vietnam, and Afghanistan.) Relating to some recent Chinese practices of referring positively to the Soviet Union's early historical record, Gorbachev continued by striking an optimistic note: "The Chinese Communists have called the victories of the U.S.S.R. and the forces of progress in World War I "a prologue to the victory of the people's revolution" in China. He flattered Beijing: The formation of people's China helped to strengthen socialism's world positions and to thwart many schemes and actions of imperialism in the very difficult postwar years. Thinking of the future, one can say that the reserves for cooperation between the U.S.S.R. and China are enormous. "(58)

The vast "diversity" of the Communist movement was an indisputable reality. Sometimes, this led to differences of opinion. The C.P.S.U. did not dramatize the fact that there was not always total unanimity among the Communist Parties, but diversity was not synonymous with disunity.

Corresponding to the conciliatory tone of Gorbachev's remarks on China, observations in Soviet dailies in 1986 on China's living conditions and economic progress have been more objective and favorable, relying partly also on more candid Chinese reports. On March 17, according to *Pravda*, China has markedly improved its working people's well-being in recent years;(59) on the other hand, her economy was "still plagued by a great many problems and difficulties." Quoting *Renmin Ribao*, *Pravda* listed "unjustifiably high rates of economic development, strained material resources," and others. The level of unemployment was still almost 2%. Similarly, *Izvestia* reported on January 31st(60) that, also according to *Renmin Ribao*, and dwelling on some unfavorable aspects of the C.P.R.'s economy, private enterprise was assuming great importance in providing employment in the cities and in utilizing surplus workers in the villages. It was expected that, in 1990 those employed in the private sector should reach fifty million.

Partly attributable to Gorbachev's new course of soft-pedalling differences with China, partly due to the continuing strained relations with the other triangular partner, the U.S.A., the Soviets attempted to stress positive aspects and improvements in the Sino-Soviet relationship. On March 19, 1986, *Pravda* reported of a meeting between the Prime Minister of the C.P.R.'s State Council and L. V. Arkhipov, First Vice-Chairman of the U.S.S.R. Council of Ministers.(61) While the latter stressed the Soviets' consistent desire to improve relations with the C.P.R. and expand multilateral cooperation between the two countries, the head of the Beijing government claimed that the two great neighboring socialist countries had "a great deal in common in their systems it would be useful to establish an economic management and to set up an exchange of experience and information in this area." Clearly, in contrast with past years when both sides did not hesitate to sharply criticize the other's domestic policies, both have come to display an eagerness to exchange pleasantries, subdue much criticism, and stress only what they allegedly held in common rather than what divided them. *Pravda* even pointed to a speech by Peng Zhen, member of the Politburo of the C.P.C., in which he pledged loyalty to Marxism-Leninism, denying that, contrary to some Chinese critics, this stance signified only conservatism and opposition to reforms. *Pravda* simply appeared pleased that he held up Marxism-Leninism, all differences in their interpretation aside: Similarly, when the first session of the Soviet-Chinese Commission on Economic, Trade, Scientific and Technical Cooperation ended in Moscow on March 22, 1986, *Pravda*, ignoring its scarce results, welcomed the increase in the volume of mutual trade in 1985 and stressed that both sides noted the existence of "considerable potential" for further Sino-Soviet scientific and technical cooperation.(62) In an interview of *Izvestia*'s correspondent with Arkhipov, after the first meeting of the joint Sino-Soviet Economic Commission, the latter disclosed that the peak of trade between the two countries had been reached back in the late 1950s when the maximum annual volume of trade turnover was approximately two billion rubles. In the late 1960s, trade and economic relations were reduced to virtually nothing. They revived, however, in 1983-1984, exceeding in 1985 1.6 billion rubles. But this, obviously, fell still short of the heights reached a generation ago!

V

CONCLUSION

Highlights in the Sino-Soviet relationship were the years 1963, when the dispute burst into the open, and the Cultural Revolution under Mao, when the hostility reached a climax. Such improvement of mutual relations, as has occurred after Mao, grew out of mutual resignation rather than of positive, pragmatically based decisions of Moscow and Beijing. Both sides, however, have come to realize that hurling insults against each other, without being followed by effective policies and measures against the adversary, produce few positive results. After a lengthy period marked by hostility, bitterness, and disappointment, if not outright shock at the rapid escalation of the rift between ideological "brothers"— deepened by the clash of strong and unbending personalities such as Stalin, Krushchev, Mao, and some of their successors-both Beijing and Moscow have toned down their acrimonious polemics. Their continuing confrontation, enhanced by an unrelenting war of words, was unlikely to further their domestic and international interests.

During the last years, the two Communist giants have reached agreements only on peripheral issues, on trade, scientific, and cultural exchange, rather than on primary issues, such as territorial, geopolitical, and military questions. An agreement on side issues may improve the climate for making further progress, but will not assure the solution of fundamental problems. On political, territorial and geopolitical issues of major importance, progress seems doubtful. Likewise, with China's nationalist and "independent" posture growing stronger, it is not likely that the C.P.R. will ever acknowledge any sort of ideological leadership of Moscow over the Communist world, especially over the C.P.R. For its prized modernization, China will depend much more on America, Japan, and the technology of Western Europe than upon Soviet technology, itself lagging behind the West.

A far as the Third World is concerned, rivalry between the two Communist neighbors is going to continue, with the Soviet union being able to hold out economic advantages especially to individual client states, both near and far away. But, in view of its aggressive moves into Afghanistan and threats in Poland, the Soviets have alienated many on account of their patent imperialist ambitions, their ruthless methods, and bullying tactics. China, having long scaled down its earlier grandiose economic plans, has become pragmatic; it is not likely to become a model of economic reforms for underdeveloped states. On the other hand, the Soviet Union, though an industrial giant, is hampered by the most serious economic problems, by bureaucratization and lack of incentives, all of which has darkened the prospects for less developed states of the Third World of following the Soviet example. On the other hand, some military leaders and dictators of the Third World are bent on retaining political control by all means. The absence of democratic and parliamentary tradition and of a solid middle class in their countries has pushed their leaders toward totalitarianism the one-party state, and toward the Soviet Union rather than toward Western models. Compared to Beijing, Moscow has been able to offer some Third World nations and organizations, professing conversion to the Communist creed, tangible economic benefits.

Moscow may not fear Beijing's raising territorial demands at present and in the near future, but the apparent unwillingness of the C.P.R. to entirely relinquish territorial claims may remain a source of irritation, if not an outright negative factor in Sino-Soviet relations. Chinese revisionism may be down-played in the immediate future, but it will remain a very divisive issue in their relationship. As a superpower, the U.S.S.R. is in no position to make significant concessions. Yielding to China would create dangerous precedents which, in the Soviet mind, would haunt the U.S.S.R. With its military might growing—disproportionately in relation to the C.P.R.—the U.S.S.R., on the contrary, may be tempted to push its boundaries and its influence beyond her present frontiers. Considering the circumstance that internal problems will not show major improvements tn the years to come, the need to appear a strong and dynamic power in international affairs will not abate. The more difficult domestic economic and social problems will become, the greater will be the temptation for Soviet adventures in foreign affairs. The major arena for foreign exploits will be the states of the Third World, where social, economic, political, and psychological unrest is rampant. The unrelenting Soviet drive for expansion, prestige, and power is not likely to lessen in any part of the globe, especially not in the regions bordering the C.P.R. The U.S.S.R. is unlikely to make far-reaching concessions, such as China still insists upon.

On the whole, Chinese criticism of Soviet domestic policy has abated since the death of Mao, but not of Soviet foreign affairs and foreign policy, which affects the C.P.R.'s interests more immediately and deeply. The same may be said of Soviet criticism of China; it also embraces sharper criticism of Chinese foreign policy and its gyrations toward the West during the last decade than of domestic policy.

While the Soviets in general have castigated Beijing's anti-Soviet political course, occasionally they have set their hopes on the fragility of the bonds linking the P.R.C. with the West.(1) In *Pravda*, I. Aleksandrov stressed the fact that Beijing is not tied to Washington by a "formal military alliance." Indeed, while for a time it appeared that Beijing had produced a 180-degree turn in its foreign policy, swinging from an anti-American stance to that of an apparently close alliance with the U.S., for a number of years Beijing's security strategy has compelled it to choose some distance from both superpowers. In view of the presence of a Soviet threat and the absence of an American threat to the P.R.C., China's position is not one of equidistance in relation to both powers—it leans now more closely toward the U.S. But Beijing is careful not to give the Soviets any excuse for an abrupt turnabout of policy and for further impairing Sino-Soviet relations.

To answer the questions posed in the subtitle of this book—"Detente, Dispute, or Conflict?"—a genuine detente between the Soviet Union and the C.P.R. is no likely prospect. Much less is the likelihood that they will become allies again in the foreseeable future. China's Vice-Premier Li Peng on April 15, 1986, told American journalists in Beijing that the two Communist neighbors "will not become allies."(2)

On the other hand, the prevailing trend since the early 1980s on both sides of the Sino-Soviet border has been a deliberate toning down of the polemics between the two states. while the divisive issues are as alive as ever and the determination of both Moscow and Beijing not to yield and retreat from their entrenched position and demands—their national interests and prestige would not permit it—neither seems interested in escalating the dispute and confrontation. The Soviets are not likely to unleash their superior military forces against the C.P.R. The Soviet Union may fear that the Chinese colossus is in the long run unbeatable and that war against the C.P.R. would soon involve the U.S. which has both European and Asiatic interests. The U.S.S.R. would thus be drawn into a two-front war and risk widespread destruction. In the event of a nuclear war, the C.P.R. undoubtedly fears unprecedented human and material losses, notwithstanding its claims to the contrary. It is also keenly aware of its own technical backwardness and military inferiority as compared to its heavily armed neighbor, and of the possibility of prolonged or permanent occupation of its vulnerable border regions.

Will the Sino-Soviet relationship remain a permanent dispute, at times abating, at other times mounting, or will it threaten to continue, as has often been the case in the past quarter of the century, as a *confrontation* threatening to escalate? It is impossible to give a precise answer to such questions. But it is more likely that the Sino-Soviet relationship will veer back and forth within this broad gray area of dispute and confrontation than to assume that the Soviet Union will take the greater risks of outright war.

FOOTNOTES

I. A.

1. For a more detailed treatment of the period 1945 to the Cultural Revolution (1966-) see A. D. Low, *The Sino-Soviet Conflict* (1976), pp. 44-336
2. Callis, H. G. *China Confucian and Communist*, 1959, pp. 383-394
3. Acheson, D. *Present at the Creation*, 1969, p. 66
4. Salisbury, H. E., *War Between Russia and China*, 1969, p. 66
5. Hinton, H. C. *China's Turbulent Quest*, 1972, p. 62
6. Clubb, E. *China and Russia; The "Great Game,"* 1964, pp. 408-409
7. *Statements by Krushchev*, Peking 1965, reprinted in *Peking Review* (subsequently *PR* or later *Beijing Review, B.R.*) Apr. 30, 1965; also *The Current Digest of the Soviet Press (CDSP)*, 8 No. 4, March 7, 1956, pp. 3-15, 29 (Translation copyright by *The Current Digest of the Soviet Press*, published weekly at Columbus, Ohio. Used by permission.)
8. *Statements*, see No. 7.
9. *CDSP*, Nr. 4. March 14,1956
10. *Pravda*, March 28, 1956; *CDSP*, Nr. 9, Apr. 11, 1956, pp. 3, 6-7
11. *People's Daily,* April 5, 1956
12. *Ibid.*; also *P.R.,*Sept. 20, 1963
13. Low, *op. cit.*, pp. 76-77
14. *Pravda*, Oct. 31, 1956, in *CDSP*, 8, No. 8, Nr. 45 (Nov. 14, 1956, pp. 10-11)
15. *People's Daily*, Peking, Nov. 2, 1956, quoted in P. Zinner, *National Communism. . .*(1956), pp. 492-495
16. Gomulka's speech, Nov. 26, 1956, quoted by J. Gittings, *Survey of the Sino-Soviet Dispute*, (1968), p. 69, also BBC *Survey of World Broadcasts*, pt 2a, no. 782
17. Reprinted in *PR*, Apr. 26, 1960
18. *Pravda* and *Izvestia*, Apr. 23, 1960, pp. 1-3 (*CDSP*, 12, Nr. 17, 1960, pp. 8-12)

19. *Pravda*, Jan. 7, 1963, pp. 1-3 (*CDSP*, 15, Nr. 1, Jan. 30, 1963, pp. 1-10, 28)

20. The Chinese letter and the June letter of the CC of the CPSU were published simultaneously in *Pravda*, July 14, 1963, pp. 1-4 (*CDSP*, 15, Nr. 28, Aug. 7, 1963, p.16 f.

21. Reprinted in *PR*, June 5, 1964

22. *Pravda*, June 12, 1965 (*CDSP*, 17, No. 24, Aug. 7, 1965, pp. 6-7)

23. *PR*, May 6, 1966, against Marshal Malinovsky; see also *Pravda*, Dec. 14, 1966

24. *Pravda* and *Izvestia*, July 4, 1968, pp. 2-3 (*CDSP* 20, No. 27, July 24, 1968, p.8)

25. *Kommunist*, No. 7, May 1968, pg 103-14 (*CDSP*, 20, No. 27, July 24, 1968, p.8); a Chinese rejoinder, *People's Daily*, June 4, 1967 (*PR*, June 9, 1967), also *Literaturnaya gazeta*, No. 16, Apr. 15, 1970, in *Current Abstracts. . .*, May 1970, p. 5

26. *Pravda*, June 6, 1967, p. 1.

27. *PR* June 9, 1967, pp 8-10

28. *People's Daily*, June 13, 1967 (in *PR*, June 16, pp. 17-18)

29. *Izvestia*, Aug. 21, 1968

30. *PR*, Aug. 23, 1968

31. *PR*, Apr. 24, 1970, p.10. Editorial Departments of *People's Daily*, Red Flag, and *Jiefangjun Bao*

32. *PR*, May 30, 1969, p. 16

33. *Ibid*.

34. *Kommunist*, No. 5, March 1969, pp. 104-116

35. Kissinger, H. *White House Years* (1979), pp. 167-168

36. *Ibid*., pp. 178-192

37. *PR*, Feb. 28, 1973, pp. 6-7; also *People's Daily*, editorial, Jan. 28, 1973

38. *PR*, Apr. 20, 1973, pp. 16-17

39. *PR*, Oct. 5, 1973, pp. 1-17

40. *PR*, September 7, 1973

41. *PR*, Dec. 21, 1973, pp. 4-5

42. *Ibid*., p. 21

43. *PR*, Jan. 9, 1974, p. 11

44. *International Affairs*, No. 7, 1973, L. Alexeiev, "Anti-Sovietism in Peking's Strategy," pp. 2lf.

45. Borisov and Koloskov, *Soviet-Chinese Relations 1945-1970 . An Outline*, (Moscow, 1972), p. 470

I.B.

1. As background for the last decade, see Jonas, Peter, and Sian Kevill (compilators), *China and the Soviet Union 1949-84* (London, 1985), chs. X and XI
2. *Pravda*, Oct. 1, 1976, A. Aleksandrov
3. Louis, V. *London Evening News*, Oct. 12, 1976
4. Brezhnev's address to the C.C. of the CPSU, Oct. 25, 1976
5. Chinese Foreign Ministry, Nov. 1, 1976
6. *Pravda*, Feb. 10, 1977, also May 14, Aleksandrov; see the Soviet note of May 19
7. Hua Guofeng's address at the Eleventh CP Congress
8. Low, *op.cit.* p. 132
9. *People's Daily*, Nov. 5, 1977
10. *Ibid.*
11. Supreme Soviet's message to Standing Committee of the Chin. National People's Congress on Feb. 24, 1978, and Hua Guofeng's report on Feb. 26
12. Conference report on Contemporary Soviet literature in Harbin, Sept. 1979, published on Dec. 20, 1979, *B.R.*, Dec. 20, 1979
13. *People's Daily*, Apr. 2, 1980
14. *Pravda*, Apr. 4, 1980
15. Beijing's note to the Soviets, Dec. 31, 1979
16. *Pravda*, Apr. 7, 1980, Aleksandrov
17. Jones and Kevill, *op. cit.*, p. 140
18. *Ibid.*, p. 143
19. *Pravda*, Sept. 24, 1973
20 . *L'Unità*, Jan. 8, 1982
21. Outer Mongolia's note to Beijing, Apr. 12, 1978; see also Tsedenball at Eighteenth Congress of the MPRP, May 26, 1981
22. *Pravda*, Feb. 28, 1979
23-24. Jones and Kevill, *op. cit.*, pp. 165-69
25. *Pravda*, Dec. 1, 1984, p.4 (in CDSP, XXXIV, Nr.48, pp. 10-11)
26. *B.R.*, Sept. 10, 1984, vol. 27, Nr. 37; see also Yu Sui, *B.R.*, Sept. 10, 1984, "Soviet Union's Diplomacy tends toward Rigidity"
27. Quoted by Jones and Kevill, *op. cit.*, p. 169, and for the following

28. *Pravda*, March 25, 1982, Brezhnev, March 24
29. Chinese Foreign Ministry, March 26, 1982, *B.R.*
30. *Pravda* May 20, 1982
31. Hu Yaobang, Report to the Twelfth Party Congress, Sept. 1, 1982, and *B.R*, Aug. 8, 1982
32.-33. Zhao Ziyang, Sept. 27, 1982
34. *Pravda*, V. Afanas'yev, Tokyo, Nov. 16, 1982
35. *New Times*, Moscow, Jan. 14, 1983
36. *Tass* commentary, Apr. 29, 1984
37. *B.R.* Jan. 21, 1985, vol. 28, Nr. 3, pp. 12-13
38. *B.R.*, March 25, 1985, Nr. 12, p. 6
39. *B.R.*, Oct. 12, 1984, Nr. 42, p. 15
40. *B.R.*, Dec. 2, 1985, p. 30
41. *Ibid.*
42. *B.R.* Jan. 28, 1985, Nr. 4, p. 30
43. *Izvestia*, Apr. 6, 1985, p.5; *Pravda*, Apr. 8, p. 4 *Pravda*, May 1, 1985 (*CDSP*, June 12, 1985)
44. *B.R.*, Yao Yilin, July 16, 1985 ; see also *CDSP*, vol. 37, Nr. 28, Aug. 7, 1985, p. 11; *Pravda*, July 11, 1985, p. 4
45 . *CDSP*, Nr. 26, July 24, 1985, and July 12, p. 1
46. *Pravda* and *Izvestia*, June 30, 1985, pp. 1-2
47. Li Peng to Amer. journalists in Beijing, Apr. 15, 1986 *B.R*, vol. 29, Nr. 16, Apr. 21, 1986

II. A.

1. *Krushchev Remembers* (1974), pp. 235-92
2. *Ibid.*, p. 241
3. Adenauer, K. *Erinnerungen*, vol., II,; see also Griffith, *Ostpolitik.* . ., pp. 78, 71-72
4. Krushchev, *op. cit.*, p. 246
5. *Ibid.*, p. 284
6. *Ibid.*, p. 286
7. *Ibid.*, p. 287
8. *Sekai Shuno*, Tokyo, Aug. 11, 1963, quoted in Doolin, *Territorial Claims in the Sino-Soviet Conflict* (1963), pp. 43-44
9. Krushchev, Sept. 15, 1964, in *CDSP*, 15, Oct. 14, 1964: "Concerning Mao's talk with a group of Japanese Socialists," *Pravda*, Sept, 2, 1964, p. 2 (*CDSP*, 16, Nr. 34, Sept. 16, 1964, pp. 3-7)

10. *Pravda* on Mao's foregoing interview, Sept. 2 and Sept. 16, 1964

11. *Pravda*, ibid.

12. *Ibid.*

13. *Ibid*

14. *Ibid*

15. *Journal of International Studies*, 1981, Li Huichun, quoted also in *B.R.*, vol. 24, Nr. 30, pp. 12-17

16. *Journ. of Internat. Studies*, 1981, Li Huichan, (*B.R.*, Nr. 15, 1981), quoting the Statement of China, Sept. 4, 1923, and also the Agreement on General Principles for the Settlement of Questions between China and the Soviet Union, May 19, 1924

17. Li Huichan, "The Crux of the Boundary Question," *Journ. of Internat. Studies*, reprinted in *B.R.*, Aug. 3, 1981, vol. 24, Nr. 31, pp. 13-16; also *B.R.*, Nr. 37, Sept. 14, 1981, pp. 21-23 and 13-16

18. In view of these differences it is hardly surprising that subsequently there was also a Sino-Soviet disagreement whether there existed "disputed areas" at all, (*B.R.*, Nr. 30, July 19, 1981, p. 17)

19.-20. *Ibid.*

21. Gittings, J. *The World and China 1922-1972* (1974), p. 256, 264-65, 268

22. Hinton, H.C., "Sino-Soviet Relations: Background and Overview," in Stuart and Tow, *China, the Soviet Union and the West* (1982), especially pp. 13, 16, and 19-21. On one hand, Hinton dismisses the territorial issue, though on the other he is unable to deny its permanency and speaks of the "highly sensitive border issue" and of Beijing's being deeply resentful of the Soviet "bullying." He believes that the "real issue is political tension"(16) and China's rejection of a "semisatellite status".(21) Actually, the border question is intrinsically linked with all of this, but also a factor *sui generis*.

23. Kissinger, H. *White House Years*, p. 166

24. Hinton, *op. cit.*, pp. 20-21

25. See 23.

II. B.

1. *Krushchev Remembers* (1974). pp. 245-57 and 283-89

2. *Ibid.* (1970 ed.), pp. 461 and 476

3. Borisov and Koloskov, *Sino-Soviet Relations* (Moscow, 1975), p. 330
4. Aspaturian, V.A. "The Domestic Sources of Soviet Policy toward China," in Stuart and Tow, *op. cit.*, pp. 39f
5. *Krushchev Remembers* (1974), p. 258
6. *Ibid.*, pp. 260-61
7. *Ibid.*, p. 263
8. *Ibid.*, pp. 275-77
9. For the following, *ibid.*, pp. 277-79
10. See 4 p. 45; see also the many works listed in the Bibliography on nationalities in the Soviet and Chinese border regions.
11. *Ibid.*
12. Gittings, *Survey.* . .(1968), p. 167; about Mao and Mongolia, see Krushchev, *op. cit.* (1974), p. 285
13. Bialer, S. "Soviet Perspectives," In Ellison, H., *The Sino-Soviet Conflict* (1982), p. 40, and D. Treadgold, "Alternative Western Views. . ."*ibid* , p. 352
14. Low, A.D., "Soviet Nationality Policy and the New Programm of the CPSR," *The Russian Review*, Jan. 1961, pp. 3-29, and "The Sino-Soviet Confrontation since Mao. . ." *Canadian Review of Studies in Nationalism*, IX, 2, fall 1982, pp. 183-199
15. *B.R.*, March 3, 1972
16. Mao, Feb. 1957; see also *Selected Works of Mao Tsetung*, vol. V (1977), p. 406; both nationalisms are "harmful."
17. Tsedenball, Moscow Conference, July 1969
18. Rakhimov T., "The Great Ppower Policy of Mao. . .and his Group on the Nationalities," *Kommunist* 1967, Nr. 4
19.-20 *B.R.*, Lu Yun, "Minority People living in the Capital" vol. 28, Nr. 52, Dec. 30, 1985
21. *B.R.*, Lu Yun, "Believers Pray for World Peace," vol. 29, Nr. 28, July 18, 1986, pp. 23-24
22. see 14., *Russian Review*
23. *B.R.*, "Soviet Hegemonists. New Tsars inherit the Predecessors' Mantle," Nr. 17, Apr. 27, 1979, pp. 13-14
24. *Pravda*, Feb. 27, 1979, Sladkovsky, "Great Chinese Chauvinism in Action," *CDSP*, XXXI, Nr. 8, pp. 8 and 9f.
25. *CDSP*, XXXI, 1979, Nr. 9, p. 4
26. *Pravda*, June 21, 1985, O. Vladimirov, pp. 10-12 (*CDSP*, XXXVII, Nr. 25, pp. 3-4)

II. C.

1. *Journal of International Studies*, Beijing, Nr. 4, 1982, p. 3 (in *B.R.*)
2. *Ibid.*, 1983, Nr. 1, (in *B.R.*, May 9, 1983, Nr. 14, pp. 14-19, and 26)
3. *B.R.*, vol. 28, Nr. 24, June 17, 1985; see also *B.R.*, Nr. 31, Aug. 27, 1975, Juhui J., "Reagan's Diplomacy"
4. *Izvestia*, Aug. 28, 1975, p. 4; see also *B.R.*, Nr. 31, Aug. 27, 1975, "Brezhnev at Helsinki"
5. *Izvestia*, July 5, 1975
6. *Voprosy istorii*, L. S. Peremolov, "Mao. . ., and Confuciamism," 1975
7. *Ibid.*
8. *Izvestia*, Apr. 28, 1975, Kudryavtsev, p. 2 (*CDSP*, Nr. 17, May 21, 1975, p. 13)
9. Quoted by Garrett and Glaser, *op. cit.*, p. 58
10. Quoted, *ibid.*, p. 62
11. *FBIJ-H* 6, 23, 1981
12. *Sixiang Zhanxian* 4, 8/20, 1981, Si Mu "The Present Internat. Situation," quoted by Garrett and Glaser, *op. cit.*, p. 71
13. *B.R.*, Jan. 9, 1984
14. *New York Times*, Feb. 8, 1983
15. Interview quoted by Garrett and Glaser, *op. cit.*, p. 86.
16. *B.R.*, Jan. 18, 1983, Nr. 2, Zhao Ziyang
17. *Ibid.*
18. *Ibid.*
19. *Pravda*, March 19, 1975
20. *Pravda*, A. Petrov, Feb. 1, 1979, p. 5
21. *Journal of International Studies*, Beijing, Jan. 1, 1982; *FBIJ*-China, March 1, 1982
22. *B.R.*, 34, Aug. 22, 1983
23. *B.R.* Nr. 47, Oct. 3, 1983 "Current US Policy toward China,"
24. *FBIJ*-China, Sept. 10, 1982 and Mei Monong, "China's Future Role in Asia," quoted by Garrett and Glaser, *op. cit.*, p. 99. See this study also for the following
25. *Ibid.*, p. 105
26. *Ibid.*, p. 108
27. *Ibid.*, pp. 128-29

28.-29. *Ibid.*, pp. 133-34

30. *Pravda*, V. Baikov, "Dangerous Partnership," Nov. 21, 1981, (*CDSP* Nr. 47, p. 6)

31. *Pravda*, Dec. 6, 1981, S. Barakhta, "Why they are opening the doors?" p. 5

32. *Pravda* Jan. 20, 1984, p. 5 (in *CDSP*, XXXIV, Nr. 3, Feb. 15, 1984) V. Ovchinnikov, "Concerning Zhao Ziyang's Visit in Washington"

33. *Kommunist*, 10, July 1971, Vladimirov and Ryazauov "Fifty Years of Communist China," especially pp. 87-90

34.-35. *B.R.* 1983, interview with Deng, June 8, 1983

36.-37. Interviews, quoted by Garrett and Glaser, *op. cit.*, pp. 21-22

38.-39. *Tass* summary of Y. Bazhanov, *Motive Forces.* . ., June 1, 1982

40. Kissinger, H. *Years of Upheaval*, ch. 3.

41. *Pravda*, Aleksandrov, June 29, 1981

42. Bazhanov, see 38, *Tass* survey, June 1, 1982; also Garrett and Glaser, *op. cit.*, pp. 35-36, and for the following

43. Arbatov, G. "U.S. Foreign Policy. . ." USA, April 1980

44. *Izvestia*, Bovin, Jan. 31, 1982

45.-46. *Pravda*, May 20, 1982, "On Soviet-Chinese Relations"

47.-49. Bazhanov quoted by Garrett and Glaser, *op. cit.*, pp. 38-40

50. *Krasnaya Zvezda*, Sept. 27, 1983

51. *N.Y. Times*, Jan. 30, 1980

i2. *Orbis*, spring 1981, Conference Report "Issue in Soviet-American Relations"

53. Interview, Feb. 1981, quoted by Garrett and Glaser, *op. cit.*, pp. 45-46

54. *Ibid.*, p. 46

55. *Pravda*, Aug. 27, 1983

56. Ukraintsev, *Problems of the Far East*, 2, 1989, "Soviet-Chinese Relations"

57. *Krasnaya Zvezda*, Jan. 18, 1984

58. Interview quoted by Garrett and Glaser, *op. cit.*, p. 55

59. *B.R.*, vol. 29, Nr. 18, May 25, 1986, pp. 10-11

II. D.

1. Amalrik, A. *Will the Soviet Union survive until 1984?* (1970), pp. 48-49
2. Kissinger, H. *White House Years*, espec. pp. 46-49. 51-55, 70-71.
3. Gittings, J. *The World and China, 1922-72* (1974), p. 254
4. Ellison, H. ed. *The Sino-Soviet Conflict* (1982), p. VIII
5. *Ibid.*, pp. 352 and 382
6. Gong, G. W., "China and the Soviet Union," In Gong, A. E, Stent and R. W. Strode *Areas of Challenge for Soviet Foreign Policy inn the 1980s*, Bloomington, pp. 53-87. Robinson, Th. W. in Stuart and Tow, *op. cit* ., (1982), p. 176.
7. *Krushchev Remembers* (1974), p. 242
8. *B.R.*, vol. 29, Nr. 2, Jan. 3, 1986, An Zhigno, p. 4
8b. *B.R.*, Nr. 36, Sept. 8, 1986, pp. 14-15
9. Gittings, J. *op. cit.*, pp. 223, 226
10. Mao Zedong, "Summing Up," 1955, p. ; "On Intellectuals", 1950, p. 228, both in *Selected Works*, vol. V (1977)
11. Mao Zedong, "In Memory of Sun Yat-sen,"1956, *ibid.*
12. *Gittings, op. cit.*, pp. 231-33
13. *Ibid.*, pp. 236-37
14. Mao' speech, 1958, p. 246
15. Löwenthal, R. in Stuart D. and W. Tow, *China, the Soviet Union, and the West* (1982). pp. 59 and 70
16. *B.R.*, Ye Jiamjing, 22, Oct. 5, 1979
17. Löwenthal, R., "Development or Utopia" in Chalmers Johnson, ed. *Change in Communist Systems* (l97O), pp. 33-106, espec. 69-70
18.-20. *Kommunist*, 8, 1978; see also *ibid.*, Shachnazarov, Cult. Revol. in China,"Nr. 3, 1967 also "Maoist Regime grows tougher" Nr. 8, 1978 *Izvestia*, March 3, 1980, "How Maoism Nourishes Revisionism"
21.-22. *Pravda* and *Izvestia*, June 6, 1979; Aleksandrov on Soviet Foreign Ministry memorandum of June 4, 1979
23. *Kommunist*, 8, 1978
24. *Pravda*, July 31, 1982, B. Barakhta (*CDSP*, XXXIV, Nr. 31, 1982, pp. 18-19)
25. *Pravda*, Yakovlev, July 14, p. 5 (*CDSP*, Nr. 28, p. 4)
26. *B.R.*, vol. 29, Nr. 14, Apr. 7, 1986, pp. 13-14

27. *Pravda*, Jan. 30, 1982, p. 5 (CDSP, XXXIV, March 3, 1982, Nr. 5, pp. 20 See also Peng on Mao, *B.R.*, Nr. 36, Sept.8, 1986, p.14-15

28. *Pravda*, reprints series of articles in Hong Ji, in 1981

29-30. *Pravda*, July 5, l98l (*CDSP*, XXXIII, Nr. 27, Aug. 5, 1981), Sixth Plen. Sess. on CPC history

31. *Krushchev Remembers* (1970), p. 292

III. A.

1. *Izvestia*, Apr. 28, 1976, p. 2, Kudryavtsev

2. Quoted by *B.R.*, Nr. 20, June 11, 1975

3. *B.R.*, Nr. 41, Oct. 12, 1979, U.N. General Assembly, Han Nianlong's address of Sept. 27, pp. 13-21

4. Zhao to the Canadian Parliament, *B.R.*, Jan. 30, 1984, pp. 16-18

5. *Journal of International Studies*, Beijing, 1981, reprinted in *B.R.*, March 1982,"Diplomacy of Zhou Enlai"

6. *B.R.*, Sept. 13, 1982, pp. llf.

7. *B.R.*, June 24, 1985, p. 34

8. *Ibid.*, p. 32

9. *B.R.*, vol. 29, Nr. 27, July 7, 1986

10. *Ibid.*

11. *B.R.*, March 8, 1982, Nr. 10, pp. 11-12

12. *B.R.*, Nr. 12, March 23, 1981, p. 13

13. *Partinava Zhizn* Aug. 1981, Nr. 16, pp. 21-27 (*CDSP* 1981, Nr. 38, p. 6)

14. *B.R.*, Oct. 12, 1979, Nr. 41, pp. 8-11

15. *B.R.*, Nr. 42, Oct. 18, 1982, pp. l4f., reprints "Some Observations on Soviet Detente," by Zhang Zhen and Rong Zhi, *Journal of Internat. Studies*, Nr. 4, 1982,

16. See 15., pp. 18-19

17. *Ibid.*, p. 20

18. *Ibid.*

19. *Ibid.*, p. 22

20. *B.R.*, Jan. 21 and 28, 1985, vol. 28, Nr. 3, p. 14, and Nr. 4, p. 25 (Jan. 28), an abridged article from *Journal of Int. Studies*, Nr. 1, 1985

21. *B.R.*, vol. 29, Nr. 19, May 12, 1986, pp. 12-13, Chen Yicun

22. *B.R.*, Sept. 1981, Nr. 39, pp. 23-25, Shen Yi

23. *B.R.*, June 15, 1979, Nr. 24, pp. 20-22
24. *B.R.*, Sept. 1981, Nr. 39, pp. 23-25, Shen Yi
25. *B.R.*, Nr. 38, Sept. 14, 1979
26. *B.R.*, Dec. 2, 1985, pp. 15-17

III. B.

1. *B.R.*, July 1, 1983, vol. 28, Nr. 26, Tong Dalin and Liu Ji
2. U.N. address, Sept. 23, 1981, in *B.R.* Nr. 40, pp. 3-24 and 29
3. *B.R.*, vol. 28, Nr. 28, July 15, 1985, p. 13
4.-5. *B.R.*, Nr. 41, Oct. 12, 1981, p. 10 and 13-14
6. *B.R.*, Oct. 26, 1981, Mu Youlin
7. *B.R.*, Nr. 3, Jan. 19, 1979, "Soviet Imperialist Strategy in Asia"
8. *B.R.*, vol. 27, Nr. 51, Dec. 17, 1985, "Washington-Moscow. How the Strategic Focus Shifted?" by Wang Baoquin
9. *B.R.*, on Gorshkov's article in *Krasnaya Zvezda*

III. C.

1. *B.R.*, March 23, 1979 reprints article in *Renmin Ribao*, March 17, 1979
2. *B.R.*, Nr. 18, May 4, 1979, pp. 10-17
3. *B.R.*, Nr. 19, May 11, 1979, "Vietnam Hegemonism Causes Tension in South Vietnam," pp. 19-21
4. *B.R.*, Nr. 23, June 8, 1979, pp. 24-25
5. *B.R.*, Nr. 9, March 2, 1979, pp. 19-22
6. *B.R.*, March 2, 1979 Chen Chu in UN Security Council, Feb. 23, 1979
7. *B.R.* Nr. 12, March 23, 1979, pp. 19-21
8. *Ibid.*, pp. 21-23, Xinhua correspondent
9. *B.R.*, Nr. 3, Jan. 19, 1979, "Soviet Imperialist Strategy in Asia"
10. *B.R.*, Nr. 6 and 7, Feb. 10, 1986
11. *B.R.*, Nov. 23, 1981, pp. 10-11
12. *B.R.*, Nr. 31, Aug. 4, 1986, Yin Chongjing, pp. 12-19
13. *B.R.*, Nr. 6, Feb. 9, 1979, Deng's visit, pp. 3-4, and 8-14
14. *B.R.*, Nr. 6, Feb. 9, 1979, p. 12, also 8-11
15. *B.R.*, interview with Deng, Feb. 16, 1979, pp. 17-20
16. *Ibid.*, p. 26

17. *Ibid.* Sept. 21, 1979
18. *Ibid.*, pp. 25-26
19. About Cuba's "integration" with the Soviet Union, *B.R.*, Mei Ping, Nr. 28 July 14, 1978, pp. 23-25
20. *B.R.*,"Cuba-Soviet Military Stronghold in Latin America," Feb. 22, 1982, pp. 11-12
21.-22. *B.R.*, on the Israeli-Egyptian Peace treaty, Nr. 13, March 30, 1979, pp. 25-28
23. *B.R.*, Nr. 15, Apr. 13, 1979, "Birth of the Republic in Iran," pp. 18-20
24.-25. *Renmin Ribao*, Apr. 16, 1986, in *B.R.*, vol. 29, Nr. 17, Apr. 28, 1986, pp. 6 and 11-12
26. *B.R.*, Nr. 16, Apr. 21, 1986, p. 7; also *ibid.*, Nr. 14, pr. 7
27. *B.R.* vol. 28, Nr. 22, pp. 11-12
28. Scalapino, R. A., "Containment and Counter-containment," in Stuart and Tow, *China, the Soviet Union, and the West* (1982), pp. 165-66
29. Robinson, Th. W., *ibid.*, p. 178
30. *B.R.*, 1986, Nr. 39, pp. 12-13
31. *B.R.*, Nov. 19, 1985, Nr. 46, pp. 13-14
32. *B.R.*, Jan. 27, 1986, Nr. 4, pp. 5-6, "Policy of Peace Prevails in World Affairs"
33. *B.R.*, Jan. 27,, 1986, Nr. 4, pp. 10-11, "USSR-Japanese Territorial Dispute Remains."
34. Joint Communique USSR-Japan, *ibid.*
35. *B.R.*, Nr. 4, Jan. 27, 1986, pp. 10—11
36. *B.R.*, Nr. 4, Jan. 27, 1986, p. 11, "Vietnam's Peace becomes Hanoi's latest Hoax"

IV. A.

1. *B.R.*, Apr. 21, 1986, p. 30
2. *Russian Studies in China* (1973)
3. *Problemy dalnego*. . . Ot redaktsii, Nr. 1, p. 19, in *Jt. Publication Res. Service*, Nr. 56711
4. *Problemy*. . .1972, Nr. 1, p. 9, transl. *ibid.*
5. Rozman, Gilbert, "Soviet Interpretations of Chinese Social History, Search for the Origins of Maoism," *Journal of Asian Studies*, XXXIV, Nr. 1, pp 49-72
6-7. *Kommunist*, 1973, 5, pp. 55-56

8. Rothenberg, M. *Whither China*; *The View from the Kremlin* (1977), p. 261

9. Victor Louis, *France Soir*, Oct. 14, 1976

10. *Pravda*, March 21, 1978, (*CDSP*, vol. 30, Nr. 12)

11. *Kommunist*, 1977. Nr. 12, "Kitai posle Mao. . ." (China after Mao. . .)

12. *Ibid.*, 1977; Nr. 12. about the suppression of the Tibetans, see W. A. Bogoslavskii, Tibetskaya raion KNR (Moscow, 1978

13. *International Affairs*, 1978, Nr. 1, Semyonov

14. *Ibid.*, 1977, Nr. 7, p. 64

15. *Krasnaya Zvezda*, Apr. 3, 1979, Mirski

16. *Novyi Mir*, Burlatskii, pp. 217-42 (transl. *Jt. Publ. Res. Serv.*, Nr. 72443)

17. *Ibid.*, espec. p. 261 and 281

18. *Pravda*, editorial, May 18, 1975

19. *Pravda*, July 9, 1975, p. 5

20. *Izvestia*, Aug. 28, 1975, p. 4, "Asian Collective Security. . ." Kudryavtsev, also *Pravda*, Apr. 7, 1976, p. 5 (*CDSP*, May 5, 1976)

21. *Kommunist*, editorial, Nr. 12, 1975

22. *World Marxist Review*, 1981, p. 71

23. *Abstract*, Gurevich (*Istoriia SSSR*, Nr. 2, March-April, pp. 192-210)

24. *World Marxist Review*, Aug. 1981, pp. 71-73, S. Maung, "Beijing's Territorial Claims"

25. *Pravda*, Feb. 1, 1979, p. 1, "Concerning Deng Hsiao Ping's interview

26. *Pravda* and *Izvestia*, Feb. 2, 1979

27. *Pravda*, Feb. 4, 1979, B. Orekhov

28. *Izvestia*, Feb. 10, 1979, "Dangerous Course"

29. *Pravda*, Feb. 10, p. 5 (*CDSP*, March 7, 1979, Nr. 6)

30. *Pravda*, Feb. 18, 1979, Korionov V., p. 4 (*CDSP*, XXXI, Nr. 6, "Dangerous Game")

31. *Pravda*, Nr. 6, p. 4, and Feb. 12, 1979, p. 4

32. *Pravda*, Feb. 20, 1979, p. 5 (*CDSP*, XXXI, Nr. 7, March 18, 1979)

33. *Pravda*, Feb. 21, 1979, Kabharov, Y., p. 5

34. *Pravda*, Feb. 21, 1979, p. 3, "Hands off Vietnam"

35. *B.R.*, Nr. 14, May 2, 1979

36. *B.R.*, Sept. 28, 1979, Nr. 39, p. 23

37. *Ibid.*
38. *Corriere della Sera*, report from Moscow Sept. 9, 1979; see
36. *B.R.*, Sept. 28, 1979 pp. 23-24
39. *Pravda*, Aleksandrov, July 11, 1979, pp. 4-5 (*CDSP*, Nr. 28, Aug., p. 11)
40. *Izvestia* (*CDSP*, XXXV, Nr. 40, Nov. 2, 1983, pp. 23-24)
41. *CDSP*, vol. XXXV, Nr. 46, Dec. 14, 1983
42. *Izvestia*, Nov. 15, 1983, p. 3, Tikhinsby
43. *Soviet Foreign Policy Today*, ed. Schulze, 1983, p. 25 and 1-2 (quoted from *CDSP*, XXXIII, Nr. 8, p. 6; *Pravda* and *Izvestia*, July 5, 1981
44. *Ibid.*, p. 107; *Pravda* May 20, 1982, pp. 4-5 (*CDSP*, XXXI, Nr. 21, pp. 14-15 and 23)
45. *B.R.*, Sept. 26, 1979
46. *Pravda*, Sept. 24, 1979
47. Note to CPR Embassy, *Pravda*, July 27, 1979, p. 4 (*CDSP*, Nr. 30, p. 4)
48. *Pravda*, May 26, 1980, Aleksandrov, p. 4 (*CDSP*, XXXII, Nr. 21, pp. 8-9)
49.-50. *Izvestia*, A. Bovin, "Partnership with Trust," Jan. 31, 1982 (*CDSP*, XXXIV, Nr. 5, p. 14)
51. Low, *op. cit.* p. 336
52. Amalrik, *Will the Soviet Union survive in 1984?* (1970), espec. 44-67 and Rothenberg, A., *The Heirs of Stalin*. .(1972), pp. 301-12, espec. 305
53. Amalrik, *op. cit.*, p. 45
54. *Ibid.*, p. 48
55. *Ibid.*, pp. 57-58
56. *Ibid.*, pp. 63-64
57. Victor Louis, *The Coming Decline of the Chinese Empire* (1979)
58. *Ibid.*, H. E. Salisbury, introduction
59. Solzhenitsyn, A. "Letter to the Leaders," in Agursky, M. *What awaits the Soviet Union?* 1984, also Scammel, *Solzhenitsyn*, 1982, pp. 864-880
60. See 59. Letter. . .
60b. V. Louis, see 57., p. 185
61. Conquest, R. *The Nation Killers. The Soviet Deportation of Nationalities* 1970, and Kolarz, W. *Russia and her Colonies*, 1952.
62. V. Louis, *op. cit.*, pp. 186-187

IV. B.

1. *Pravda*, Oct. 31, 1982, *CSDP*, XXXIV, Nr. 16, p. 5, and Nr. 46, Dec. 15

2. Fejto F., "France and China..." in Halpern, A. M., *Policies toward China; from Six Continents*, N.Y. 1965, pp. 42-76

3. *Manchester Guardian*, Nov. 1, 1979 4. Joan Barth Urban, "The Impact of the Sino-Soviet Dispute on Western Europe," in H. J. Ellison, *The Sino-Soviet Conflict* (1982), pp. 295-322

5. Brandt, W. *A Peace Policy for Europe* (1969), pp. 94-95

6. Kevin Devlin, "The Challenge of the 'New Internationalism,'" in Ellison, ed. *The Sino-Soviet Conflict,* 1982, pp. 146-71, espec. 147

7. *L'Unità*, Oct. 26, 1973

8. *Ibid.*, Jan. 22, 1964

9. See 6, p. 150

10. *L'Unità*, Sept. 4, 1964, and *Pravda*, Sept 10, 1964

11. See 6, p. 157

12. *L'Unità*, Dec. 9, 1971

13. See 6, p. 170

14a. *Ibid.*, p. 171

14b. *B.R.*, vol. 29, No. 36, Sept. 8, 1986, p. 9

14c. *Ibid.*, No. 40, Oct. 6, 1986, p. 9

14d. *Ibid*, No. 41, Oct. 13, 1986, p. 1

15. *Pravda*, Aleksandrov, June 27, 1981

16. *Far East Economic Review*, Moscow, March 7, 1981 (*CDSP*, 1982, Nr. 3, pp. 15-24)

17. *B.R.*, Li Xiannian, Jan. 8, 1981

18. Brezhnev, Tashkent, March 24, 1982

19. Legvold, "The Soviet Union and Eastern Europe," in Griffith, W. E., ed. *The Soviet Empire; Expansion and Detente*, (1976)

20. *Pravda*, Afanas'yev, Nov. 16, 1982

21. Arnold, A. *Afghanistan. The Soviet Invasion in Perspective* (1981), p. 98

22. *Ibid.*, pp. 10lf.

23. *Pravda*, Dec. 9, 1978

24. *B.R.*, Xin Changlin, "Afghanistan in Turmoil," vol. 22, Nr. 24, June 15, 1979

25. *Pravda*, Dec. 31, 1979, Petrov A. (*CDSP*, XXXI, 1979, Nr. 52, pp. 5-7)

26. *Pravda*, Dec. 31, 1979

27. *Pravda* and *Izvestia*, Jan. 13, 1980, p. 1 (*CDSP*, XXXII, Nr. 5, pp. 2-4)

28. *Literaturnaya gazeta*, March 12, 1980, p. 9 (*CDSP*, XXXII, 1980, Nr. 10, p. 7)

29. *Pravda*, June 25, 1980 (CDSP, XXXII, Nr. 25, June 25 pp. 2-4)

30. *B.R.*, vol. 29, Nr. 20, May 19, 1986, pp. 10-11; also April 27, 1986

31. *CDSP*, XXXII, Nr. 8, 1980, pp. 27-32

32. *Ibid.*, p. 25

33. *Pravda*, Jan. 8, 1986, p. 5 (*CDSP*, XXXVIII, Nr. 1, 1986, p. 20)

34. *Tass*, Jan. 24, 1985, "From a hostile stand," and *B.R.*, March 4, 1985, p. 16

35. *Pravda*, March 29, 1984 (*CDSP*, XXXVI. Nr. 13, p. 12)

36.-37. *Pravda*, May 30, 1984, "On Reagan's Visit to China"; also *Izvestia*, May 5, p. 4

38. For the aftermath of Reagan's journey to China, see *Izvestia*, July 1984 (*CDSP*, XXXIV, Nr. 30) and *Izvestia*, July 25, 1984, "Eastern Front against the USSR?" Also *Pravda*, July 26, 1984, V. Ovchinnikov

39.-40. *Izvestia*, July 25, 1984

41. *Pravda*, July 15, 1979, M. Nikitin (*CDSP*, XXXI Nr. 28, pp. 4-5)

42. *Pravda*. A. Petrov, Aug. 11, 1979, p. 4 (*CDSP*, Nr. 32, Sept. 5, 1979, p. 8)

43. *Pravda* and *Izvestia*, March 3, 1979, p.2 (*CDSP*, XXXI, 1979, Nr. 9, p. 4)

44. *Pravda*, Feb. 24, 1979 p. 4, Aleksandrov, and *B.R.*, Nr. 9, p. 6

45. *Pravda*, 1979, Nr. 9, p. 6.

46. *Pravda*, March 5, 1979, p. 4, Yuri Zhukov

47. *Izvestia*, Polit. Commentator, March 23, 1979, p. 5 (*CDSP*, No. 12, Apr. 18, 1979)

48. *Izvestia*, Aug. 8, 1980, p. 5, M. Ilyinsky

49. *Pravda*, Aug. 21, 1979, p. 4, S. Dmitriyev, "Facing a Choice," (*CDSP*, Sept. 19, 1979, p. 10)

50. Griffith. *Sino-Soviet Rapprochement*, 1963 (*CDSP*, vol. 32, Nr. 2, pp. 20-29)
51. *Pravda*, and *Izvestia*, Nov. 23, 1982, pp. 1-2 (*CDSP*, XXXIV, Nr. 47, p. 6)
52. *CDSP*, XXXII, Nr. 39, Oct. 24, 1984, A. Gromyko
53. *Pravda*, Sept. 28, 1984 pp. 4-5
54. *Pravda*, Oct. 27, 1984, p. 2 (*CDSP*, Nov. 21, 1984)
55. *B.R.*, vol. 29, Nr. 25, June 23, 1986
56. *Ibid.*, pp. 15-16
57. *CDSP*, XXXVIII, 1986, Nr. 8, pp. 27-32
58. *Ibid.*, p. 30
59. *Pravda*, (*CDSP*, XXXVIII, 1986, Nr. 11, p. 16)
60. *Izvestia*, Jan. 31, 1986
61. *Pravda*, (*CDSP*, 1986) Nr. 11, p. 4
62. *Pravda*, March 22, 1986, p. 4 (*CDSP*, Nr. 12, Apr. 19, p. 29; see also *Izvestia* correspondent, "Gains in China-USA Economic Ties Cited," Nr. 17, 1986, p. 5)

V. Conclusion

1. *Pravda*, May 26, 1980, Aleksandrov, "Beijing... Whipping up Tension"
2. *B.R.*, Vice Premier Li Peng, Apr. 15, 1986; see also Gorbachev's conciliatory words, but hardly meaningful suggestions in his speech in Vladivostok in August 1986, stressing Soviet willingness to discuss with China new measures "to create an atmosphere /!/ of good-neighborliness" (*CDSP*, Aug. 27, 1986, Nr. 30, p. 7).

SELECTED BIBLIOGRAPHY

A. *Dailies, Journals, and Digests*:

American Political Science Review
Annals of the American Academy of Politicai Science
Asian Survey
Beijing Review (B.R., formerly Peking Review, P.R.)
Canadian Review of Studies in Nationalism
China Digest
China Reconstructs
China Quarterly
Current Abstracts of the Soviet Press
Current Background (American Consulate General) Hongkong
Current Digest of the Soviet Press (CD5P)
Current History
Department of State Bulletin
Encounter
Far Eastern Economic Policy
Foreign Broadcast Information Service Daily Report (FBIS)
Issues and Studies, Taipei, Taiwan
Izvestia
Joint Publications Research Service
Journal of Asian Studies
Foreign Affairs
The Hindu, Madras
International Affairs
Kommunist, Moscow
Krasnaya Zvezda
Literaturnaya gazeta
Mirovaia ekonomika i mezhdunarodnaya otnochenia
Le Monde, Paris
Narody Azii i Afriki
Neues Deutschland
The New China News Agency, Beijing
New Times (Novoe vremia)
New York Times
Observer, London

Pacific Affairs
Partiinaya Zhizn
Pravda
Problems of Communism
Problems of Peace and Socialism
Problemy dalnego vostoka
Red Flag (Hongqui), Beijing
Review of the Hongkong China Press
The Russian Review
Selections from the China Mainland Press (US Consulate, Hongkong)
Slavic Review
Soviet News
Soviet Studies in History
Studies in Comparative Communism
Sovietskoe kitaevedenie
Times
L'Unità (Milan)
Voprosy istorii
Voprosy filosofii
Washington Post
Die Welt
World Marxist Review
Yearbook of World Affairs
Za rubeshom

B. *General Works* (some of the books listed here include collections of primary sources):

Adenauer, K. *Erinnerungen*, vol. 2, Rhondorf, 1984
Agursky, M. *What awaits the Soviet Union*, 1974

Albright, D. E., ed., *Communism and Political Systems in Western Europe*, Boulder, 1974

An Tai-sung, *The Sino-Soviet Territorial Dispute*, 1973

An Analytical Survey of Moscow-Peiping Relations, World

Anti-Communist League, Taipei, Taiwan, 1971
From Anti-Imperialism to Anti-Socialism, Moscow, Prague,
1974

Ashley, R. K., *The Political Economies of War and Peace.
The Sino-Soviet-American Triangle*, N. Y., 1980

Aspaturian, V. V., et al. *Eurocommunism between East and
West*, Bloomington, 1980
Aspaturian, V. V., et al. "Diplomacy in the Mirror of Soviet
Scholarship," in *Contemporary History in the Soviet Mirrorv*
eds. J. Keep and L. Busby, N.Y., 1964

Astaf'ev, G. V., Nikiforov V. N., and Sladkovsie, eds.
Noveishaie historiia Kitaia, 1917-1970gg (Contemporary
History of China 1917-70), Moscow, 1970

Barnett, A. D., *China and the Major Powers in East Asia*,
Washington, 1977

Bazhanov, B. G., *Motive Forces of US Policy Toward China*,
Moscow, 1982

Behbehani, H. S. H., *China's Foreign Policy in the Arab
World*, 1955-75 Boston, London

Beloff, Max, *Soviet Policy in the Far East 1944-51*, London,
1953

Bialer, Seweryn, ed. *Domestic Context of Soviet Foreign-
Policy*, Boulder, 1981

Bialer, Seweryn, ed. *Stalin's Successors; Leadership, Stability
and Change in the Soviet Union*, Cambridge Univ. Pr., 1980

Borisov, 0., Rakhmanin and Koloskov, B. T., *Sovietskoi-
kitaiskie otnosheniia 1945-1970. Kratki ocherk* (Sino-Soviet
Relations 1945-70. A Brief Outline), Moscow, 1975

Borkenau, F., *World Communism. A History of the
Communist International*, N.Y., 1939

The Boundary Question between China and Tibet, Peking, 1940

Brandt, Willy, *A Peace Policy for Europe*, N. Y., 1974

Brzezinski, Z. H., *The Soviet Bloc; Unity and Conflict*, Cambridge, MA, 1967

Burlatskii, F., *Mao Tsze-dun* Moscow, 1976

Byrnes, R. F., *After Brezhnev. Source of Soviet Conduct in the 1980s*, Bloomington, 1983

Callis, H. G., *China, Confucian and Communist*, N.Y., 1959

Caroe, Olaf, *The Turks of Central Asia and Stalinism*, London, 1953

Caroe, Olaf, *The Soviet Empire*, London, 1953

Caroe, Olaf, *The Chinese Armed Forces Today*, London, n.d.

Choudbury G. W., *Chinese Perception of the World*, Durham, 1977

Clubb, O., *China and Russia; The "Great Game,"* N.Y., 1977

Conally, Violet, *Siberia today and tomorrow*, London, 1975

Conquest, Robert, *The Great Terror. Stalin's Purge of the Thirties*, N. Y., 1968

Conquest, Robert, *The Nation-Killers. The Soviet Denortation-of Nationalities*, N.Y., London, 1970

Conquest, Robert, *Power and Policy in the USSR*, London 1962, also 1967

Conquest, Robert, *A Critique of Mao Tse-tung's Theoretical Conceptions, Moscow, 1972*

Dallin, A., ed. Diversity in International Communism, 1963

Dallin, David J., *Soviet Russia and the Far East*, New Haven, 1948

Dedijer, V., *Tito Speaks*, London, 1953

Degras, Jane, ed. *Soviet Documents on Foreign Policy*, 3 vols, London, 1951-53

Deutscher, I., *Russia, China and the West. A Contemporary Chronicle 1953-66*, ed. by F. Halliday, London, 1970

Djilas, Milovan, *Conversations with Stalin*, London, 1962

Domes, Jűrgen, *Chinese Politics after Mao*, Cardiff Univ. College, 1979

Domes, Jűrgen, *The Internal Politics of China, 1949-72*, London, N.Y., 1973

Domes, Jűrgen, *Politische Soziologie in der Volksrepublik China*, Wiesbaden, 1980

Donaldson, R. H., *Soviet Policy toward India; Ideology and Strategy*, Cambridge, 1974

Dupree, Louis, *Afghanistan*, Princeton, 1973

Eckstein, Alexander, *China's Economic Revolution*, N.Y., Cambridge, 1977

Editorial Collegium: L. P. Delyusin, M. A. Persits, A. B. Rezhikov, Prof. R. A. Ulyanovskii, chief ed. *Komintern i Vostok*. (The Comintern and the Eastern Struggle for the Leninist Strategy and Tactics of the National Liberation Movement), Moscow, 1969

Elegant, Robert S., *China's Red Masters*, N.Y., 1951

Eran, Oded, *The Mezhdunarodniki, Ramat Gan*, Israel, 1979

Fairbank, J. K., *East Asia; The Modern Transformation*, Boston, 1965

Fairbank, J. K., *The Chinese World Order*, Cambridge, 1968

Feis, H., *The Chinese Tangle. The American Effort in China from Pearl Harbor to the Marshall Mission*, Princeton, 1953

Fejtő, F., *Chine-USSR; de l'*alliance au conflit: 1950-1977 Paris, 1978

Feuerwerker, A., ed. *History of Communist China*, Cambridge, Ma., 1968

Fischer-Galati, Stephen, ed. *The Communist Parties of Eastern Europe*, N.Y., 1970

Fitzgerald, C. P., *Flood Tide in China*, London, 1958 *Chinese View of their Place in the World*, London, N.Y. 1969

Floyd, D., *Mao against Kurshchev*, N.Y., 1964

Friedmann, Lawrence, *The West and the Modernization of China*, London, 1979

Friters, G. M., *Outer Mongolia and its International Position*, London, 1951

Garaudy, R., *Le grand tournant du socialisme*, Paris, 1969

Barrett, Banning N. and Bonnie S. Glaser, (*War and Peace; The Views from Moscow and Beijing*), No. 20 of Policy Papers, Internat. Affairs, Berkeley, 1984

Gates, R. A., *Soviet Sinology*. Unpublished PH. D. Dissert., Georgetown Univ., 1974

Gati, Charles, ed. *The International Policies of Eastern Europe*, N.Y., 1976

Gelman, Harry, *The Soviet Far East build-up and Soviet Risk-taking against China*, Rand Corp., Santa Monica, 1982

Ginsburgs G. and C. F. Pinkele, *The Sino-Soviet Territorial Dispute, 1949-64*, N.Y., 1978

Gittings, J., *The World and China 1922-1972* N.Y. 1974

Gong, G. W., "China and the Soviet Union," in Gong, A. E. Stuart, and R. V. Strode, *Areas of Challenge for Soviet Foreign Policy in the 1980s*, Un. of Indiana Press, Bloomington, pp. 53-87

Gorside, Roger, *Coming Alive; China after Mao*, N.Y., 1981

Griffith, William E., *Ostpolitik of the Federal Republic of Germany*, Cambridge, 1978

Griffith, William E., *The Soviet Empire; Expansion and Detente*, Lexington, 1976

Griffith, William E., *The West European Left*, Lexington, 1979

Halperin, Morton, *Bureaucratic Politics and, Foreign Policy*, Washington, 1974

Halperin, Morton, *Sino-Soviet Reiations and Arms Control*, Cambridge, 1967

Halperin, Morton, *China and the Bomb*, N.Y., 1965

Halpern, A. M., ed. *The Policies toward China*, N.Y., 1965

Hanrieder, W. R., ed. *West German Foreign Policy 1949-79*, Boulder, 1980

Heaton, W. R., *A United Front against Hegemonism*, Washington, D.C., 1980

Haykal, Mohammed, *Sphinx and the Commissar; the rise and fall of Soviet influence in the Arab World*, London, 1978

Hinton, H. C., *The Bear at the Gate*; China's *Policy-making under Soviet Pressure*, Washington, D.C., 1971

Hinton, H. C., *Three and a Half Powers, The New Balance*, Ind. Press, 1975

Hinton, H. C., *History of Economic Relations between Russia and China*, Moscow, 1957

Hoetzsch, Otto, *Russland in Asien. Geschichte einer Expansion*, Stuttgart, 1966

Hoffmann, Stanley, *Decline or Renewal of France since the 1930s*, N.Y., 1974

Hough, Jerry F., *Soviet Leadership in Transition*, Washington, 1980

Hyland G. G., *"The Sino-Soviet Conflict; A Search for New Security Strategy,"* in *Asian Security in the 1980s; Problems and Policies for a Time of Transition*, Rand Corp., Santa Monica, 1979

International Institute of Strategic Studies. *The Military Balance 1979-1980*, London, 1981

Ivanow, O., *Soviet-Chinese Relations Surveyed*, Moscow, 1975

Jackson, W. A. D., *The Russo-Chinese Borderlands*, N.Y., 1962

Jacobsen, C. G., *Sino-Soviet Relations since Mao. The Chairman's Legacy*, N.Y. . . .1982

Jacoviello, Alberto, *Capire la Cina* Milano, 1972.

Jacoviello, Alberto, *Cina due anni dopo*, Milano, 1975

Jarvis, R., *Perception and Misperception in International Relations*, Princeton, 1976

Peter, Jones and Sian Kevill, *China and the Soviet Union, 1949-1984*, Facts on File Publications, London, 1985

Kapitsa, M. S., *Sovetsko-kitaiskie otnosheniia v 1931-45* (Sino-Soviet relations, 1931-1945), Moscow, 1956

Karnow, Stanley, *Mao and China from Revolution to Revolution*, introduction by J. K. Fairbank, N.Y. 1972

Kau Ying-mao, *The Lin Piao Affair*, White Plains, N.Y., 1975

Kaw Marita Co., *Post-Mao Soviet Anaysis of China's Economic Development, 1949-69*, unpubi. Diss. Univ. of Washington, 1977

Kirby. E. S., *Russian Studies of China*, Toronto, 1975

Kissinger, Henry, *White House Years*, Boston, Toronto, 1979, *Years of Upheaval*, Boston, 1982

Kiuzadsham, L. S., *Ideologicheskie Kampanii v KNR 1949-l960* (Ideological Struggles in the People's Republic of China 1949-60) Moscow, 1970

Klochko, M. A., *Soviet Scientist in Red China*, N.Y., 1954

Kolarz, W. A., *Peoples of the Soviet Far East*, N.Y., 1954

Kolarz, W. A., *Russia and her Colonies*, London, 1952

Kolodzicy, E. A., *France's International Policy under De Gaulle and Pompidou*, Ithaca, 1974

Kraus, Willy, *Wirtschaftliche Entwicklung and Sozialer Wandel in der Volksrepublik*, Berlin, 1979

Kraus, Willy, *Krushchev Remembers*, Boston 1970 (also 1974), Strobe Talbott, ed.

Kulski, W. W., *The Soviet Union in World Affairs*, Syracuse, 1973

Lamb, Alastair, *The China-Indian Border*, London, Oxford, 1964

Larkin, B. D., *China and Africa l949-1970. The Foreign Policy of the People's Republic of China*, Berkeley, 1971

Lattimore, Owen, *Inner Asian Frontier of China*, N.Y. 1951
Lattimore, Owen, *The Mongols of Manchuria*, N.Y., 1934

Lattimore, Owen, *Nationalism and Revolution in Mongolia*, N.Y., 1955

Lenin i problemy sovremennego Kitaia (Lenin and the Problems of Contemporary China) Moscow, 1971 (1968)

Leninskaia politika v otnoshenii Kitaia (Leninist Politics and Relations with China) Moscow, 1971

Lieberthal, K., *Central Documents and Politburo Politics in China*, Ann Arbor, Un. of Mich., 1978

Lieberthal, K., *Mao Tse-tung's Perception of the Soviet Union as Communicated in 1969*, Santa Monica, Rand P-5726, 1976

Lieberthal, K., *The Sino-Soviet Conflict in the 1970s. Its Evolution and Implications for the Strategic Triangle,* Santa Monica, Rand R 2342-NA, 1978

Lobanov-Rostovsky, A. *Russia and Asia*, Ann Arbor, 1951

Longo, Luigi, *Opinione sulla Cina*, Milan, 1977

Louis, Victor, *The Coming Decline of the Chinese Empire. With a Dissenting Introduction by H. E. Salisbury. N.Y., 1979*

Low, A. D., *Lenin on the Question of Nationality*, N.Y., 1958

Low, A. D., *The Sino-Soviet Dispute. An Analysis of the Polemics*, Rutherford, 1976

Lőwenthal, R., "*Development vs. Utopia in Communist Policy*, in Chalmers Johnson, ed. *Change in Communist Systems*, Stanford, 1970

Lőwenthal, R., *Model or Ally. The Communist Powers and the Developing Countries* N.Y., 1977

May, E. R. and Thomson, J. C., Jr., *American-East Asian Relations*, Cambridge, Ma. 1972

Mao Tse-tung, *Little Red Book* (Quotations from Chairman Mao), Beijing, 1967

Mao Tse-tung, *Selected Works of Mao Tse-tung*, vol. V, For. Langu. Press, 1977

Mao Tse-tung, *Selected Writings from the Works of Mao*, Beijing, 1967

McLane, C. B., *Soviet Strategies in Southeast Asia; An Exploration of Eastern Policy under Lenin and Stalin*, Princeton, 1966

Mehnert, Klaus, *China Returns*, 1971 (1972)

Mezhdunarodnye Otnosheniia na Dal'nem Vostoke 1870-1945 (International Relations in the Far East 1870-1945) Prepared by the Sov. Academy of Sciences, Moscow, 1951

Michael, Franz, *Mao and the Perpetual Revolution*, N.Y., 1977

Middleton, Drew, *The Duel of the Giants*, 1978

Mitchison, Lois, *The Overseas Chinese*, London, 1960

Nikiforov, V. N., *Sovietskie istoriki o problemakh Kitaia* (Soviet Historians about the Problems of China), Moscow, 1972

North, R. C., *The Foreign Relations of China*, Duxbury, Ma., 1978

North, R. C., *Moscow and the Chinese Communists*, Stanford, 1953 (1963)

Ocherki Istorii Kitaya (Outlines of the Most Recent History of China) Moscow, 1959

Ojha, I. C., *China's Foreign Policy in an Age of Transition*, Boston, 1969

Oksenberg M. and R. B. Oxman, eds. *Dragon and Eagle. US-China Relations Past and Future*, N.Y., 1978

Padick, Clement, and others. *Russia and China. Non-Ideological Aspects of their Relationship*, L.A., 1966

Payne, Robert, *Portrait of a Revolutionary: Mao Tse-tung*, N.Y., 1961

Piao, Lin, *The Polemic on the General Line of the Communist Movement*, Beijing, 1965

Pillsbury, M., *Salt on the Dragon; Chinese Views*, Santa Monica, Rand Co., 1975

Pipes, R., *The Formation of the Soviet Union; Communism and Nationalism 1917-23*, Cambridge, 1954

Pollack, J. D., "Sino-Soviet Relations. . ." in Stuart and Tow, eds. *The Soviet Union, and the West*, Boulder, 1982, pp. 275-92.

Pomerennig, Horst, *Der chinesisch-sowjetische Grenzkonflikt*, Freiburg i.b. 1968

Pope, R. R., *The Soviet Affairs Specialists*. Unpublished PH., Dissert., Un. of Pennsylvania, 1975

Purcell, Victor, *The Chinese in Southeast Asia*, 2nd ed., London, 1965

Pye, Lucien W., *The Dynamics of Chinese Politics*, Cambridge, Ma., 1981

Pye, Lucien W., *The Spirit of Chinese Politics. A psychocultural study*. Cambridge, Ma, 1968

Pyn Min, *Istoriia Kitaisco-sovetskoi druzhby* (History of the Sino-Soviet Friendship), Moscow, 1959

Quested, R. K. I., *Sino-Russian Relations. A Short History*, Sydney, London, 1984

Ramachandrau K. N., *Power and Ideology; The Sino-Soviet Disputes,* 1977

Rees, D., *Korea. The Limited War*, N.Y., 1964

Remnek, Richard *Soviet Scholars and Soviet Foreign Policy*, Durham, 1975

Riasanovsky, N. V., *A History of Russia*, N.Y., 1963

Rice, E. E., *Mao's Way*, Berkeley, 1972

Ronchey, Alberto *The Two Red Giants*; *An Analysis of Sino-Soviet Relations*, N.Y. 1965

Rothenberg, Morris *Whither China*; *The View from the Kremlin*, Un. of Miami, 1977

Rowe, D. N. *Modern China*, Princeton, 1959

Rozman, Gilbert, ed. *Soviet Studies of Modern China. Assessments of Recent Scholarship*, Ann Arbor, 1984

Rubinstein, A. Z., *The Forein Policy of the Soviet Union*, N.Y. 1960, *Soviet and Chinese Influence in the Third World*, Boulder, 1975

Rumiantsev, A. M., *Istoki i evolutsiia "idei Mao Tszeduna."* (The origins and the evolution of the Ideas of Mao), Moscow, 1972

Rupen, R. A. and Farrell, R., eds., *Vietnam and the Sino-Soviet Dispute*, N.Y. 1967

Salisbury, H. E., *War between Russia and China*, N.Y., 1969

Samokhin, A., *Kitaiski krug Rossii* (The Chinese Encirclement of Russia), Frankfurt a. M ., 1981

Sandles, G. A., *Soviet Images of the People's Republic of China 1949-1979*, Ph.D. Dissert. 1981

Saran, V., *The Sino-Soviet Schism. A Bibliography 1956-64*, Bombay, 1971

Scalapino, R. A., ed. *Foreign Policy of Modern Japan*, Berkeley, 1977

Scammel, M., *Solzhenitsyn. A Biography.*, N.Y., London, 1984

Schram, Stuart R., *Mao Tse-tung*, N.Y., 1967 (1969)

Schram, Stuart R., *Political Thought of Mao Tse-tung*, N.Y., 1963 (1969),

Schram, Stuart R., *Quotations from Chairman Mao Tse-tung*, N.Y., 1969

Schwartz, Benjamin I., *Chinese Communism and the Rise of Mao*, Cambridge, Ma. 1958

Schwartz, Harry, *Tsars, Mandarins, and Commissars. A History of Chinese-Russian Relations*, Philadelphia, 1964

Schwartz, Morton, *Soviet Perceptions of the US*. Berkeley, 1978

Sergeichuk, S., *Throuh Russian Eyes,*; *American-Chinese Relations*, Arlington, 1975

Seton-Watson, Hugh, *From Lenin to Malenkov*, N.Y., 1953

Shabad, Theodore, *China's Changing Map*, N.Y. 1956

Simon, S. W., *The Broken Triangle*; *Peking, Djakarta, and the PKI*, Baltimore, 1968

Simmons, R. R., *The Strained Alliance* N.Y., 1975

Simmons, R. R., *The Sino-Russian Crisis*, Nanking,

Skachkov, P. E., *Bibliografiia Kitaia* (Bibliography of China), Moscow, 1960

Skilling, H. G. and Griffith, Franklyn, eds., *Interest Groups in Soviet Politics*, Princeton, 1971

Snow, E., *Mao's* Autobiography, N.Y., 1939 *Red Star over China*, N.Y. 1944 (London, 1951), *The other Side of the River*, N.Y. 1962 (London, 1963)

Sokolovski Marshal V. D., *Soviet Military Strategy*, 3rd ed., N.Y., 1975

Solomon, E. H., ed., *Asian Security in the 1980s*; *Problems and Politics*, Cambridge, *The China Factor in Sino-American Relations and the Global Scene*, N.Y. 1981

Sonnenfeldt, Helmut, *"The China Factor in Soviet Disarmament Policy,"* in Halperin, M., *Sino-Soviet Relations*, 1974

Sovietsko-Kitaiskie otnosheniia 1917-1957 (Soviet-Chinese Relations), Moscow, 1957

Stalin, I. V., *Sochineniia* (Collected Works), 13 vols., Moscow, 1946-51; China especially vols. 8 and 9, 1948 and 1949.

Stuart, Douglas and Wm. Tow, eds., *China, The-Soviet Union and the West. Dimensions for the 1980s*, Boulder, 1982

Sulzberger, C. L., *The Coldest War, Russia's Game in China*, N.Y, 1974

Swearingen, Rodger, *The Soviet Union and Postwar Japan*, Stanford, 1978

Tai Sung An, *The Sino-Soviet Territorial Dispute*, Westminster, 1973

Tang, Peter S. H., *Communist China Today*, Washington, D.C., 1961 (1962)

Thornton, R. C., *The Struggle for Power, 1917-1972*, Bloomington, 1973

Tien-Feng Cheng, *A History of Sino-Soviet Relations*, Washington. 1957

Tőkes, W. L., ed. *Eurocommunism and Detente*, 1978

Treadgold, D. W., ed., *Soviet and Chinese Communism. Similarities and Differences*, Seattle, 1967

Treadgold, D. W., ed., *Twentieth Century Russia*, Chicago, 1976, 4th ed.

Treadgold, D. W., ed., *The West in Russia and China*, Cambridge, 1973

Triangular Relations of Mainland China, the Soviet Union, and North Korea, Soeul, 1977

Tsien Hua Tsui, *The Sino-Soviet Border Dispute in the 1920s*, Ontario, 1983

Tuchman, Barbara, *Stillwell and the American Experience In China 1941-45*, N.Y., 1970

Ulam, A. B., *Expansion and Coexistence. The History of Soviet Russian Foreign Policy, 1917-1967*, Washington, D.C., 1974

Ulam, A. B., *The Rivals, America and Russia since World War II*, N.Y., 1972

U.S. Congress, Joint Economic Committee. The Allocation of Resources in the Soviet Union and China. Hearings, 1975 through 1980

USSR. Ministry of Foreign Affairs. *Dokumenty Vneshnei Politiki SSSR* (Documents of Foreign Poiicy of the USSR), Moscow, 1958

Van Eckelen, N. F., *Indian Foreign Relations and the Border Dispute with China* The Hague, 1964

Van Slycke, L. P., *Enemies and Friends; The United Front in Chinese Communist History*, Stanford, 1967

Vucinish, Wayne S., ed., *Russia and Asia. Essays on the Influence of Russia on the Asian Peoples*, Stanford, 1972

Watson, P., *The Frontiers of China*, N.Y., 1966

Wei, H., *China and Soviet Russia*, N.Y., 1956

Wheeler, G. E., *Modern History of Soviet Central Asia*, N.Y., 1964 (1965)

Whiting, A. S. and General Sheng, Shihts'ai, *Sinkiang; Pawn or Pivot*, East Lansing, 1958

Whiting, A. S., *The Chinese Calculus of Deterrence*, Ann Arbor, 1975

Wich, Richard, *"The Sino-Soviet Crisis Politics" A Study of Political Change and Communication*, Cambridge, Ma., 1980

Wilcox, Wayne et. al. eds., *Asia and the International System*, Cambridge, 1972

Wilson, Dick, *The People's Emperor*, Garden City, 1980

Wittfogel, K. A., *Oriental Despotism. A Comparative Study of Total Power* New Haven, 1957

Wu, Aitchen K., *China and the Soviet Union. A Study of Sino-Soviet Relations*, N.Y., 1950

Yahuda, M. B., *China's* Role in World Affairs, London, 1978

Zablocki, Clement, ed., *Sino-Soviet Rivalry; Implications for US Policy*, Washington, 1966

Zagoria, D. S., ed., *Communist China and the Soviet Bloc*, Philadelphia, 1963,

Zagoria, D. S., ed., *The Sino-Soviet Conflict 1956-1961*, Princeton, 1962 *Vietnam Triangle*, N.Y., 1967 ed.,

Zagoria, D. S., ed., *Soviet Policy in East Asia*, New Haven, 1982

Zimmerman, W., *Soviet Perspectives on International Relations*, Princeton, 1969

Zinner, Paul E., ed., *National Communism and Popular Revolt in Eastern Europe*; a selection of documents, N.Y., 1956

C. *Periodical Articles*:

(Articles which were published in *Beijing Review* (formerly *Peking Review*) and in *Pravda* and *Izvestia*, or reprinted in the *Current Digest of the Soviet Press* (*CDSP*) are not listed here; nor are articles from other journals which were reprinted in the foregoing journals. All these articles—meaning the great majority of sources—are listed only once, in the footnotes).

Alexeiev, L., "Anti-Sovietism in Peking's Strategy," *International Afffairs*, No. 7, 1973, p. 22

Apalin, G., "Peking. A Policy inimical to Peace, Democracy, and Socialism," *ibid.*, Nr. 33, 1973, pp. 22-28

Berton, P., "Background to the Territorial Issue," *Studies in Comparative Communism*, Nrs. 3-4, July-Oct. 1969

Borisov, Z. K., "Threat and Opportunity in the Communist Schism," *Foreign Affairs*, 40, Nr. 3 (Apr. 1963), pp. 513-26

Current History, several issues yearly devoted to China and the USSR

Godwin, P. H., "China and the Second World: The Search for Defense Technology," *Contemporary China*, fall 1978, pp. 3-9

Griffith, W. E., "Sino-Soviet Rapprochement," *Problems of Communism*, Mr. 2, 1983

Hall, Gus, "The Dangerous Doctrine of World Domination," *World Marxist Review*, Nov. 1981

Hough, Jerry, "The Generation Gap and the Brezhnev Successors," *Problems of Communism*, July-Aug. 1979, pp. 1-16

Hyland, W., "The Sino-Soviet Conflict: A Search for New Security Strategies," *Strategic Review*, 7, fall 1979

Johnson, C., "Cultural Revolution," *Far Eastern Economic Review*, 1968, p. 187f.

Karmal, Babrak, "Indissoluble Unity with the People," *World Marxist Review*, N. 6, 1981, p. 23f.

Kovalev, E. F., "A New Step in the Study of Sino-Soviet
Relations," *Voprosy istorii*, No. 11. 1972

Klatt, Werner, "China's Economy in 1975. A Review."
Internat. Affairs, Oct. 1979, p. 586f

Kapchenko, N., "Threat to Peace from Peking. Hegemonistic
Policy", *ibid.*, 2, 1979, pp. 66-77

Low, A. D., "Soviet Nationality Policy and the New Program
of the CPSU," *The Russian Review*, Jan. 1961, pp. 3-9,

Low, A. D., "The Sino-Soviet Confrontation Since Mao.
Marxism-Leninism, Hegemony, and Nationalism." *Canadian
Review of Studies in Nationalism*, Vol. IX, No. 2, fall 1982,
pp. 183-199

Luttwak, E., "Against the China Card," *Commentary*, Oct.
1978, pp. 37-43

Mancall, N., "Soviet Historians and the Sino-Soviet Alliance,"
China Quarterly, 53, Jan.-March 1973, pp. 80-97

Maung, S., "Peking's Territ. Claims," *World Marxist Review*,
Aug. 1981, pp. 71f.

Mirski, Z., "Aggressivnost Kitaia" *Krasnaya Zvezda*, Apr. 3,
1979

Peng Pingshan, "Lenin and the National Liberation Movement," *Hongqi*, No., 8, Apr. 16, 1980, in *FBIS*, Republic of
China, May 12, 1980, pp. C3-C8

Rozman, G., "Moscow-China Watchers in the Post-Mao Era:
The Response to a Changing China," *China Quarterly*, June
1983

Schram, S. R., "The Party in Chinese Communist Ideology,"
China Quarterly, Apr.-June 1969, pp. 1-16

Seton-Watson, H., "Differences in the Communist Parties,"
Annals of the Amer. Aca. of Polit. and Soc. Science, May
1958, pp. 1-7

Sonnenfeldt, H.,, "Implications of the Soviet Invasion of
Afghanistan for East-West Relations," *NATO Review,* 28,
Apr. 1980, pp. 1f.

Tikhvinski, S. L., "On Prohlems in Recent History of China,"
Voprosy istorii, No. 2, fall 1973, pp. 3-58.